Cultural Analysis and Bourdieu's Legacy

Cultural Analysis and Bourdieu's Legacy explores the achievements and limitations of a Bourdieusian approach to cultural analysis through original contributions from the most distinguished international scholars.

This edited collection offers sustained critical engagement, substantiated by new empirical work and comparative analysis, and also presents concrete evidence of alternative analyses of culture in Britain, France and the USA. Discussions are situated in relation to current debates about cultural analysis, in particular the vibrant and extensive disputes concerning the applicability of Bourdieu's concepts and methods. Subsequently, implications for the future of research work in cultural analysis – both theory and methods – are drawn. The contributing authors offer key interpretations of the work of Bordieu, arguments for alternative approaches to cultural analysis, and critical applications of his concepts in empirical analysis.

This book is essential reading for graduate students of sociology, cultural studies, social anthropology or cultural geography, providing great insight into the work of one of the most eminent contemporary scholars in the field of cultural analysis.

Elizabeth Silva is Professor of Sociology at the Open University. She is a member of the project team of Cultural Capital and Social Exclusion (CCSE) and of the Centre for Research on Socio-Cultural Change (CRESC). She has published various sole-authored and co-authored articles using CCSE material. Her publications include: *Technology, Culture, Family: Influences on Home Life* (Palgrave 2010); *Culture, Class, Distinction* (Routledge 2009, with Tony Bennett, Mike Savage, Alan Warde, Modesto Gayo-Cal and David Wright); and *Contemporary Culture and Everyday Life* (Sociology Press 2004, co-edited).

Alan Warde is Professor of Sociology at the University of Manchester. He is a member of the project team of Cultural Capital and Social Exclusion and has authored and co-authored several articles using its data. His publications include: *Trust in Food: an Institutional and Comparative Analysis* (2007, with Unni Kjaernes and Mark Harvey); *Eating Out: Social Differentiation, Consumption and Pleasure* (2000, with Lydia Martens); and *Consumption, Food and Taste: Culinary Antinomies and Commodity Culture* (1997).

Culture, Economy and the Social
A new series from CRESC – the ESRC Centre for Research on Socio-cultural Change

Editors
Tony Bennett
Open University

Penny Harvey
Manchester University

Kevin Hetherington
Open University

The *Culture, Economy and the Social* series is committed to innovative contemporary, comparative and historical work on the relations between social, cultural and economic change. It publishes empirically based research that is theoretically informed, that critically examines the ways in which social, cultural and economic change is framed and made visible, and that is attentive to perspectives that tend to be ignored or side-lined by grand theorising or epochal accounts of social change. The series addresses the diverse manifestations of contemporary capitalism, and considers the various ways in which the 'social', 'the cultural' and 'the economic' are apprehended as tangible sites of value and practice. It is explicitly comparative, publishing books that work across disciplinary perspectives, cross-culturally, or across different historical periods.

The series is actively engaged in the analysis of the different theoretical traditions that have contributed to the development of the 'cultural turn' with a view to clarifying where these approaches converge and where they diverge on a particular issue. It is equally concerned to explore the new critical agendas emerging from current critiques of the cultural turn: those associated with the descriptive turn, for example. Our commitment to interdisciplinarity thus aims at enriching theoretical and methodological discussion, building awareness of the common ground that has emerged in the past decade, and thinking through what is at stake in those approaches that resist integration to a common analytical model.

1 **The Media and Social Theory (2008)**
Edited by David Hesmondhalgh and Jason Toynbee

2 **Culture Class Distinction (2009)**
Tony Bennett, Mike Savage, Elizabeth Bortolaia Silva, Alan Warde, Modesto Gayo-Cal and David Wright

3 **Material Powers (2010)**
Edited by Tony Bennett and Patrick Joyce

4 **The Social after Gabriel Tarde (2010)**
Debates and Assessments
Edited by Matei Candea

5 **Milk, Modernity and the Making of the Human (2010)**
Richie Nimmo

6 **Cultural Analysis and Bourdieu's Legacy (2010)**
Edited by Elizabeth Silva and Alan Ward

7 **Creative Labour (forthcoming)**
Media Work in Three Cultural Industries
Edited by David Hesmondhalgh and Sarah Baker

8 **Rio de Janeiro (forthcoming)**
Urban Life through the Eyes of the City
Beatriz Jaguaribe

Centre for Research on Socio-Cultural Change

Cultural Analysis and Bourdieu's Legacy

Settling accounts and developing alternatives

Edited by Elizabeth Silva and Alan Warde

Routledge
Taylor & Francis Group

LONDON AND NEW YORK

First published 2010 by Routledge
2 Park Square, Milton Park, Abingdon, Oxon, OX14 4RN

Simultaneously published in the USA and Canada
by Routledge
270 Madison Avenue, New York, NY 10016

Routledge is an imprint of the Taylor & Francis Group

© 2010 Elizabeth Silva and Alan Warde; individual chapters, the
contributors

Typeset in Times New Roman by
Pindar NZ, Auckland, New Zealand
Printed and bound in Great Britain by
The MPG Books Group

British Library Cataloguing in Publication Data
A catalogue record for this book is available from the British Library

Library of Congress Cataloging in Publication Data
Cultural analysis and Bourdieu's legacy : settling accounts and developing
alternatives / edited by Elizabeth Silva and Alan Warde.
    p. cm.
  Includes bibliographical references and index.
  1. Culture. 2. Sociology. 3. Bourdieu, Pierre, 1930-2002—Criticism and
interpretation. I. Silva, Elizabeth Bortolaia II. Warde, Alan.
  HM621.C84 2010
  301.092—dc22   2009035626

ISBN10: 0-415-49535-0 (hbk)
ISBN10: 0-203-87862-0 (ebk)

ISBN13: 978-0-415-49535-6 (hbk)
ISBN13: 978-0-203-87862-0 (ebk)

Contents

Contributors

Tony Bennett is Professor of Sociology at the Open University and co-Director of the ESRC Centre for Research on Socio-Cultural Change (CRESC). His publications include: *Pasts Beyond Memory: Evolution, Museums, Colonialism* (2004); *Accounting for Tastes: Australian Everyday Cultures* (1999 with J. Frow and M. Emmison); and *Culture: A Reformer's Science* (1998).

Fiona Devine is Professor of Sociology at the University of Manchester. Her publications include: *Doing Social Science: Evidence and Methods in Empirical Research* (2008 with Sue Heath); *Class Practices: How Parents Help Their Children Get Good Jobs* (2004); *Social Inequalities in Comparative Perspective* (2004 edited with M. Waters); and *Social Class in America and Britain* (1997).

Rick Fantasia is a Professor of Sociology at Smith College, Northampton, USA. He frequently conducts research in France, and his research interests include the interaction between labor and culture in the United States and France. He was particularly influenced by the French sociologist Pierre Bourdieu. His publications include: *Cultures of Solidarity* (1988); *Bringing Class Back In: Historical and Contemporary Perspectives* (1991 co-authored with Kim Voss); *Hard Work: Remaking the American Labor Movement* (2004); and *The Magic of Americanism: French Gastronomy in the Age of Neo-Liberalism* (in preparation).

Michael Grenfell is Professor of Education at the School of Education in the Faculty of Law, Arts and Social Sciences at the University of Southampton, UK. He has a special interest in research methodology; in particular, employing the work of Pierre Bourdieu. He is author of *Bourdieu and Education* (Falmer 1998) and *Pierre Bourdieu: Agent Provocateur* (Continuum 2004); *Art Rules* (Berg 2007); and *Bourdieu: Education and Training* (Continuum 2007).

Antoine Hennion is Director of Research at the École des Mines de Paris. His recent publications include a collective book on music lovers (*Figure de l'amateur* (2000)); a book on the use of J. S. Bach in nineteenth-century France (*La grandeur de Bach* (2000), with J-M. Fauquet); and a forthcoming translation of *La passion musicale. Une sociologie de la mediation* (1993).

Michèle Lamont is Robert I. Goldman Professor of European Studies and Professor of Sociology and African American Studies at Harvard University. Publications include: *Cream Rising: Finding and Defining Excellence in the Social Sciences and the Humanities* (forthcoming); *Money, Morals, and Manners: The Culture of the French and the American Upper-Middle Class* (1992); *Cultivating Differences: Symbolic Boundaries and the Making of Inequality* (co-edited, 1992); and *The Dignity of Working Men: Morality and the Boundaries of Race, Class, and Immigration* (2000).

Frédéric Lebaron is Maître de Conférences at the University of Picardie, France. He is also a researcher at the Centre de Sociologie Européenne (Collège de France, École des Hautes Études en Sciences Sociales et CNRS). He works on economic sociology and sociology of sciences. His publications include *La croyance économique. Les économistes entre science et politique* (2000) and various contributions in collaboration with Pierre Bourdieu: 'Et si on repensait l'économie? Un entretien avec Pierre Bourdieu et Frédéric Lebaron' (*Le Nouvel Observateur* – N°1852, 04/05/2000).

Diane Reay is a sociologist, and is Professor of Education at Cambridge University. She is also interested in broader issues of the relationship between the self and society, the affective and the material. Her work includes research in education, which develops Pierre Bourdieu's conceptual framework in order to understand gendered and racialized class processes. Publications include: *Degrees of Choice: Social class, race and gender in higher education* (2005, with M. David and S. Ball); and *Class Work: Mothers' involvement in children's schooling* (1998).

Mike Savage is Professor of Sociology at the University of Manchester and Director of the ESRC Centre for Research on Socio-Cultural Change (CRESC). Publications include: *Globalization and Belonging* (2005, with G. Bagnall and B. Longhurst); *Renewing Class Analysis* (2000, with F. Devine, R. Crompton and J. Scott); and *Social Class and Social Transformation* (1999).

Andrew Sayer is Professor of Social Theory and Political Economy at the Department of Sociology, University of Lancaster. His publications include: *Microcircuits of Capital* (1988, with K. J. Morgan); *Method in Social Science* (1992); *The New Social Economy* (1992, with R. A. Walker); *Radical Political Economy: A Critique* (1995); *Realism and Social Science* (2000); and *The Moral Significance of Class* (2005).

David Swartz is Assistant Professor of Sociology at Boston University, USA. He is the author of *Culture & Power: The Sociology of Pierre Bourdieu* (1997) and *After Bourdieu: Influence, Critique, Elaboration* (2004, co-editor with V. L. Zolberg). His research interests include the study of élites and stratification, education, culture, religion, and social theory and he is currently writing a book on the political sociology of Pierre Bourdieu.

Acknowledgements

This book arises from the Final Symposium for the research project 'Cultural Capital and Social Exclusion: A Critical Investigation (CCSE)' funded by the ESRC (R000239801) which we organized. The event was funded partly from the ESRC award and co-funded by the Department of Sociology at the Open University and the Centre for Research on Socio-Cultural Change (CRESC). We gratefully acknowledge this financial support. Tony Bennett and Mike Savage, our co-holders of the award for the CCSE research project, deserve our first thanks, as we shared work, ideas and taking turns with disseminating our engagement with Bourdieu's work. Thanks also to our other co-researchers David Wright and Modesto Gayo-Cal. All contributors to the book participated at the Symposium and we thank them all, together with other participants: Lisa Adkins, Georgina Born, Hugo Ceron Anaya, Angela Dale, Eiko Ikegama, Camilla Kennedy-Harper, Nobumi Kobayashi-Hillary, Brigitte Le Roux, Nick Prior, Hélène Snee, Jason Toynbee, Janet Wolff, Kath Woodward and David Wright (again). We benefited from Karen Ho's excellent administrative support, and from Margaret Marchant's assistance in compiling the book.

1   The importance of Bourdieu

Elizabeth Silva and Alan Warde

Pierre Bourdieu was probably the most eminent sociologist, of the final quarter of the twentieth century, in the world. He was also probably the most controversial. He had long aroused fierce passions within French sociological circles. There he had become increasingly well-known from the 1960s, and his eminent position in the French sociological field was marked by his election to the most prestigious of professorships in sociology at the Collège de France in 1981.[1] The personalized tensions and oppositions that typically fracture the intellectual field in France, which result in clan-like solidarities, stoke the fires of hostility and controversy. No account of his impact in France would be adequate without some understanding of the personalized bases of intellectual alignments and allegiances, with Alain Touraine and Raymond Boudon providing Bourdieu's main competitors and antagonists (Robbins, 2000; Grenfell, 2004b; Fuller, 2006). As a prominent figure in the French intellectual field, he personally inspired mixed emotional reactions, with some very negative judgements expressed by his adversaries, as for example captured in a recent biography by Marie-Anne Lescourret (2008), which accuses him of being arrogant and dismissive. His undoubted self-confidence irritated fellow sociologists unsympathetic to his work. Bernard Lahire (1999: 11), a sociologist who engaged closely and critically with Bourdieu's work, took the view that Bourdieu 'like many other researchers in social sciences refuses to recognize his adversaries and remains deaf to all refutation'. Natalie Heinich (2002: 45), a former student of Bourdieu's, described the situation as one where 'the real enemies are not those with whom one debates but those with whom we no longer speak'. As Bourdieu's *Homo Academicus* (1988 [1984]) makes clear, the French academic world is a competitive one where strategic manoeuvring for reputation and rewards are the norm, with the ensuing rivalry within the field sometimes becoming bitter and acrimonious.

However, while Bourdieu divided the French sociological community on personal and intellectual grounds, he had limited impact internationally until the 1990s, when arguably he came to be acknowledged as the world's most eminent sociological theorist. Before then, outside France, aside from widespread acclaim for *Distinction* (1984 [1979]) and a niche in the sociology of education, he was not very highly regarded in the international social scientific community. Critics variously pronounced his already extensive works obscure, inconsistent, limited and derivative (e.g. Jenkins, 1992). More recently, Bourdieu has appealed very widely across the social sciences and humanities, inspiring work in anthropology, sociology, geography, literature, feminist studies and cultural studies. It is worth reflecting on what changed on the international scene.

Most obviously, there was the publication of some new substantial works. Alongside the battles for territory, resources and reputation came an outpouring of substantive studies of the highest quality including *The Rules of Art* (1996a [1992]), *Homo Academicus* (1988 [1984]) and *The State Nobility* (1996b [1989]). That these were accompanied by an extensive programme of translation into English was by no means coincidental. Bourdieu benefited from the good offices of Polity Press which rapidly (and more or less comprehensively) published not only his theoretical books but also his empirical studies of French institutions in English. At the same time he also produced some more accessible and popular essays and interviews, of varied provenance by date, in collections like *Practical Reason* (1998b [1994]), *The Field of Cultural Production* (1993c) and *In Other Words* (1990c). Now entering the final phase of his career, from about 1990 onwards, he devoted a good deal more attention to public affairs, being well recognized as a public intellectual opposed particularly to the excesses of neo-liberal economic management. This did not stop him from producing major sociological works, and one – *The Weight of the World* (1999c), which examined contemporary sources of distress, misery and disappointment as captured in personal biographies – became a popular bestseller.

More exposure for his major sociological works was accompanied by a rapid growth of increasingly positive secondary commentary which all helped bring him widespread acclaim. Among these was a book of essays edited by Craig Calhoun, Edward LiPuma and Moishe Postone (1993) which explored Bourdieu's work in cultural anthropology, linguistics, media studies, ethnomethodology, philosophy and feminism, centred on explorations about the notion of 'reflexivity', 'systems of classification' and the relations between practical knowledge and universal structures. David Swartz (1997) produced a very sophisticated, clear and balanced account of his sociological work particularly as it related to power and culture. This served to systematize Bourdieu's position and to present sympathetically his approach to a series of longstanding major sociological dilemmas. Richard Shusterman's edited collection (1999) assessed Bourdieu's philosophical theories, revealing dimensions of his thought relevant for philosophy of today. It suggests that limits to his theory may be overcome in alliance with discussions in social sciences. Bridget Fowler (2000) compiled a collection of essays centred on debates in the humanities to consider Bourdieu's theory of practice through his work as an ethnographer and cultural theorist, philosopher and sociologist assessing theoretically his theories as working tools.

Meanwhile scholars from many places beyond the borders of France were making attempts to apply his concepts – often not very authentically – to their own empirical problems. Jeffrey Sallaz and Jane Zavisca (2007), in a crisp analysis of the impact of Bourdieu on American sociology, indicate the increasing diffusion of his work over the last 25 years, with accelerating application of his concepts in new empirical research. Calling it, after Imre Lakatos (1978), a progressive research programme, they identify many works, and some key and highly regarded studies, which indicate inventive modes of appropriation, of which Bourdieu would probably have approved (for he said theories were to be used, not debated), with key concepts being applied to problems of political, economic and cultural sociology. They show a leap in the citation of works by Bourdieu in the leading American sociological journals during the 1990s. Something similar happens in the UK, where Halsey (2004: 173) reports Bourdieu as the second-most cited author in the three major British sociological journals in 2000, having not been in the top ten in 1990. Probably data for other European countries would indicate the same.

Bourdieu's growing impact within sociology may have arisen from something of a change of strategy on his part. Unusually for a very successful and prominent sociologist, he eschewed purely theoretical work and made his contribution to the building up of concepts and methods through empirical studies of modern French society. In his sociological phase he had insisted on theory and theoretical concepts being subordinate to substantive sociological analysis. Derek Robbins (2000) makes the case well. Robbins sees Bourdieu's work as an outgrowth of his trajectory within the French academy, a matter of dispositions changing as a result of competition and struggle in the intellectual field. Bourdieu's career had three separate stages, as cultural anthropologist, scientific sociologist and public intellectual, each exhibiting different preoccupations, intellectual developments being a matter of pragmatic and strategic response to changes in position with concepts devised for immediate application rather than formalization. However, towards the end of the 1980s, Bourdieu seemed to begin to present his work as a systematic corpus. Perhaps encouraged by Loïc Wacquant, the four most prominent key concepts that frame all his work – habitus, capitals, field and practice – concepts which had been used often in diverse ways, were consciously brought together, giving shape to and making more accessible a conceptual and theoretical core. *Invitation to Reflexive Sociology* (Bourdieu and Wacquant, 1992) was a major step in systematising concepts previously employed in a more *ad hoc* manner. *Invitation to Reflexive Sociology* nevertheless still proclaimed that '"Theories" are research programs that call not for "theoretical debate" but for a practical utilization that either refutes or generalizes them' (ibid.: 77). The utility, validity and applicability of these four key concepts have been one of the most controversial aspects of debates about Bourdieu's work, and – unsurprisingly – some of the chapters in this collection engage closely with them.

Perhaps more important though in the elevation of Bourdieu's reputation was the changing external environment of the social sciences. The promotion of interdisciplinarity and internationalization had significant implications.

For a good deal of his career Bourdieu devoted himself specifically to promoting sociology, defending its intellectual autonomy and the distinctiveness of its methods (Robbins, 2006: 6–9). His concern with the craft of sociology, and with the central issues of sociological debate never left him. *Pascalian Meditations* (Bourdieu, 2000d [1997]) is one fine example of his late re-working of older debates central to the discipline. Nevertheless, with a general turn to interdisciplinarity, Bourdieu's work became of increasing interest to a wide range of scholars. In the field of consumption, for example, his work – particularly *Distinction* – uniquely provided common ground across anthropology, geography, marketing, media studies and sociology (see Miller, 1995). His extensive empirical research in the fields of art, literature and photography also positioned him well in relation to 'the cultural turn'. So despite having only a short-lived interest in cultural studies and having no time for postmodern thought, his substantive contributions to the analysis of cultural production drew his work into the field of the fine arts, and indeed also into some of the more popular arts (e.g. Brown and Szeman, 2000). Emergence from the sociological ghetto was as good for his reputation as was his increased exposure as a public intellectual (see Swartz, Chapter 4 of this volume).

At the same time, sociology itself was in the process of becoming more broadly internationalized. During the twentieth century it was possible to analyse sociology in terms of largely exclusive national traditions of thought. The reduction of language barriers as English increased its dominance in social scientific communication, the challenge to the view that 'society', understood as coterminous with the nation-state, should be the primary object of sociology, and greater international academic association and co-operation (not to mention globalization, migration and tourism) dismantled an older sociological parochialism. Besides translation of all his major works into English, trans-Atlantic mobility brought young scholars to study at the *Centre de Sociologie Européenne* (including contributors in this volume: Rick Fantasia, Michael Grenfell and Michèle Lamont). They, and others like them, in turn spread Bourdieu's influence, particularly in the sociology of culture in the United States (see Bennett, *et al.*, 2009; Lamont, Chapter 10 this volume; Sallaz and Zavisca, 2007).

Of course, none of these factors would have been of the remotest importance without the existence of a corpus of work of the highest intellectual quality and relevance. The range of Bourdieu's work, as the essays in this book testify, was prodigious. He wrote about most of the substantive domains of sociological focus – from schooling to art, stratification to housing, masculinity to élite formation. He made significant contributions also to the philosophy of method, social and sociological theory, methodology and empirical analysis. The future will no doubt hold substantial intellectual biographies seeking to evaluate the originality and coherence of his work. But for now we seek, in a more modest way, to determine what the legacy is for sociology and for cultural analysis in particular. How are social scientists currently making use of Bourdieu? Which elements of his work are proving fruitful, how might they contribute to the shaping of cultural analysis, and what parts are being dismissed?

We are far from being the first to address these questions. Since his death in 2002 several volumes have been devoted to evaluating Bourdieu's contribution, including a number of high-profile engagements. David Swartz and Vera Zolberg's (2004) collection of essays, drawn in large part from a special edition of *Theory and Society* published a year earlier, offers many insights into Bourdieu's work on religion, economic models, educational research, French literature and politics. The volume offers a deeper understanding of the work of Bourdieu, mainly sympathetic and focusing on theoretical and conceptual matters. A special edition of *Cultural Studies* (2003) reviewed his impact on cultural studies in America especially, with a focus on the use of his key concepts and on the role of intellectuals. Another significant contribution is the volume edited by Lisa Adkins and Beverly Skeggs (2004) exploring the ways in which Bourdieu's social theory opens up rich possibilities for engagement by contemporary feminism. Contributions focus on Bourdieu's concepts of symbolic violence and habitus to creatively focus on discussions about gender, the body, affect, sexuality, as well as class and social change. Robbins (2006: 1), when introducing a special edition of the journal *Theory, Culture & Society* (*TCS*), noted the publication of several other volumes in the manner of *Festschriften* honouring the man and his works and appealed for more creative uses of Bourdieu's legacy. The *TCS* collection explored the origins of Bourdieu's thought across different disciplines particularly in relation to philosophy and science studies. Meanwhile, however, many journal articles were published taking inspiration from and applying Bourdieu's concepts. Whether it is necessary to take on all of Bourdieu's concepts in order to fruitfully apply his insights is disputed (see, for example, the reflection of Swartz (2008) on the programme of research on organizations espoused by Mustafa Emirbayer and Victoria Johnson (2008)). Manifestly, concepts of capital, habitus and field have had inspired applications from scholars who are not faithful subscribers to the Bourdieusian schema (see Sallaz and Zavisca, 2007, for some instances; also Crossley, 2001; Ferguson, 2004; Lawler, 2008; Lizardo, 2005; Savage, *et al.*, 2005).

The contributions in this book are informed by the preceding discussions on the application, implications and limitations of Bourdieu's work to social theory and cultural analyses. We seek to add to this body of literature by bringing together some distinguished sociologists whose work has been influenced in one way or another by Bourdieu. The essays in this book come from a symposium held in 2006 to review some of the implications of an empirical study of cultural taste, knowledge and participation in the UK which was nearing completion. *Cultural Capital and Social Exclusion* (CCSE) engaged closely with Bourdieu's theoretical and methodological perspectives on the understanding of culture and social divisions in contemporary society while asking similar questions to those of *Distinction*.[2] The analysis of the empirical material, perhaps typically and instructively for such ventures, indicated that while Bourdieu can be a source of great inspiration, it is not possible to simply adopt his concepts or straightforwardly endorse his substantive findings (see Bennett, *et al.*, 2009). Because of the origins of this book in relation to the CCSE project, reference to Bourdieu's work on culture, and to the central notion of cultural capital, is a strong, though this is not an exclusive focus of the ensuing chapters.

The book presents different approaches to cultural analysis using the work of Bourdieu as an anchor point. Culture, cultural change and methodological engagements to capture the relations of the cultural within other spheres are given prominence in the essays. While concerned with Bourdieusian approaches to cultural analysis, 'culture' is here understood as a theoretical category that serves to deal with questions of how cultural differences are patterned and bounded in space and time. For the contributing authors, culture is understood to entail a wide range of life involvements. They span culture as a category of social life in which learned behaviour is implicated; as an institutional sphere, or field, where meaning-making is produced; as practice, both in the sense of performativity and repertoire for action; and as a partially coherent landscape with shifting but bounded procedures and schemes applied to social life. Engagement with Bourdieu's work implies that, while using a notion of culture to get at meaningful human action, a particular conception of the relationality of the social is addressed, including cultural repertoires involving banal activities but also going beyond the description of everyday conduct of ordinary people, involving a topological approach.

Contested relations to a legacy

Bourdieu remains a highly controversial figure. The contributions to this book take one of four different positions. First, some offer a defence of his legacy and expanded claims for his authority, a position taken (broadly speaking) by Michael Grenfell, Rick Fantasia and David Swartz. It is clearly possible to work with his concepts and organizing principles in order to conduct vibrant, powerful and persuasive pieces of social analysis. A second response might be described as a partial appropriation, where some parts of the theoretical or methodological corpus are accepted and then applied, along with other concepts or approaches, to offer empirically based explanations. The chapter by Mike Savage, Elizabeth Silva and Alan Warde, and that by Diane Reay are instances of this kind of engagement. Arguably Bourdieu, at least in his earlier work, would approve of this strategy, insofar as he suggested that concepts and theories were not to be objectified, but used to illuminate and explain particular puzzles in sociological analysis. Thus the same concepts might not always be appropriate, new ones need to be formed, or new insights may be drawn from elsewhere, in the face of an explanatory puzzle. A third position, illustrated by Andrew Sayer and Tony Bennett, arises from extensive engagement with Bourdieu's work. Such a position offers admiration, albeit sometimes grudging, for the inspiration that Bourdieu has brought to sociological analysis, and also for his productivity, range and flexibility. Bourdieu is recognized as a major contributor to social science in the second half of the twentieth century, but there are significant parts of his work that are unacceptable, and it is argued that it would be best to abandon the framework and many of the assumptions that underpin it. This coming to terms, most clear in Sayer, may recognize and share some of Bourdieu's distinctive solutions to the problems of sociology, but without wanting to use those, or integrate them, in future analysis. Finally there is repudiation. Illustrated by the chapters of Antoine Hennion and Michèle Lamont, it is maintained that the positions that Bourdieu took were never satisfactory, and it is contended, outrightly by Hennion and in a more nuanced way by Lamont, that there would be little point in working with the concepts or the associated problematic. Better, then, to forget than to mine for nuggets that might contribute to future analysis.

Defending the legacy

Michael Grenfell insists that while there is much that Bourdieu did not do, there is much profit to be had from thinking 'with' Bourdieu and through his methods to consider the implications of adopting his approach. He outlines the development of Bourdieu's concepts and their employment, taking issue with what he calls 'misuses' (misinterpretations and misapplications) by academics in varied appropriations of his work. Grenfell notes a number of misplaced critical strategies including the making of 'false accusations', claiming that there is nothing special in Bourdieu's approach by reducing it too much, claiming what he says has always been known anyway, further embroidering his original concepts to suit one's purposes, and using his work as an orthodoxy simply to be replicated. While these misuses do not apply singularly to Bourdieu, they are found frequently among his reviewers. These strategies unfairly account for his contribution, in particular as it regards his (1) structured approach and (2) the possibilities of moving on from his work.

The structured approach is relevant for the three stages of methodology that Grenfell outlines from Bourdieu's practice. Firstly, the construction of the research object is always started afresh, making the normal conspicuous by reconceptualising it in relational terms. Secondly, an account of the field is constructed via an examination of the relation of the field with other fields, its 'mapping' of the volume and configurations of various forms of capital and the analysis of the habitus of the agents in the field. These levels are never discrete but always mixed up, the homologies between field, capitals and habitus being central to the understanding of the approach. Thirdly, a reflection about the social conditions of thinking derived from the position of the researcher in social space is particularly important for the ongoing practice of research. If one were to follow this Bourdieusian approach one would necessarily always move beyond Bourdieu since his method is offered as interpretation of social processes in flux.

The Bourdieusian approach is very closely followed by Rick Fantasia who concentrates on the exploration of the field, a concept which became increasingly important to Bourdieu in the course of his career. Through an account of the transformation of French gastronomy, Fantasia demonstrates how the concept of field can be creatively and constructively deployed in contemporary institutional analysis, in ways similar to Bourdieu's explorations of the literary and the art fields. He shows that *haute cuisine* becomes consecrated through the activities of professional chefs, aided and abetted by cultural intermediaries, from early in the nineteenth century. The literary and philosophical apparatus associated with gastronomy gives the field a degree of autonomy, making it appear to be, and actually to be, governed by aesthetic rather than economic impulses. It is this which conferred a special relationship between food and French self-identity, becoming early a basis for the celebration of French national cuisine.

Fantasia argues that the relationship to industrial culinary organization from the 1970s – a shift occurring much later in France than in the US or the UK – brought about a change in the relationship between gastronomy and the operations of

the economic field. While popular representations still place industrial production – especially fast food – as totally at odds with the worlds of *haute cuisine*
and *Michelin*-starred restaurants, an increasingly seductive accommodation is
occurring. Big industrial corporations have purchased sometimes the restaurants,
but (more importantly) the symbolic capital of consecrated celebrity chefs – particularly those who have three *Michelin* stars – for their own business empires or
products. The most successful chefs have exploited these business opportunities
(shifting from *chef de cuisine* to *chef d'entreprise*, as Fantasia neatly describes it)
as they endorse products, open shops, as well as opening new, much less fancy
restaurants, and sometimes chains of restaurants. Their success depends upon their
reputations for the quality of their cooking in their flagship restaurants. However,
this clearly may have dangerous consequences, as the dalliance with the logic of
the economic field may easily undermine the sanctity of the artisanal and artistic
justifications upon which *haute cuisine* and its restaurants were established. The
distance between the logic of McDonald's and the magic of *Haute Cuisine* in
France is not as great as is often imagined.

Moving into the field of power and politics, David Swartz neatly dissects the
different aspects these have, and their meanings as found in Bourdieu's work.
He contrasts the relatively unproblematic, but not much exploited, potential for a
sociology of politics to be derived from Bourdieu's work, with a much less stable
and persuasive version of how sociology might be used politically. During his
career Bourdieu shifted his position on the latter issue without entirely satisfactorily reaching a final resolution. Swartz indicates the shifts, the virtues of different
positions and their incumbent problems. An uncompromising insistence to the
end on the need to defend scientific autonomy and independence accompanied a
conviction that science should be articulated with political activism. The tension
was never satisfactorily resolved and grew more problematic over time.

Having tried out many different solutions, Bourdieu came to consider that the
new political circumstances of the later part of his life – of neo-liberalism and
growing media power – changed the appropriate role for the sociologist. Swartz
notes that Bourdieu's view of the intellectual role moved close to Foucault's
idea of the 'specific intellectual', one who intervenes on issues of her specialized
knowledge which permits her to speak with authority and disturb the ways people
think. Latterly Bourdieu advocated 'scholarship with commitment' (2002a: 465–9
in Swartz this volume), a condition where the roles of scholar and political activist
are less sharply distinguished.

Partial appropriation

Building on Bourdieu's analysis of stratification, Mike Savage, Elizabeth Silva
and Alan Warde examine the implications of the distinction between objective and
subjective class location with reflections about issues of class dis-identification
and identity of class, on the basis of an empirical study employing quantitative
and qualitative methods. The discussion is particularly relevant in the context of
contemporary debates in the UK about the salience of class.

Recent research notes that while class is widely understood as a feature of social inequality, class identities do not appear to be meaningful to individuals. In the context of globalization and individualization processes, researchers have identified decline in class consciousness and awareness. Emotional frames of a more individualized kind have been noted at the same time that class hierarchies are found to inform everyday life in new ways. Joining the debate on 'dis-identification', the authors consider the limits of class identity and the ways in which powers of classification are expressed in the 'talk' of research participants.

The findings indicate lack of direct class identification, with references to class pertaining to the external world rather than to personal experience. Both the deployment and the avoidance of idioms of class reveal an awareness of the power of classifying. Ambivalence towards class is thus actively produced and dis-identification often hides awareness of distinctive privileges.

Also working with frameworks of class stratification, Diane Reay defends the usefulness of the concept of habitus and makes a neat empirical demonstration of the way in which it can be used, in relation to the concept of field, to understand class experiences of education. She argues that disjunctions between field and habitus may well be positive and generative, as well as causing difficulties in some instances. It often depends upon what resources the individual has. She identifies and analyses a telling class-based asymmetry in situations where habitus and position in the field are not aligned, indicating that it is harder for the working-class child to overcome the problems of joining a middle-class field – e.g. the university education one – than vice versa.

Working-class children do often overcome their lack of cultural resources, adopting a flexible and open orientation towards the demands of an inherently middle-class educational system for which they are previously unprepared. The implication of the argument and the evidence is that it is much harder for working-class children to take advantage of a disjuncture between habitus of origin and a non-congenial field setting. Such a situation is likely to be anxiety provoking and also, presumably, they are more likely to fail as a result. This is shown by the tendency of working-class children to be excluded from the arena of higher education. However, this exclusion is not absolute and it is manifestly overcome (sometimes with some difficulty) by a segment of the working class. Reay contrasts this situation with that of middle-class children when they are inserted into an unfamiliar field – like the working-class comprehensive school. They may find their circumstances difficult, and actually learn very little about working-class culture and its virtues. Yet, they may learn something positive – an added capital resource for them – about ethnic diversity, remaining largely confident about themselves and the middle-class culture from which they hail and to which they will return.

The differences Diane Reay identifies in how students from different social classes make sense of choices indicates that if habitus is helpful for understanding the ingrained assumptions of the middle-class it is less helpful in understanding the processes experienced by working-class applicants to university. For the working class the pre-reflexive has to become reflexive and their 'natural' predispositions need converting into new dispositions. The dis-alignment between habitus and field has certain costs. Nevertheless, Reay disputes Bourdieu's view about the burdens of a 'divided habitus' and its creation of instabilities and neuroses.

Critical revisions

Andrew Sayer's essay cogently and persuasively identifies elements of a theory of action or conduct which draws upon and acknowledges virtues in Bourdieu's theory of habitus while at the same time identifying some of its shortcomings. Some elements raised in Reay's essay are here probed through a different focus. Sayer identifies several weaknesses in Bourdieu's account, including insufficient attention to the ethical dimension of conduct, neglect of the role of emotions in the process of reasoning, and disregard for connections between conduct and an ever-present moral concern with the well-being of self and others. None of these extensions or objections is at odds with the basic concept of the habitus, with its emphasis on learned dispositions and the capacity to act in ways that short-circuit or eliminate reflection. The consequence, arguably, is a much more positive view of human action, according lay ethical reasoning the authenticity that it deserves. At the same time, the tendencies of many sociologists besides Bourdieu to imagine that only they reflect and understand the causes of action, while others (lay persons) act automatically, in line with convention, or on the basis of self-interest, are problematized.

Sayer argues that Bourdieu does not allow for disinterested action and therefore does not grapple with the issue of the importance of how to live. He reduces social life to the pursuit of power and advantage even though he recognizes the deeply evaluative character of social actions: the value of people, practices and objects. Bourdieu's individuals, notes Sayer, pursue only external goods. Moreover, internal goods obey logics that are not entirely social, but Bourdieu makes no concessions to biological or psychological factors which also inform the habitus. Interestingly, while his academic theorizing does not include comments on human well being, his political writings do. In this regard, Swartz's claim for attention to Bourdieu's political sociology (Chapter 4) would perhaps provide a finer understanding of Bourdieu's insights into unjust social processes, with the identification of what is 'wrong' and what is 'right'.

Concerned with how culture operates as a mechanism for the exercise of power, Tony Bennett contrasts Bourdieu with Foucault. He seeks to identify how their approaches can complement each other but suggests that Foucault's governmentality approach to the relations between culture and the social exposes shortcomings in Bourdieu's concepts of field, cultural capital and the habitus.

Bennett claims that Bourdieu fails to meet the challenges that Foucault's assumptions pose for his concepts of field and habitus. Regularities and irregularities in the field of discourse, and the discontinuities in historical analysis, cannot be treated as relational struggles for profits or cumulative historicity, respectively. *Contra* Bourdieu's account of the unified construction of the habitus, Foucault's formulation of the technologies of the self and the technologies of power produces pluralized spaces and practices of self-formation, which result in a self with divisions and cracks produced by the varied techniques of subjectification through which different authorities work to order the self. Bourdieu's attribution of universal validity to the roles of the economy and the social in affecting the cultural is further challenged by Foucault's principle of historically specific 'transactional realities'. The ordering of 'transactional realities', historically informed and produced through governmental practices, reveals gender and ethnicity to be elements in governing, not 'add-ons' to the primacy of class relations.

While Foucault and Bourdieu appear closer in their perspectives concerning the roles of cultural knowledge in distinctive forms of power, Bennett remarks that the unity of action derived from a pre-given structure based on class relations, implicit in Bourdieu's logic of the 'space of possibles', does not resonate with Foucault's account of the dispersal of discursive options that informs his account of the field of 'strategic possibilities'. The position-taking of actors in social space that informs Bourdieu's 'space of possibles' rests, contrary to Bourdieu's own account, on a quite different logic. On the basis of his comparison, Bennett suggests that cultural-capital theory can itself be viewed as a specific form of cultural governmentality that is only too evidently marked by its associations with post-war French cultural and education policies.

Repudiation

Antoine Hennion's contribution is a revision and translation of an earlier article (published in 1985) which reviewed the publication and reception of *Distinction* in France. It continues to have resonance because the nature of Bourdieu's scientific practice continues to arouse controversy today. If Grenfell seeks to establish a sympathetic account of Bourdieu's intellectual practice and analytic strategy, and Swartz depicts its progress through several stages, Hennion seeks to demonstrate that it should be seen instead as a rather complex illusion. When Bourdieu shows pictures of people in their houses, their furniture, clothes and bodily hexis, is he merely appealing to the existing knowledge of his readers? Would not they otherwise fail to find this evidence of Bourdieu's theory, and thus acclaim his theoretical and interpretive achievement? In this lies the sleight of hand which is associated with his strategy of pretending that people do not know – they misrecognize – what they patently already do know. Hennion's is a somewhat characteristically Gallic polemic – ironic, intriguing, elliptical, teasing. He seems to suggest that since the public can only be constructed from a series of practical activities which are inevitably the province of intermediaries, the process of that construction is something that should be made transparent. The rhetorical component of Bourdieu's works is evident in his setting up the social world as a stage upon which, behind a drawn curtain, order and structure are established, subsequently to be revealed to applause by an audience enthralled by the clever exposure by the sociologist/director of the plot after the curtain rises. Drawing a parallel between the producer or manager of an aspiring young pop star, he illustrates the parallel involved in Bourdieu's acting as intermediary in the revelation of the order of the world as universal knowledge to a section of society whose understanding is nothing but partial. The promise or hope that the public (or an authentic popular public) can be reached out to is denied by the very techniques which intercede in the quest to engage it.

Hennion's reading and critique of Bourdieu's work sets out his own espousal of a theory of knowledge of 'theoretical theatricality' to argue, against Bourdieu, that science is not pure and that it is stage-managed. He suggests that it is essential to find the intermediary in the process of knowing people – or the popular – in culture.

The ways in which Bourdieu's work has generated new questions is particularly evident in Michèle Lamont's account. As the 'outsider within', over a number of years Lamont applied Bourdieu's work in the different and more diverse national context of the United States. We asked her to reflect on her academic journey. She remarks upon the early impact of Bourdieu's engagement with micro-level social relationships and roles in daily interactions as not separated from the symbolic violence of material world or aesthetics. Lamont's national comparative perspective led her to emphasize the fit between context and cultural object. Resonating with some of Sayer's concerns she asks in which conditions value is created.

Lamont's critical stance towards Bourdieu has produced new thinking in two main areas. Firstly, examining classification systems comparatively and *in situ*, she questioned the applicability of *Distinction* to the US. Was command of high culture central for high status everywhere? Empirically her work has addressed differences between cultural centre and cultural periphery, the permeability of group boundaries, the relationship between social and symbolic boundaries, that differentiation does not translate into exclusion, and that available cultural repertoires and macro-structures shape the habitus as well as orientations to culture. Secondly, moving further from Bourdieu, she investigated the role of moral values in boundary production, with ethno-racial boundaries a principal concern. She offered an innovative analysis of the production of boundaries in taste and the creation of differences and worth using cross-national comparisons to expose competing criteria of evaluation. Latterly, applied to the academic field, she elaborates on the social and emotional aspects associated with judgement in processes of rule formation.

The sheer range of responses to Bourdieu's work represented in the essays in this book makes clear the difficulty associated with delivering a decisive evaluation of his legacy. Appealing arguments are made for a comprehensive embrace of his framework, for its use as a source of inspiration to be worked against, and for its abandonment. Partly because intellectual relationships with Bourdieu are so varied and contested, we invited Frédéric Lebaron and Fiona Devine to reflect on the essays in this volume in order to provide additional insights into his overall contribution. Their wise observations precede a short epilogue which summarizes some of the factors likely to affect Bourdieu's influence on the subsequent development of sociological approaches to cultural analysis.

Notes

1 The Collège de France is not a university but functions as the crowning of university careers.
2 The project was funded from March 2003 to February 2006 by the ESRC (Award no R000239801). Many papers and a book were published from this project: see Bennett, *et al.* (2009) and Chapter 5 in this book. The project's website address is: http://www. open.ac.uk/socialsciences/cultural-capital-and-social-exclusion/project-summary. php?

2 Working with *habitus* and *field*

The logic of Bourdieu's practice

Michael Grenfell

This chapter comprises four main sections and offers a positive appraisal of Bourdieu's approach in the light of various applications and criticisms of his work. The first section gives a very brief outline of the influence of Bourdieu in a range of academic fields; for example, education, cultural studies and art. It focuses on the way his conceptual tools emerged and were employed. It then lists in a fairly systematic way what I have termed 'misuses' of Bourdieu; briefly, a range of academic strategies which misinterpret or misapply Bourdieu, and the consequences of each. The third section sketches out the key stages in any Bourdieusian approach to empirical analyses. The aim here is to consider the essential features of theory and practice in Bourdieusian methodology against which various applications may be compared. The chapter is built around an intention to think 'with' Bourdieu. However, the last section aims to extend this approach. Rather than insist on a Bourdieusian orthodoxy, the discussion concludes with a consideration of some of the issues involved in adopting such a method.

This chapter sets itself within a body of my work undertaken over a twenty-five-year period to develop and apply the potential of Bourdieu's theory of practice within a range of social sciences settings: language/sociolinguistics (Grenfell, 1993), linguistics (Grenfell, 2003), teacher education (Grenfell, 1996), education and classroom language (Grenfell, 2004a, 2007), and art and aesthetics (Grenfell and Hardy, 2007). During this period, the place of Bourdieu's work within the academic field has changed: from one of being peripheral, to a general acknowledgement of him having set an agenda that challenges a range of research issues across these fields. The chapter takes a generally positive approach to the work. Clearly, there is much that Bourdieu did not do. However, my concern here is firstly to avoid entering into the sort of discussion so common in the social sciences, one which aims to show what Bourdieu 'fails', 'avoids', 'ignores', 'sidesteps', 'overlooks' to do. Bourdieu's ideas are themselves now part of an academic struggle, which inherently carries the *interests*[1] of those expressing them. Part of what I write relates to the types of strategy common in approaching Bourdieu. There is also illustration of ways in which his concepts have been over-extended. Finally, I set out some guiding principles in undertaking social science research from a Bourdieusian perspective. My approach is not intended to have a go at social science research, but rather to raise issues of reflexivity in challenging the reader to consider their own use of Bourdieu (see also Bourdieu, 2007 [2004]; Grenfell, 2008a: postscript). Before taking these points forward, I want first to consider how Bourdieu's axioms emerged, and secondly the way they have been 'misused' as part of the academic discourse.

Using and misusing Bourdieu

On various occasions, Bourdieu argues for a 'sociogenetic' reading of his work (for example, 1993c). Here, he emphasizes the need to place what he has written within the social context of its production in order to avoid a 'de-historic' reading of his publications. It is difficult to overestimate the impact of the socio-historic climate on the emergence of Bourdieu's methodological approach: most noticeably, in the Béarn and in Algeria (see Grenfell, 2006). Both contexts furnished Bourdieu with examples of societies in transition – the contrast between traditional communities and the modern (urban) world – and the resultant social suffering to which this gave rise. Bourdieu's early ethnography, or social philosophy, was preoccupied with the nature and consequences of change as it affected the two regions with which Bourdieu was most intimately connected (arguably, the same preoccupation inspired *La misère du monde* (1999d [1993]) thirty years later). Primary, empirical, personal experience was therefore at the core of Bourdieu's interpretations in these early field studies, and fundamental to the formation of his ideas. Indeed, some decades later he wrote of the personal 'revolution' in thinking that was required on his part to see the world (and thus understand it) from the perspective of the Algerian worker (2000a). He approached the two major topics of his studies in the 1960s – education and culture – with a similar need to *break* with standard inter-pretations of them as social phenomena. This 'rupture with the pre-constructed' is described as the main motive for studying and publishing analyses on Algeria, and in order to elucidate a topic that was poorly understood by the majority of French men and women (see Bourdieu and Grenfell, 1995: 4). Similarly, his work on edu-cation came partly from a wish to understand 'what it was to be a student' (ibid.), itself part of a self-objectification of academic life. However, these studies were also mounted against a background of intense intellectual debate in the immediate post-war period in France. Existentialism and Structuralism were the dominant trends, and both came under the influence of Soviet Marxism and Communist theory in a climate which sought to establish an alternative to both Fascism and Capitalism. An appreciation of this background is important for any subsequent use of Bourdieu's method.

It is clear that Bourdieu was active in dialogues with various political groups and individuals at the time; for example, his involvement with conferences such as the 'Week of Marxist Thought' (9–15 March 1966) and the *Cercle Noroit* (June 1965) (see for example 2008 [2002]: 34). These set out to address issues surrounding the social transformations which had taken place in France and elsewhere since the Second World War; in particular, the unequal distribution of profits and sharing which had resulted in these changes. The logical conclusion arising from these debates was that education could be an instrument of change, if not liberation.

However, Bourdieu's work on education also focused on the significant role that cultural elements played as an implicit arbitrator of what was and was not acceptable (and thinkable) in scholastic discourse; hence, his other main topic of research in the 1960s – culture. His subsequent work on museums, photography and taste (Bourdieu, *et al.*, 1990a [1965], Bourdieu, *et al.*, 1990b [1966]) also implied questions about the liberating potential of culture: an issue that is particularly pertinent in France with its strong traditions of *éducation permanente, personalism* and *maisons de la culture* (see Grenfell, 2004b: Chapters 3 and 4). The idea of 'culture' as the vehicle for personal emancipation was also to become a popular notion in Britain in educational writings in the 1970s and 1980s where alternative cultural forms were held up as equal, valid and valued, and (somewhat under the influence of Gramscian Marxism), as a challenge to a dominant culture, which was seen as essentially hegemonic. Indeed, Bourdieu's academic profile rose significantly at this time through publications on education – *Reproduction* (1977a) and the chapters included in the collected volume *Knowledge and Control* (Young, 1971).

The point I am wishing to emphasize is that Bourdieu's work was, at the same time, both intensely personal and very public: personal, to the extent to which it arose from his own immediate experiences and surroundings; public, in that it addressed the key issues dominating the social discourse of the day. However, Bourdieu's perspective is more than dispositional – it is also methodological. He often makes the point that he 'never theorises as such', but rather developed theoretical statements to explain the relations he saw after deep immersion in empirical data. It was in this way that his key concepts were developed. Thus,

> the concept of *habitus* which was developed as part of an attempt to account for the practices of men and women who found themselves thrown into a strange and foreign cosmos imposed by colonialism, with cultural equipment and dispositions – particularly economic dispositions – acquired in a pre-capitalist world.
>
> (Bourdieu, 2005 [2000]: 2)

A concept such as *habitus* consequently emerged from an empirical engagement with a particular social phenomenon – inductive rather than deductive. Other concepts were formulated in a similar fashion.

> [T]he concept of *cultural capital* which, being elaborated and deployed at more or less the same time as Gary Becker was putting into circulation the vague and flabby notion of 'human capital' (a notion heavily laden with sociologically unacceptable assumptions), was intended to account for otherwise inexplicable differences in academic performance with children of unequal cultural patrimonies and, more generally, in all kinds of cultural or economic practices; the concept of *social capital* which I had developed, from my earliest ethnographical work in Kabylia or Béarn, to account for residual differences, linked, broadly speaking, to the resources which can be brought together *per procurationem* through the networks of 'relations' of various

sizes and differing density ...; the concept of *symbolic capital*, which I had to construct to explain the logic of the economy of honour and 'good faith' and which I have been able to clarify and refine in, by and for the analysis of the economy of symbolic goods, particularly of works of art; and lastly, and most importantly, the concept of *field*, which has met with some success.

(Ibid.)

A key point to note here is that, methodologically, Bourdieu's approach sees social phenomena in terms of *structural relations* – both cognitive and social. Things are understood in terms of their *relational* context – how they acquire sense in relation to their position with respect to other phenomena which share the context (see Bourdieu, 1998b: 3–6). This way of thinking is contrasted, by Bourdieu, with the *substantialist* approach, where things are treated as 'pre-existing entities' – with essential properties. For Bourdieu, 'the real' is relational because reality is nothing other than *structure*, a set of relationships, 'obscured by the realities of ordinary sense-experience' (Bourdieu, 1987: 3). Yet both the empirical and relational aspects of Bourdieu's work are often overlooked by his critics and users.

Misusing Bourdieu

A range of identifiable strategies have been employed in social science research to interpret and critique Bourdieu. Each can be seen as characterizing a specific technique within the academic discourse, and therefore the position of the particular researcher employing such strategies within it.

First, for example, there is what might be called the 'false accusations' based on partial and superficial readings of Bourdieu's work. For instance, his approach is wrongly construed as being deterministic, overly structural, and lacking in the possibility of resistance to socio-cultural hegemonies. Thus, he 'failed'. This argument leads to the charge that there is no scope for change in Bourdieu's theories – which would be true if the original interpretation were true – even though it might well be argued that his theory of practice is all about change.

The second strategy is based around the academic ploy of setting up the one who is to be shot down. The approach here is to give what Bourdieu has written a certain (partial) interpretation and then use that interpretation to show what Bourdieu does not do – leaving the way open for the writer to come to his aid, thus demonstrating his or her own superior insight. This strategy often comes with language which suggests Bourdieu deliberately avoided, overlooked or ignored specific themes chosen as pertinent by the critic. The problem here is that the critic rarely contrasts their own position and substantive intent with Bourdieu's (even in terms of discipline, philosophy, or cultural context), and so dismisses or overlooks anything that does not fit their own interpretative framework.

The third strategy is a form of reductionism. Here, conceptual terms such as 'habitus', 'field' and 'reflexivity' are reduced to 'agency', 'context' and 'self-awareness'. As these latter are common in the social sciences, this argument leads to the claim that Bourdieu does nothing special: what he does, they all do – what he shows, they already know. Thus, the dynamic between these concepts, which is at the centre of a Bourdieusian approach, is underplayed and the methodological potential undermined.

The fourth strategy can really be understood as a form of theoretical and empirical amnesia. Here, the writers claim that what Bourdieu showed is merely something that was always known. For example, the main insights behind *Distinction* are taken to be blindingly obvious: as if an understanding of the social construction of taste predates Bourdieu's studies. This strategy results from an a-temporal reading of his work and what came next, and is exacerbated by the length of time between the publication of texts in French and their subsequent appearance in English (in the case of *Photography*, this was almost 25 years). So, the work is read *out of its time* and subsequent discussions are then used to show where the original 'failed'.

The fifth strategy is rather more prosaic. Here, Bourdieu's key concepts – *habitus*, *field*, for example – are simply thrown at ethnographic data where some of them stick. This strategy is used to give apparent depth and theoretical rigour to the analysis, and as a way of *metaphorizing* the data: simply re-describing social data through Bourdieusian narrative language. For example, the biographical and individual context of social agents are simply presented in terms of their *habitus* and field, without any of the components of a proper 'field analysis' (see below). In this case, Bourdieu is hardly needed at all other than to give the empirical a theoretical gloss.

The sixth strategy extends the prose form to the poetic. Here, the concepts are embroidered and develop hybrid forms. *Habitus* become *field* and *field* becomes *habitus*. There is no distinction between sites, networks, social spaces and fields. Any human attribute can be put in front of habitus: pedagogic, emotional, psychological, organizational, national, and so on. *Capital* similarly proliferates; for example, technological, physical, aesthetic, journalistic, decorative, and managerial. Indeed, many of these terms are sometimes attached to all three – *habitus*, *field* and *capital*. One of the key qualities of Bourdieu's theoretical tools, on the other hand, is that they are kept to a minimum – as necessary and sufficient to the data – and not to be added to when another existing concept is sufficient.

In the seventh strategy, Bourdieu is referenced to in an oblique way; for example, in a footnote, as an academic gesture of acquaintance and comprehensiveness.

And, of course, there is an eighth strategy to be added: for those who believe they are the holders of the true theoretical inheritance and are keen to establish a Bourdieusian orthodoxy as part of his academic legacy. This final strategy is doomed since the concepts will survive only so long as they are used rigorously in academic communities to analyse present day socio-cultural data.

In fact, all of these strategies (and others) are common enough in academia where each scholar is struggling to assert their own interpretation of the social world. Such strategies might be found in connection with critiques of any major (and minor) thinker. Bourdieu is not being singled out for special treatment. However, there is an issue here about *interest*: what is the research that is being written about? How and why is it important? Clearly, there are also questions about politics, activism, and both the how and the why of social science research.

A structured approach

Bourdieu was nervous about any reference to his work which also alluded to 'structure', since he was attempting to distance himself both from structural linguistics, anthropological structuralism and, later, post-structuralism. Nevertheless, he did himself refer to his approach as 'structuralist constructivism' or 'constructivist structuralism' (1989c) to highlight the dynamic of structural relations noted above. *Structure* is important in his theory of practice as it allows for the interplay between the 'subjective' and 'objective' on which the whole approach is based. For Bourdieu, the primary act is one of cognition; that is an individual engaging in their social (material and ideational) environment. The response of social agents is both empirical and naïve at its origin, but increasingly conditioned by the pre-given – what has been experienced before. That internalization, for Bourdieu, is both mental (cognitive) and corporeal – embedded in the *being* of social agents. Bourdieu sought to *break* with this primary empirical state in disclosing the meanings which lie beneath social action. However, this break is itself mounted in terms of further 'breaks' from different forms of knowledge derived from within the philosophical field; namely, subjectivist and objectivist knowledge (see Grenfell, 2004b: 174 for further discussion) – a dichotomy which Bourdieu sees as 'fundamental and 'ruinous' (1990 [1980]: 25). On the one side is the 'objective mode' with its representations of reality as things thrown into sharp relief; on the other is the 'subjective mode', where agents manipulate their self-image in presenting themselves to a world that is experienced as a series of spontaneous events. Bourdieu places Marx and Durkheim on the objective side, and Schütz, Merleau Ponty and phenomenology on the subjective side. Thus, there is, for Bourdieu, a dialectic between the social and the cognitive, which is expressed in and as structural relations. Social and cognitive structures are always seen as being both *structuring* and *structured*. This issue is central to Bourdieu's thinking since, in effect, it represents a struggle over our very perceptions of the social world, and is therefore pertinent to both the object of research and to the researcher investigating it. It is an issue which permeates all aspects of his research practice and underpins his methodology. Next, I consider the key aspects of that methodology in terms of three key conterminus stages:

1   the construction of the research object;
2   a three-level approach to field study;
3   participant objectivation.

I shall say something on each of these stages.

1 The construction of the research object

As noted, much of Bourdieu's work needs to be understood as an attempt to break with the pre-given. This is as true for the example of Algeria as a nation-state as it is for the role of education, aesthetic taste, and the freedom of neo-liberal economics.

In each case, an accepted practice, form or concept is deconstructed in terms of the structured dynamic that Bourdieu finds in his empirical analyses. But, as I have argued above, these analytical representations are not simply descriptions of primary everyday reality. They are also conveyed in a specific language: conceptual terms, theories, rationales. There is consequently a struggle over what terms, or language, are adopted in representing the object of study: Which version? And what do such terms implicitly include and exclude? A crucial first responsibility of the would-be social science researcher is therefore *the construction of the research object*. Indeed, Bourdieu refers to the construction of the research object as 'the summum of the art' (1989c) of social science. He does not accept that the weight of a particular research tradition can be judged simply in terms of the importance of its objects of study; indeed, he argues that some of the most important objects of study have been dealt with using very poor academic approaches. His alternative is to 'begin again': to scrutinize the research object in terms of how its field of study represents it – What are its keys terms? What are the dominant explanatory concepts, rationales and theories? What academic traditions represent it? Whilst doing this reconstruction, the research object is reconceptualized in relational terms. The question is then: what are the best terms to represent this relational construction? Clearly, this is where concepts such as *habitus* and *field* are useful. Sometimes, a change in language of representation is crucial to *re-viewing* a particular research object. At one point, Bourdieu does in fact warn the would-be researcher to 'beware of words' (Bourdieu and Wacquant, 1989: 54) because of the way they are the repository of all sorts of 'historical assumptions' (ibid.), silent confusions, impositions, and academic interests. The very language of the constructed object of research is therefore scrutinized for these embedded meanings. Making the 'normal' conspicuous, and examining the mundane and banal, were further important parts of the construction of a 'scientific object', giving rise to specific forms of questions and enquiries.

Once this stage had been accomplished, Bourdieu's method proceeds in terms of a 'Field analysis'. What is this?

2 A three-level approach to field study

When asked explicitly by Loïc Wacquant (Bourdieu and Wacquant, 1992: 104–7) to sum up this methodological approach, Bourdieu described it in terms of **three distinct levels**:

1   analyse the position of the *field vis-à-vis* the field of power;
2   map out the objective structure of relations between the positions occupied by agents who compete for the legitimate forms of specific authority of which the *field* is a site;
3   analyse the *habitus* of agents; the systems of dispositions they have acquired by internalizing a deterministic type of social and economic condition.

For Bourdieu, society should be understood as 'structured space', and multidimensional in terms of its objective and ideational structures as represented within the social and cognitive. For analytical purposes, however, he draws a distinction between the actual structure of the social system in its multidimensional stratification and the symbolic products which arise from it: 'In reality, the space of symbolic stances and the space of social positions are two independent, but homologous, spaces' (1994 [1987]: 113). Bourdieu describes his method as attempting to reconstruct the *space of differences*, or differential positions, and only then accounting for these positions in terms of the differential properties (categories) of that social space. Such properties are eventually defined in terms of *capital*: that is, what is symbolically valued. Regions are then 'cut up' to see the operation and the placing – *capital* configurations – of a range of social groupings. These groupings may be of any kind – race, gender, geographical, political, class – although, increasingly in his work, the settings he investigated were conceptualized as *fields* – for example, education, media, politics – as bounded sites of social activity.

At the *first level* of a *field* analysis, the relationships between the *field* and other fields – in particular, the *field* of power – are established. In a way, this is part of the process of the 'construction of the research object', since it considers the structural positioning of the *field* of enquiry within a network of fields. It is also probably one of the most difficult stages to operationalize, since it is at this level that most will have been written (and thus pre-representing the field). There is, consequently, most *interest* in maintaining the orthodox view of its form and function.

At the *second level*, the *field* itself is 'mapped' in terms of its morphology, taxonomy, and the positions occupied within it. Moreover, the symbolic forms of the field *capital* – its currency – are also identified together with their generating logic of practice – defining what is and is not valued in the specific field. Bourdieu further argues that, in his empirical studies, the 'primary' principles of differentiation can be attributed to both the *volume* and the particular *configuration* of (*cultural*, *social* and *economic*) *capital*. Individuals and groups define themselves by how much *capital* they hold and by the balance of capital types within that holding. A further crucial point is how the social trajectories of individuals and groups differentiate themselves from one another. For Bourdieu, a particular 'social class' title as a differentiating principle is, for example, never a 'thing' in itself, but a heuristic used to uncover the generational processes within the social space. The emergence of such a concept has to be a product of method, not its 'starting point'. This approach sets up definitions for social classes 'on paper' which relate to what exists in reality. To the extent to which various individuals hold similar *capital* volumes and configurations (i.e. share material conditions) in conjunction with others, they will constitute a homogeneous, and thus identifiable, group. They thus hold a similar position in the overall structure of the *social space*, and also share similar *habitus* and consequent dispositional characteristics.

In the *third level* of the analysis, it is necessary to analyse actual agents in the field in terms of their *habitus*: background, trajectory and positioning. Here, we are not so much concerned with their individual characteristics and idiosyncrasies as with their attributes in relation to the *field* under study (including its logic of practice and symbolic systems). *Habitus* shapes individual responses (directs individuals) and defines their positions in the *field* in terms of the *capital* they hold.

Bourdieu never presented *field* analyses in terms of these three discrete levels; in much of his work, they are mixed up. However, each level is included. There are various other points to emphasize. Firstly, there is the need to distinguish between *social space, fields*, site contexts and concepts such as 'class', and the relationships between each. Secondly, there is the aforementioned contrast between *social space* and symbolic space. *Social space* is multidimensional and too complex to capture in its totality, even empirically; only the organization of that space and the symbolic positions within it can be mapped. Thirdly, it is necessary to include all aspects of all three levels in *field* analyses. It is not enough to offer an analysis of the *field* in itself; it is crucial that links are made with the (structural) relations between the *field* and other *fields*; for example, the art *field* and the *fields* of politics, commerce, the media, and so on. There is also the question of the direction of analysis: from the relations between *fields* (level 1), to the *field* itself (level 2) and then *habitus* (level 3). This order has the advantage of involving 'the construction of the research object' at an initial conceptual stage and hence removes the possibility of simply over-extrapolating on the basis of biographical data (the product of level 3). It is indeed useful to operate a 'bottom-up' approach to research, and biographical and ethnographic data do allow for inductive analyses. However, in the hands of other researchers, such data are often used simply to create a Bourdieusian-type narrative around what is a straight biographical or ethnographic one. *Field* can even be ignored altogether; whilst the exact interaction between habitus and field – which is crucial to a Bourdieusian analysis – is overlooked. Instead, it is necessary to map the structure of the *field*, its logic of practice, and the principles of differentiation underpinning such logic. Moreover, it is necessary to identify positions within structured *social space* (both within and across *fields*); either organizational and/ or symbolic. Indeed, the homologies between these social dimensions are a critical aspect of understanding field operations.

The concept of *capital – economic, social*, and *cultural* – is available to navigate the *social space* and to identify both the symbolic forms and the defining principles of its value-system. This is why other inventions such as 'institutional habitus' or 'gendered habitus' can be so confusing. They mislead by implying that 'institutions', or universal genders, rather than individuals, have *habitus*, thus conflating the subjective and objective resources of the theory of practice. If we understand institutional habitus as the way that institutions endow certain aspects of habitus on those who pass through it, there is still a methodological and practical confusion. The sources of institutional differences are objective and are therefore to be found in its structured space and the capital forms that are prevalent there – its *cultural capital* – not in the '*habitus*' of the institution. The institutional aspects that any individual's *habitus* carries are therefore best understood as an endowment of what Bourdieu calls 'institutionalized *cultural capital*'. Such *capital* is here a kind of site-specific social incarnation of what is valued in the *field*. We cannot and must not turn *habitus* into *capital* or vice versa.

As noted, Bourdieu's own empirical approach to his research was to begin with an immersion in primary data and the structural relations he encountered there. Here, it is important that there is a particular practical phenomenon, or research question, at the point of initiation in Bourdieu's work – not a conceptual motif or theoretical gloss. He says so quite explicitly on several occasions and, in the Foreword to *Reproduction* (1977 [1970]: xviii), goes out of his way to insist that, although the book is divided into two parts – the first theoretical, and the second empirical – really their provenance should be understood as being the other way around, from practice to theory; in other words, to come up with a set of propositions for the research which were '*logically required* as a ground for its findings' (my emphasis). Here, the mapping of the *social space* precedes the use of concepts – as in the case of 'social class'. The alternative is to put a theoretical cart before an empirical horse, which can lead to both a substantiation and a reification of theoretical tools, and a confusion of what to understand from the results of the study. Bourdieu writes:

> It is because the analyses reported in *Distinction* are read in a realist and substantialist way (as opposed to a relational one) – thus assigning directly this or that property or practice to a 'class', playing soccer or drinking *pastis* to workers, playing golf or drinking champagne to the traditional *grande bourgeoisie* – that I am taken to task for overlooking the specific logic and autonomy of the symbolic order, thereby reduced to a mere *reflection* of the social order. (In other words, once again, the charge of reductionalism thrown at me is based on a reductionist reading of my analyses.
>
> (Bourdieu, 1994 [1987]: 113)

Here, in methodological terms, the relational is again asserted over the substantialist. It may be perfectly possible to create new concepts, but surely this should only occur where an existing one cannot be used, and is necessary from directly observable structural relations identified in data. Anything else amounts to a form of scholastic indulgence which, as well as leading to a confusing and prosaic fragmentation of theoretical tools, undermines the integrity of the original concepts themselves. This point connects with the third principal stage or component of a Bourdieusian methodology: 'Participant objectivation'.

3 *Participant objectivation*

If the 'construction of the research object' is a way of making evident the assumptions, suppositions, and constructions embedded in topics of research, and the ways they are represented and thought about, 'participant objectivation' calls for a similar reflexive process to focus on the individual conducting the research. Such reflexivity is not merely the exaggerated form of self-awareness which has become popular in some social science research in recent decades, especially in its postmodernist leanings. For Bourdieu, this ultra 'self-awareness' is little more than the illusion of the transcendence of thought by thought itself – 'return of thought onto itself' (2000d [1997]: 10) – of the sort of assumed mental omnipotence popular amongst neo-Kantian philosophers. Instead, Bourdieu is interested in an objectification of the social conditions of the thinking which set the limits on thought.

Such an objectification of the 'social conditions' of thinking itself necessarily calls for the objectification of the academic field itself, with all its practical and epistemological biases. The position of the researcher in this social space is consequently critical in understanding what can and cannot be thought in terms of the orthodoxies (*doxa*) of the *field* itself.

Furthermore, researchers, by definition, have 'free time' to develop a different relationship to the world of which they are a part. Bourdieu argues that this position liberates them from the exigencies of acting in certain domains of the empirical world. However, it can also lead to a type of scholastic fallacy where 'the things of logic are confused with the logic of things' (see Bourdieu and Wacquant, 1992: 123). Bourdieu terms this 'free-time' *skholè*, and as analogous to the Kantian 'pure gaze' – the idea that there is a transcendent truth beyond social construction. The only way to avoid this scholastic fallacy is to adopt a reflexive approach to the social sciences. This undertaking entails, firstly, operating an objectification of the object of study: why it was chosen and what brought it about. Such an objectification is particularly important where State sponsorship of research funding influenced outcomes. Secondly, there is the need to position the particular terms of the discipline used in the research; how the object of research is constructed therein and the limits of the terms employed. This objectification also implies an 'epistemological reading' of research. Rather than 'crush one's rivals' through an alternative paradigmatic position, there is the need to read it in *its own terms* or contest those terms with alternatives. Finally, there is the recognition of *skholè*, or leisure, inherent in scholastic *fields*, and its effect in terms of separating out practical from theoretical knowledge. The latter is produced in an academic space which infuses it with the symbolic values, and thus the structures and dispositions dominant within that space (see Grenfell, 2004b, Chapter 7 for further discussion). This form of reflexivity necessarily involves turning the tools of analysis of the research object – in this case, *field, habitus, capital* and others – back on the researchers themselves. Bourdieu argues that this is the only way to partially escape from the social, economic, political, and philosophical determinisms which are necessarily at work in any knowledge field. Few social scientists seem yet to have grasped what Bourdieu intended by reflexivity in his approach, still less how it operates in his work. Very few then seem able to operationalize it for themselves, and yet it is a critical element in his project and the basis of his claim that 'the truth is, truth is at stake' (2001b: 31).

Clearly, Bourdieu sees this type of reflexivity as a *personal* responsibility and, indeed, a necessity rather than an option. However, it is also, and perhaps above all, a *collective* acknowledgement and commitment (the issue being the extent to which a knowledge field is a 'community of truth' or simply an arena for individual competition and contestation). The personal and collective are the subjective and objective ends of the same process. How does he do this? In *Homo Academicus* (1988 [1984]) Bourdieu undertakes a process of objectifying his own academic space (*objective*). However, it was only much later that this process necessitated a public declaration with the inclusion of a *subjective* counterpart in his work, most noticeably brought together in his final lecture at the Collège de France, and the posthumously published *Sketch for a Self-Analysis* (2007 [2004]). This aspect of

Bourdieu's practice should not be considered as a bolt-on, after-the-event undertaking, but as a necessary part of the ongoing research process itself: And one which is disclosed! Not to do this is to accept 'field truth', with all its inherent *interests*, as *the* truth: to misrecognize the interests of the *field* to serve these interests – a kind of act of methodological *mauvaise foi*.

Beyond Bourdieu?

There is a kind of paradox. Setting out these guiding methodological principles as above might be seen as a form of prescription, as a way of imposing a Bourdieusian orthodoxy. Indeed, there can be a kind of intellectual totalitarianism about Bourdieu's sociology, since it seems to suggest that it should be adopted in its totality if it is going to work. This aspect is clearly antithetical to an intellectual process which favours a certain form of synthetic eclecticism. Yet, at the same time, caution also needs to be exercised in *making too much* of Bourdieu. Earlier, I wrote of the dangers of treating his concepts in too broad a manner. I suggested that this *metaphorizing* of data amounted to little more than embroidering them with various conceptual terms, which leads to a weak form of constructivism. Here, a conceptual term is simply imposed on a piece of data and allowed to speak for itself, giving it a prosaic rather than an analytical meaning. For example, to extend his concepts to the sphere of emotions moves from the representation of dispositions formed from positions in the social space to individual psychologies. We need to note that Bourdieu was always careful to distinguish between sociology and psychology, and it is arguable that it was only in his later work that he began to explore the psychological possibilities of his approach. See, for example, his comments on the 'clinical' possibilities of his work (2000c) and his account of the father-son relationship in the *Weight of the World* (1999d [1993]: 508). Here, he shows how the 'unconscious desire' of the family to reproduce itself can lead to a 'burden of inheritance' for offspring. The son is consequently caught in the 'double bind' of satisfying his father's expectation of inheritance and lineage, while defining his own 'being in the world' – whether to preserve his father's genealogical 'project' or to define his own. Such is a structural analysis of the effects of *conatus* (see Fuller, 2008 for further discussion). However, if all we do is to change emotions into 'emotional capital', what we are in effect doing is again to confuse the subjective and the objective. Emotional responses may well be dispositional (subjective), and clearly, they are passed on between parent and child. However, *capital* is a *field* concept (objective), valued and operational in the *field* which is its medium of operation. The whole point of Bourdieu's approach is to avoid dichotomising between the subjective and objective. Yet, if emotions are indeed 'capital' – valued resources (for example, support, patience, commitment) – one needs to ask in what *fields* (and which logic of practice) these operate and carry symbolic value in terms of position taking and how they link with other *fields*. What is necessary, rather, is a teasing out of the exact structural relations between individual dispositions, their actions, and the structure of the *field* – including its dominant logic of practice and forms of *capital* – and how this can be traced back to the *field* of power.

A further paradox involves the very language of these concepts. If we are going to use them, we should at least use them accurately and within a methodology that is congruent with the type of practical approach that gave rise to them in the first place. Yet, as noted, on more than one occasion Bourdieu did warn the would-be researcher to 'beware of words'. Part of the role of Bourdieusian language is indeed to provide a vehicle for this new way of seeing the world – what he referred as *metanoia*, or a 'new gaze' (Bourdieu and Wacquant, 1992: 251) and, in this chapter, I have emphasized the way his concepts were formed in the intensity of analyses collected in empirical settings. To this extent, they are not just a 'useful theoretical toolkit' but 'epistemologically charged' matrices which carry with them a range of theoretical perspectives – philosophies, sociologies, anthropologies – in an integrated fashion. One function they have is to *make the world strange* and bring the mundane into analytical discourse. They offer a language which breaks with everyday language – the empirical – but also one which challenges the orthodox terms of academic discourse – the scientific. In doing so, they provide a consensual point of reference or focus for those working within this paradigm. Indeed, terms like *habitus*, *field*, and *capital* might similarly be considered as *a language of association* (what the philosopher Richard Rorty would term a 'final' vocabulary), which collectively might offer the bases for what Bourdieu referred to as the *libido sciendi universel* – itself a constitution of a 'corporatism of the universal' – the *raison d'être* of which has to be ultimately political. Yet, Bourdieusian language itself can also ensnare. Just as there is little to be gained in proving Bourdieu 'right' or 'wrong', to adopt his own terms of analysis too easily is to pass over the essential empirical process of relational construction. Bourdieu's world view is after all his own: a French intellectual, born in the twentieth century, acting to understand the world that surrounded him at that time. Why should we want to interpret our own world through his lens and language? Why indeed? It would be a sorry situation were Bourdieu himself to become more important, or of more interest, than the objects of research themselves, or if concepts always intended to be relational were substantiated – ironically, the very opposite to Bourdieu's intent. To this extent, it may be as well to take a step back from the key concepts themselves and to again consider the 'theory of practice' which underpins them. Such a move would require a re-reading – and possibly reinterpretation – of the philosophies which justified it in the first place. We need to work with Bourdieu – but *without* Bourdieu. Rather than making the concepts too rigid or too malleable, we might return to empirical questions of research construction and the sorts of philosophies of science which might help us build on Bourdieu's methodological legacy.

Any such endeavour will, however, amount to little if the practical agenda does not include an engagement with issues of reflexivity and the reflexive researcher, which are so central to a Bourdieusian approach. Bourdieu himself anticipated the cries of outrage that will go up if the standard 'rules' of a field are called into question, together with the *interests* they serve. For example, with respect to taste and culture, belief in transcendent aesthetics can be abandoned only at the personal cost of 'symbolic capital' (a little like the academic act of disclosure mentioned above). That is why it is simply easier, and serves more *interests*, to maintain a commitment to what Bourdieu calls 'Heideggerian-Hölderlinian revelations' (1996a [1992]: 1), with their faith in 'miraculous virtues', 'pure interest' and 'pure form'. A consequence of this position is that it is, in fact, simply easier (and a useful academic ploy) to show what Bourdieu did not do and where and how he 'failed' than to develop a substantive alternative. This approach to using Bourdieu will always exist in a field where individual academic status is prioritized over 'knowledge communities', and will continue so long as the interests of this research field are not objectified as part of a reflexive method. Bourdieu's alternative is to argue for the provision of social conditions which will allow for what he terms 'rational dialogue', or a *Realpolik of reason* (see, for example, Bourdieu (1999b: 226ff.) and (1998b [1994]: 139, 144)), to describe the social conditions necessary for the exercise of reason, albeit of Bourdieu's practical, reflexive form.

There is much that Bourdieu *did not do*. Some of his work was clearly only introductory. For example, his comments on the relations between function and form in individual art objects, and the potential for 'objective art' through an application of his reflexive method on the part of artists themselves (see Grenfell and Hardy, 2007: Chapters 7 and 8 for further discussion). What Bourdieu *did do* was offer a method to develop a sociological interpretation of social processes in flux, of which culture and art were a part. This project should not be seen as a sociological deconstruction of art and culture, but more as a complementary social analysis of them in terms of 'trans-historical fields' (i.e. social spaces which extend over time, whose outward forms evolve whilst retaining their own characteristic logic of practice) and the 'expressive impulses' (of individual dispositions) (1993c: 188) to be found within them. For Bourdieu, the 'cultural arbitrary' was just that – arbitrary. However, although arbitrary, it was logical in terms of the (practical) interests it served – the nature of which it is the business of social science to disclose. He further argued that such a mission is perhaps more reassuring than the leap of faith that is required for the belief in talent and aesthetic uniqueness (the latter itself homologous with expressions by those from a certain section of the social space to legitimize their own dominance and supremacy). By extension, what is at stake in terms of approach and method is certainly of greater importance than the strategies of a particular sub-section of the academic field based around their own individual *scholastic libido* and *interests* – the 'dominated of the dominant' (see Bourdieu, 1989a): i.e. those forming part of the dominant social groups but dominated within the overall *field* of power because of lack of autonomy; for example, intellectuals and academics. The potential of Bourdieu's method is rather to define an alternative approach and a different form of scientific knowledge – one which ultimately has practical, political consequences. This mission was central to Bourdieu's own endeavours and surely remains one worth fighting for.

Note

1   It is my personal practice to put Bourdieu's key concepts (with their implied epistemological bases) in italics in order to differentiate them from the common, everyday sense of the words.

3 'Cooking the books' of the French gastronomic field

Rick Fantasia

Insofar as he was less a High Priest of social theory than a Master Craftsman of social research, Pierre Bourdieu's analytical legacy should properly be understood in terms of its ability to uncover the logic and practice of particular social worlds. In this chapter, the universe of French gastronomy is considered as a distinctive field of practices. Drawing upon Bourdieu's analytical methods I seek to demonstrate in a schematic (rather than systematic) way, the changing logic of the field of gastronomic practices in France. To do so I trace key aspects of its changing organizational structure and forms of representation through the two crucial periods of its development. In the first I outline the process by which the gastronomic field developed as an autonomous domain in the latter decades of the nineteenth century, achieving a sufficient coherence of practices, institutions, and representations to sustain itself as a distinctive social field. The second traces the process of erosion of that autonomy a century later, pointing to the new institutional arrangements and relations that have emerged to keep it afloat.

By 'field' we refer to a distinctive social microcosm that carries its own characteristic practices, rules, forms of authority and standards of evaluation (Bourdieu and Wacquant, 1992: 101–2). As Bourdieu asserted and demonstrated, a field is a structured space of positions that is, at once, a field of *force* operating upon those within it, and equally a field of *struggles* through which social agents act to preserve or transform the distribution of resources within it. Fields are, as one key practitioner has put it: 'historical constellations that arise, grow, change shape, and sometimes wane or perish, over time' that emerge with a certain degree of *autonomy*, which is essentially the capacity to insulate itself from external influences and to uphold its own criteria of evaluation over and against those of neighboring or intruding fields (Wacquant, 1998).

Roots of a French gastronomic field

In her analysis of the genesis of gastronomy as a cultural field in the nineteenth century, Priscilla Ferguson (1998) places gastronomic literature at its very foundation. She argues that through gastronomic writers (Grimod de la Reynière, Carême, Brillat-Savarin) as well as through dominant literary figures from other cultural domains who wrote about gastronomy (Balzac in literature and Fourier in philosophy), the emergent 'gastronomic field' received symbolic fortification from more firmly established cultural fields. Thus with gastronomic writing accepted as good literature, the emergent gastronomic field acquired a measure of cultural legitimacy. Brillat-Savarin played a particularly important role in this process, according to Ferguson, because unlike most of the food writing produced by journalists and chefs, his was a non-instrumental viewpoint and his writing transcended the domain of gastronomy, placing it 'within a larger intellectual and social universe':

> For Brillat-Savarin, the text was its own end, a status hardly altered by the few recipes included in the work. The often noted stylistic qualities of the *Physiology of Taste* – the anecdotal mode, the witty tone, the language play – give this work an almost palpable literary aura.
>
> (Ferguson, 1998: 616–17)

Ferguson's focus on literature in the emergence of the gastronomic field is insightful, but we might add two notes of caution. The first has to do with limiting a social analysis of the gastronomic field to literary practices alone. While literature was undoubtedly crucial in creating a symbolic foundation for the gastronomic field, in the ways that have been indicated and as Ferguson has shown, a fuller grasp of the social logic of the field would seem to require that the means of its symbolic construction be conjoined to a broader range of social practices.

The second hesitation has to do with the relations between fields, and in particular with Ferguson's idea that the relative strength of a field (its 'cultural resonance' and 'cultural resistance' in her terms) is a function of its dependence on its connections to other cultural fields (or in relation to the 'larger society' in her words) (ibid.: 602). Despite the fact that this would need to be demonstrated empirically and not simply asserted, one would expect the strength of a field to rest not so much on its dependence on other fields as on the degree of relative autonomy it enjoys *from* other fields. In other words, its strength would seem to reside in its ability to operate in terms of its own proper rules and principles of regulation and on its own internal evaluative criteria. Its autonomy ensures a certain fortification in relation to principles of evaluation and regulation introduced from other fields, such as in various cultural fields (U.S. cinema, for example) where the governing rules and principles have been increasingly superseded, if not overwhelmed, by the standards imposed by the economic field.

While in the early stages of its formation gastronomy may indeed have acquired a level of social prestige through the links it was able to forge with more established fields, such as literature and philosophy, as it has gained a certain autonomy (the phase of what Ferguson terms 'consolidation'), it has come to assert itself as something more than a branch of either, and therein lies its strength as a field. Its capacity to maintain and assert its own rules and its own standards of evaluation over and above those of competing or neighboring or dominant fields is the effective source of its power in the society. Of course the independence of a field is always relative and a function of its historical trajectory (whereby fields come to be located hierarchically, in relation to one another) but achieving independence does not consign a field to 'the cultural equivalent of solitary confinement' as Ferguson fears. On the contrary, it can be viewed as a measure of its maturation.

Over the first half of the nineteenth century, Brillat-Savarin's meditations on taste, the body and the aesthetics of food; Grimod de la Reynière's symbolic construction of a French 'public' for restaurants; and the chef Antonin Carême's celebration of the culinary arts, taken together, can be seen as having symbolically constructed the foundation for a distinctive design for living, the 'art of eating well,' whereby the act of properly nourishing the body simultaneously accomplishes the proper nourishment of the soul. It was a form of perception that, among other things, abandoned the traditional dietetic/medicinal principles of cooking that had governed culinary practice for several hundred years, in favor of a kind of pure gastronomic aesthetic, a stance equivalent to that of 'art for art's sake' that emerged contemporaneously in the fields of artistic practice (Bourdieu, 1996a [1992]: esp. Part I, Chapter 1 and Bourdieu, 1993c: Chapter 5). In the seventeenth century the fine arts borrowed the metaphor of *taste* from the culinary domain, where it had long been central to the dietetic principle, because taste is what determined the age and toxicity of foodstuffs, and served to match specific foods to the temperament and the body of the individual (Flandrin, 1999: 429). It can be seen as having been part of a process of symbolic labor through which the *gastronome* became distinguished from (and elevated above) the *gourmand*. As Ferguson recounts, we see constructed the discriminating *connoisseur*, raised to 'the lofty position of high priest for this new cult,' the *gastronome* was thereby discursively differentiated from the sinful and indulgent *gourmand*, the glutton who 'only knows how to ingest' (Ferguson, 1998: 608–9). The development of a pure gastronomic disposition was an expression of a distinctive 'art of living,' the basic aspiration of all acts of cultural distinction and a (barely) misrecognized assertion of bourgeois dominance in the society. As Bourdieu has put it:

> At stake in every struggle over art there is also the imposition of an art of living, that is, the transmutation of an arbitrary way of living into the legitimate way of life which casts every other way of living into arbitrariness.
>
> (Bourdieu, 1984 [1979])

Thus was *haute cuisine* elevated by an ethos of 'cuisine for cuisine's sake', a kind of 'pure gastronomic aesthetic' in which the sublime (in the act of consumption) was posed against the practical task of 'cooking to eat' (as a biological necessity). A complement to this process unfolded within the realm of production, as the artistry of culinary creation achieved dominance over cooking as a commercial practice.

The conquest of autonomy

If the symbolic construction of the field of French gastronomy took place over the course of the first half of the nineteenth century, its material infrastructure was largely put into place in the decades of the second half. Although French scientists had made crucial advances in food preservation techniques (including

Pasteur's discoveries of the scientific bases of food sterilization that served as the foundation) the fact that France was a heavily agricultural society, with southern growing seasons that lasted virtually year-round, meant that the institutional foundations for industrial food processing were developed more slowly in France than elsewhere (Pedrocco, 1999: 487–8). Throughout Europe, advances in food production, processing, preservation, distribution, and storage were underway, but rapid urbanization and population growth generated requirements for food production that could not be met by European agricultural capacity alone, thereby creating an opening for American firms. Aided by technical innovations in refrigeration techniques, American firms successfully entered the European market during an agricultural depression of 1873 with exports of substantial quantities of fresh and processed foods. The mass production of preserved foods began in the 1860s in the U.S., where canning factories developed rapidly with the outbreak of the Civil War and companies like Campbell and Heinz and Borden had success with advertising techniques that would come to be employed in Europe (ibid.: 489). Once Europe's agricultural crisis lifted, European agricultural interests were able to compete against U.S. industry, but its facility with industrial and commercial techniques in the food preservation industry implanted the 'American model' in the domain of food ways, a fixture synonymous with the industrial logic of efficiency, high volume, and standardization, the very embodiment of industrial modernity.

It was a model that introduced a thin fissure into the gastronomic domain that would later be expanded. On one side stood entrepreneurs, managers, and industrialists, seeking to maximize profit and expand their enterprises. On the other stood professional chefs, who responded to the industrial imperative (toward large-scale enterprise, product standardization, and routinization and de-skilling of the labor process) in a way that resembled that of skilled artisans everywhere, namely by a collective defense of their trade. Thus, the latter decades of the nineteenth century were punctuated by small shopkeepers and artisans in the traditional *métiers d'alimentation* (including *chefs de cuisine, cuisiniers, pâtissiers, boulangers, traiteurs*) increasingly organizing themselves into trade union associations (*chambres syndicales*) in response to the installation of large food-processing plants in the outskirts of Paris, several of which employed close to two thousand workers (Trubeck, 2000: 81).

The professional chef and the industrial manager represented social actors pursuing divergent career paths and embodying sharply different values and aesthetic dispositions with regard to food and to cuisine. Within the emerging gastronomic field were distinctive, even opposing, institutional milieux, each with its own logic of practice, each drawing into its orbit those predisposed to it, and each represented by key social agents who can be seen as having embodied these emerging divisions.[1] Thus, representative of the one side was Auguste Corthay, an industrialist who had formerly been a chef to the Italian royal family, and who had come to extol the modern virtues of preserved food ('Daily, the great factories will deliver tasty, freshly prepared and cooked food at very low prices. It will be the start of a new century!'); whose book, *La conserve alimentaire*, was published in four editions between 1891 and 1902 and whose magazine of the same title was published continuously from 1903 to 1914 (Corthay, 1902; Capatti, 1999: 495). Corthay might be regarded as the industrial counterpart to the gastronomes of the previous century.

Whereas Brillat-Savarin had presented a series of philosophic and aesthetic 'meditations' on taste, the senses, the preparation of meals, the social character of dining, the table, and the body, Corthay offered up a disquisition on the practical methods of food processing and conservation, with recipes geared not to the senses so much as to industrial preparation and preservation. Only secondarily concerned with the taste of the food, Corthay's recipes emphasized the proper amount of water, salt, sugar, oil, or carbonate of soda added to the various steamed vegetables, or fruit *confit*, or canned fish or meats that were laid out in his 473-page compendium of industrial food ways. A connoisseur of haute cuisine would have seen the work as a gastronomic abomination, a meditation on tastelessness that deliberately and explicitly eschewed the skill of the chef/artisan in favor of the industrial machine and its practical possibilities. Corthay's book (1902), subtitled *Traité Practique de Fabrication*, eulogized the machinery of industrial production and emphasized practical matters of quantity (weights, amount of produce – high volume being the objective of industrial production). Simultaneously a practical industrial manual and a celebratory reflection on the practical virtues of industrial technique, Corthay's book placed both visual and narrative emphasis on the organization of the industrial kitchen and on the production machinery of production deployed within it (including presentation of adoring images of the factory-kitchen and of food-processing machinery).

On the other side of the emerging divide between industrial food processing and the culinary arts stood the renowned chef, Georges Auguste Escoffier. His classic *Guide Culinaire* first appeared in 1902, and he came to personify French *haute cuisine* through mid-century, a period when its symbolic imprint was perhaps most pronounced. His book remains a central text in the training of professional chefs, while Escoffier continues to occupy a prominent place in the pantheon of *haute cuisine*, a legacy marked as much by his contribution to the organization of the modern restaurant kitchen as by the considerable culinary artistry he displayed within it (Mennell, 1996: 157). For generations, Escoffier's finely honed artisan skills and refined aesthetic sensibilities represented the model for all *grand chefs* of haute cuisine. He stood on the one side of the emergent division in the gastronomic field where culinary practice represented an art; with the industrial values of mechanization, standardization, time-thrift, and labor-saving techniques resting on the other (Capatti, 1999: 496).

The emergence of an industrial cuisine in the latter decades of the nineteenth century no doubt helped to delimit and to define the artisanship of the culinary arts. The professional chef was placed at the very center of the emerging gastronomic universe, as artist and artisan in contrast to the industrial practitioners of industrial cuisine, to be sure, but also as specifically *male* artisans distinct from the female purveyors of *domestic* cuisine. That is, the elevation of the professional chef was also accomplished through a necessarily hierarchical social differentiation of the culinary practices of the chef from 'mere' everyday domestic cookery performed by housewives (Swinbank, 2002). This required boring into powerful cultural bedrock that held women to be the *gardiennes du feu* and considered culinary talent a matter of female nature rather than of human cultural practice, with *haute cuisine* confronting such gender mythology by representing itself as a thing apart (and above).[2]

Supporting these transformations over the course of the same period, the increasing mechanization of publishing made possible the publication of numerous culinary journals that both aided the process of social differentiation and reflected it. There were at least twelve culinary journals founded in France between 1870 and 1900, intended either for men involved in professional cooking practice or for women engaged in food preparation or household management (Trubeck, 2000: 83). One such journal, *L'Art Culinaire*, played a particularly significant historical role in placing the chef at the center of the gastronomic field. Founded by chefs in 1883 as the journal of the *Société des Cuisiniers Français*, it was considered the leading professional journal of the day, devoted to the everyday concerns of the chef profession (with articles on qualities of various foodstuffs, on the techniques of food preparation, and on a variety of questions related to the art and science of cooking; as well as on occupational matters, such as the training of cooks and the system of apprenticeships). In contrast to other leading culinary journals, it cultivated a distinctive readership, the professional male chef (ibid.: 85). While various prominent chefs contributed as well, the recipes and menus of Auguste Escoffier were found in almost every issue of *L'Art Culinaire* and by 1890 the journal had put him well on the way to becoming the most influential chef of the Third Republic (Mennell, 1996: 174). Escoffier's rise to prominence can be seen as having marked the triumph of the professional chef in the struggle to achieve a certain 'jurisdiction' over the kitchen, but also in the triumph of the chef of the restaurant (and hotel) kitchen over the managers of both industrial and domestic kitchens.

While Escoffier played a key role in elevating the professional chef in symbolic terms, he was also responsible for institutionalizing the modern organization of the professional kitchen. With the opening of the Savoy Hotel in London in 1889 under the direction of César Ritz, Escoffier was provided with a stage upon which to work his culinary and organizational magic, thereby permanently shifting the main venue of *haute cuisine* from the upper-class household to the gastronomic restaurant; in this case to the kitchens of the luxury hotels that were opening throughout Europe. No longer were chefs mere glorified household servants, but they could now aspire to commanding spaces of their own making, spaces with an international visibility that Escoffier had helped secure for French *haute cuisine* (Dornenburg and Page, 2003: 8; Mennell, 1996: 179; Trubeck, 2000: 48).

All the important marks of professional accomplishment, major awards of recognition, and the rites of institution that would truly *matter* within the field of gastronomic practices revolved around the practices of professional chefs, their associates, and the institutions closest to them. That is, according to the evaluative criteria composed from within this universe, it would be chefs, their restaurants and their creations that would represent the principal objects of veneration, rather than the purveyors of industrial cuisine ('food service professionals' as they might be called today) for their products or processes, or indeed the family recipes and home-cooked meals prepared by the (mostly female) cooks of the domestic household.

The latter decades of the nineteenth century thus saw the consolidation of French gastronomy as a distinctive domain that was increasingly acquiring its own rules, regulations, institutional forms, and developing its own proper standards and methods of evaluation. The measure of autonomy achieved by the gastronomic field had its *social* expression in the dominance of the professional chef in the restaurant and hotel kitchen. It was increasingly a social world unto itself, having defined itself through a process of social conquest in which the professional chef had come to hold sway, a sphere dominated by men and not women (therefore a cuisine distinguished apart from the cuisine of the private household) and a cuisine that had been symbolically elevated above industrial process, and therefore a victory for professional chefs over their industrial counterparts. Thus the scale of valuation that became established in this world was one that was constructed not between craft and industry, as in the rest of the industrializing world where the skilled artisan was everywhere forced to defend his position and his traditional craft prerogatives against the encroachment of mechanized standardization and its insidious deskilling effect. Rather, the practice of the chef had come to occupy the space between art and craft, a scale of valuation that redounded to the enhancement of the position of professional chef.

Neither the centrality of the grand chef nor the transcendental quality of *haute cuisine* as a cultural object would have been possible without a system for the production and reproduction of *belief* in the virtuosity of the chef and the cultural meaning of *haute cuisine*. A proper analysis of the production of belief in French gastronomy would require systematic attention to those social agents (individual and institutional) collectively engaged in the production of this belief, including the various gastronomic guides; the trade journals and magazines; the journalists and the food critics; the foundations; the museums and monuments, including both the established figures and the rebels; the consecrators and the critics, from the more influential to the more marginal, as well as attention to the sources of social power that make them so. While these social actors may appear entirely peripheral to the cooking process in the kitchen and ancillary to the production of *haute cuisine* as a cultural object, they are central to the production of belief in both the power of the chef and the power of the cultural object.

Since the end of the Second World War, the *Guide Michelin* and its rating system can be regarded as having furnished the *nomos* of the field, to the extent that the Michelin guide asserted the dominant principles of vision and division that establish and maintain the terms and the boundaries of the gastronomic field. Its symbolic power has resided in its power to consecrate chefs and restaurants through its role as gatekeeper over one of the primary stakes in the gastronomic field, namely the monopoly of culinary legitimacy, or the power to assert (with authority) just who may legitimately be considered a 'grand chef' in France. Within the domain of *haute cuisine*, as well as across the broad realm of the French gastronomy, the *Guide Michelin* is recognized as granting the supreme measure of culinary worth, with its highest three-star rating never having been bestowed on more than 27 chefs or restaurants in any given year.

A powerful mystique envelops the Michelin rating system, one that is spun from a combination of elements. The most prominent has been the cult of *secrecy* surrounding the inspectors, who conduct the restaurant inspections, anonymously, with even the precise number of inspectors remaining a closely guarded secret.[3] Next to its legendary secrecy and anonymity, another pillar of the Michelin mystique has been its cultivated *disinterestedness*, or its seeming disregard for commercial concerns. It is a trait largely derived from the fact that for 92 of its 107 years of existence, the Michelin guide (unlike other guides) has refused to accept advertising on its pages (Mesplède, 1998). The appearance of disinterestedness creates a kind of cultural 'firewall' that appears to protect the evaluative process from any conflict of interest, at least in pecuniary terms, and the effect of this has been to lend the guide a strong measure of legitimacy, strengthening belief in the integrity of the system. Another ingredient of the Michelin mystique is the air of *timelessness* that it appears to embody, the product of the combined effect of its age as an institution (over a century), its serialized publication schedule (there is a ritualized quality to its annual publication) and the conservatism of its almost unvarying presentation, dressed in the same red cover and organized according to the same format. The elements operate in relation to one another to magnify the timelessness that it seems to exemplify, while also facilitating a ready transposition in the public imagination of the history of the *Guide* with the history of the gastronomic world that it has chronicled.[4] Its ability to evoke a sense of solidity is further augmented by its association with a venerable family-owned and -dominated industrial corporation that has been firmly implanted in the French economy for over a century (Echikson, 1995: 76–7).

The elements of secrecy, disinterestedness, and timelessness that create the Michelin mystique serve to magnify its gatekeeping powers. Its power to consecrate those seeking to enter the temple makes it an object of fear and respect among the players within the field, but it is also widely known to those outside via a popular media that sustains the popular fascination with it. There are other culinary guides in France, and some have enjoyed a fair degree of influence, but in the French gastronomic field three stars in the *Guide Michelin* is the 'holy grail' for the chef and the restaurateur and neither considers themself (or is considered) at the summit until they are in receipt of their third star. In France the publication of every new edition of the annual *Guide* is a greatly anticipated and noteworthy media event, and this air of cultural authority is both a cause and a consequence of its mystique, and is made possible by a belief in its integrity as a gastronomic arbiter. The annual 'scorecard' of winners and losers is a kind of serialized game that is an object of great interest, in a country where most three-star chefs remain virtually household names.[5] But if the Michelin mystique helps maintain a belief in the cultural power of *haute cuisine*, it is a game in which both the losers and the winners prevail, to the extent that it reinforces the central place of *haute cuisine* in the gastronomic field, and of gastronomy in French culture and society.

If the *Guide Michelin* reigns supreme among culinary guides, the process of consecration in the gastronomic field is performed by a broader configuration of social actors and institutions.[6] The *concours* has been an important form of culinary consecration, a competitive contest in which one's talent and skill in the craft is judged and authorized by one's peers, a central method of recognition within the artisan culture of the chef profession. Such *concours* are ubiquitous rituals in the domain of wine and of *haute cuisine*, and the chefs who win them hold them aloft throughout their careers as marks of pride and accomplishment.

The most coveted culinary *concours* that serves as a virtual model for all of the others has been the award of the *Meilleur Ouvrier de France* (*MOF*), created in 1924 and administered by a non-profit association that sponsors competitions for some 220 different crafts in France. Operating across a broad spectrum of occupations, including those of the building construction industry, the arts, cosmetology, among many others, the '*métiers de bouche*' ('crafts of the mouth') account for 11 different award competitions within the field of gastronomy. For example, held every four years, the *concours* for '*cuisine-restauration*' would typically commence with several hundred candidates who are then winnowed down to 30 or 40 finalists, from which emerge four or five award winners.

The *MOF* is the most prestigious award that can be accorded a worker in any of the manual or service trades in France, though it accords no explicit material rights. It is not a license to practice a craft, it affords no entry to a job site; but only accords the right of the medal winner to wear the French *tricolor* on their collar, a symbol bestowing considerable prestige among the members of a craft, including those culinary trades for which there is a competition. It is a highly coveted prize within the chef profession and is an even more exclusive 'club' than that of those who have achieved three stars in the Michelin guide (of the 38 *grand chefs* who have possessed three Michelin stars since 1990, 23 never won the *MOF*).

The entire system of culinary recognition, including the awards and competitions and the organizations that sponsor them, have operated in a more or less reciprocally confirming relationship with the gastronomic guides and magazines, their food critics and journalists, and their rating systems. They have all been bound to and have fed off the field of gastronomic practices. In doing so, they have been collectively involved in the production of value of the gastronomic field, including its dominant players and institutions, engaging one another in the struggle to impose a way of seeing through a lens in which the chef and the practices and institutions of haute cuisine have held sway. It is an arrangement that essentially mirrors the field of cultural production (Bourdieu, 1993c: 261).

The erosion of autonomy[7]

It must be said that José Bové and his tractor could not have chosen a more appropriate target for decapitation than that McDonald's outlet in South-Central France back in 1999.[8] Everything, from the company's global reach, its relentlessly formulaic organization, and its hyperbolic promotional style, to its hyper-rationalized labor process (overseen by the evil genius of a computerized accounting system capable of monitoring worker productivity at each of its cash registers, in each of its restaurants, anywhere on the planet), to its position within a carnivorous system of industrial agriculture that has devoured small farmers to the point of extinction, recommends McDonald's as the perfect embodiment of American-style neo-liberalism. But while the populist drama of the 'David' of the *Confédération Paysanne* fending off the prototypical American 'Goliath' (and in a battle waged deep in the heart of '*la France profonde*') was a brilliant piece of guerrilla theatre and a useful weapon in the struggle to overthrow the existing symbolic order, its simplified narrative obscured important parts of the story.

In a more complicated version, McDonald's might be considered in the context of a wider arena of French institutions and social forces that have developed and changed, together, and in relation to it. Here we sketch a brief and provisional outline of such a story, one that locates McDonald's on the institutional and spatial landscape of the French gastronomic field. As we step back to take in this broader view, the vision that emerges is not so much that of the unwanted interloper menacing the peaceable host, but a more counter-intuitive picture that directs our attention to the indigenous forces of 'Americanization' within the French gastronomic field. From this vantage point, neo-liberalism is not so much a boorish intruder, loudly announcing itself at the front door, but is seen slipping in more discreetly, through a gradual and nearly intangible process of erosion in which 'limited reforms' slowly trickle into the crevices and interstices of even the most traditional (and therefore least likely) institutions, practices, and locations.

Although it seems somewhat counter-intuitive, the fast-food industry in France was actually established by *French* companies that were attempting to beat the Americans at their own game. The McDonald's Corporation entered France in the early 1970s along with other American-based chain companies (hotels, commercial cleaning companies, weight-control services, tax preparation and employment agencies) that were expanding into Europe in response to rising labor costs, market saturation, and increased competition within the United States. McDonald's was not the first fast-food company to operate in France (brands with names like 'Crip Crop', 'Dino-Croc', 'Chicken Shop' and the British-owned 'Wimpy' preceded it) and, until 1982, it was forced to cede most of the French fast-food market to indigenous chains while it settled a prolonged legal dispute with its local franchisee. Only afterward was it able to reacquire its license to develop its brand in France.

It was these companies that largely fueled the fast-food industry in France in the 1970s and 1980s, opening numerous hamburger restaurant chains closely modeled on the McDonald's formula. With American-sounding names ('Magic Burger', 'France-Quick', 'FreeTime', 'B'Burger', 'Manhattan Burger', 'Katy's Burger', 'Love Burger', 'Kiss Burger') these restaurants sold hamburgers and other American foods (prepared by part-time workers along a computerized assembly-line) and essentially packaged, displayed, and marketed as 'American' goods in restaurants whose design, organization, and internal spatial symbolism borrowed heavily from the American fast-food model (Fantasia, 1995).

So, while the McDonald's name was legendary in business circles, giving it considerable symbolic power, its actual business role was fairly negligible in the early stages of fast-food growth in France, thereby providing an opportunity for

French-owned corporations and independent entrepreneurs to enter the market for fast food. That is, the domination by McDonald's over the French fast-food market has been relatively recent. As late as 1989, 80 per cent of the 777 fast-food *hamburger* restaurants that were located in France were owned by French or European firms or investor groups.[9] Once McDonald's settled its legal dispute and was able to expand in the French market, it did so steadily, installing 150 restaurants within the first seven years (1982–1989). However, since 1989 McDonald's has expanded in the French market with great force, using its enormous marketing capability to sweep most of the French firms out of market entirely, while opening roughly one new restaurant outlet every week over the course of two decades, so that by the beginning of 2009 there were 1,134 McDonald's restaurants in France.[10]

Even before McDonald's came to dominate in France, its looming presence in the international market made it difficult for small or independent companies to operate and it isn't surprising that the small independent firms very soon lost out to larger, more heavily capitalized French chains. The most active in the fast-food business were large industrial groups (*grands groupes industriels*) like SOPAD, SODEXHO, EVITAIR – conglomerates with roots in post-war service-sector industries such as tourism and hotels, catering and chain restaurants, supermarkets, and industrial food processing (called '*l'agro-alimentaire*' in French). With corporate genealogies that can sometimes be traced back to the Marshall Plan 'productivity missions' of the 1950s (that took European businessmen to the U.S. to learn American business techniques), they represent a sector that, from birth, has been suckled at the tit of the 'American model'. They tend to be firms bred in expressed opposition to the organizational, financial, and stylistic temperament of the historic family-owned enterprises of the traditional manufacturing industries in France, representing a sort of 'comprador bourgeoisie' with respect to the introduction of American forms of commercial culture generally (Boltanski, 1981).

At the level of both production and consumption, American-style fast food either introduced or provided a firm institutional structure for a range of innovations that stood in contrast to the practices of traditional restaurants in France. In the realm of production practices, McDonald's (and the French-owned firms modeled on it) brought computerized accounting systems; extreme rationalization of the food preparation labor process; an extensive use of contingent labor (mostly part-time); and a virulent opposition to unions. At the level of consumption, American-style fast food brought to the gastronomic field, and to the French service sector, various innovations in the methods of restaurant marketing and service delivery (including the extensive use of visual hyperbole in promotions and in the design of restaurants and their internal space; smooth uncovered surface textures; bright lighting levels; colorful menus that dominate the visual field; self-service practices; ordering and queuing patterns; packaging of food to be eaten by hand; tables cleared off by customers, etc.). At the level of production and consumption, fast food in France was driven by youth, with both a workforce and a customer base made up of young people and with a style that attracted them on the basis of an appearance of stylistic rebelliousness, especially in relation to traditional French cultural forms (Fantasia, 1995).

While the fast-food restaurant and experience represented a cultural break from traditional French culinary practices, the fast-food industry was only the most extreme expression of an industrialized culinary sector that emerged in France in the 1970s. This sector has included a massive, vertically organized food-processing industry (*l'industrie agro-alimentaire*); various commercial restaurant sectors, including those devoted to institutional provisions (canteens, cafeterias, and restaurants in schools, prisons, hospitals, etc.) and standardized chain restaurants ('Hippo' and 'Buffalo Grill' are two well-known brands); supermarket chains that have expanded to become massive 'selling factories' (hypermarkets) for the distribution of goods of all sorts.

What has distinguished industrial cuisine (and its various institutional affiliates) from *haute cuisine* (and its cult of artisanship) is that the industrial is governed by the principles and rules of the economic field. Its standards uphold the values of profit maximization, standardization, high-volume production, technological innovation, speed and efficiency; whereas *haute cuisine* has been governed by the logic and values of art and artisanship, with a fidelity to traditional practices, to the fabrication of unique creations, to complex and sophisticated technique, aesthetic refinement, low-volume production, formal training, the consumption of time, etc. The one extols the quantity of production; the other the quality of creation; the one is led by the managerial skills of the *chef d' enterprise*; the other by the virtuosity of the *chef de cuisine*.

It is not simply a matter of being able to recognize the domestic sources of neo-liberalism in France, for it is not surprising to find the logic of the mass market governing the activities of industrial food processing, cafeterias, supermarkets, chain restaurants, and fast-food outlets, regardless of their national origin (although the 'American model' has been viewed as a particularly harsh strain of neo-liberal practice). It is necessary to make an analytical break from the sort of realist approach that would treat fast food and *haute cuisine* as distinctive worlds, toward a view that seeks to understand the social logic operating around (and through) fast food toward the wider field of culinary practices in which it has been embedded. That is, it is necessary to look to the field of relationships that link mass cultural goods to luxury markets, mass culture to high culture; and that link regionalism and 'the local' (*le terroir*) to 'globalization' and 'Americanization'.

Crossing the firewall

When we begin to pull at the threads of industrial cuisine, we can begin to see the degree to which its logic, its institutions, and its practices have expanded well beyond their customary orbit, increasingly penetrating (and occupying) what had traditionally been considered an antipodal universe of *haute cuisine*. Of course, *haute cuisine* is able to maintain all appearances. It sustains its air of venerability and tradition through an elaborate edifice of private and public institutions that chronicle it and that consist of foundations, associations, and museums of the culinary arts. Various rites of sanctification signify who is worthy to enter its portals (through awards, prizes, ceremonies, and the all-important star system), and serve as a cosmetic to cover its increasingly commercial and promotional aims. The highly elaborated event of the *Confrérie des Chevaliers du Tastevin*, for example, is an exclusive annual dinner held in Renaissance costume at the Château du Clos de Vougeot in Beaune in Burgundy, cloaked in pomp and circumstance. The ritual is far more than symbolic, however, for it always immediately precedes the annual Burgundy wine market, where wine exporters, distributors, wine critics, and restaurant sommeliers gather to place their annual orders for Burgundy wines. A Renaissance ritual thus serves as a sacred 'cover' for a thoroughly modern commercial operation.

Helping to sustain the conviction is an army of retainers (magazines, journals and journalists, food critics) who operate as though entranced by the very magical powers that they are employed to render believable. It is a domain that has both a 'majestic' and a 'magical' quality. It is majestic in the way that *haute cuisine* represents France to the outside world and to itself: as sacrosanct, as venerable, through the cult of the lineage (Chef Vergé begets Chef Ducasse, who begets Chef Solivérès, who begets …); and in the romance of *le terroir* (a term with no English equivalent, that refers to that which is drawn from a particular soil or place, and made sublime by the traditional artisan practices of that place). The constructed majesty of *haute cuisine* stands in almost direct proportion to the constructed frivolousness of fast food, with each serving as key elements of the symbolic vocabulary by which France and the U.S. represent themselves to the rest of the world.

As is the case with all luxury industries, the principles of *haute cuisine* could not be any further from the logic of the mass market (standardization, high volume, low cost, convenience, informality) and the production requirements that make mass markets possible (rationalization, polyvalence, cheap and flexible labor, weak collective structures). In recent decades, however, the symbolic and institutional barrier that once afforded *haute cuisine* a significant degree of independence from pure commercial standards has become increasingly permeable, allowing for an ease of movement across the divide from both directions.

From one direction, the large industrial groups have reached across the divide into the domain of artisanship, to purchase some of the most venerable culinary establishments in Paris.[11] These industries now routinely engage in the practice of 'leasing' portions of the accumulated prestige of the *grand chefs* by procuring their signatures to enhance the symbolic value of their products (including lines of frozen and prepared foods, chain restaurants, as well as pots and pans, aprons, television programs, cookbooks, wines, and various 'satellite' restaurants around the world).

Not only have the large industrial groups entered what was once considered the sacred ground of *haute cuisine* in pursuit of direct profits, but they have also been involved in the maintenance and reproduction of the culinary patrimony itself. For example, they have helped to finance and govern the Fondation Brillat-Savarin (an institution created in 1980 and charged with defending against the forces of homogenization!) and have sponsored the 'Chef of the Year Award', an honor bestowed annually by *Le Chef* magazine, one of the principal organs of the chef profession. So in the same 1990 issue in which Alain Ducasse was granted an award as Chef of the Year, the magazine also featured awards granted to the industry of *l'agro-*

alimentaire by its own trade association for industrial food products (for example, awards were bestowed upon Daregal for its *herbes aromatiques surgelées*; Mikogel for its *mini-bavarois*; Sopad-Nestlé for '*entremets flans sans cuisson*', and Uncle Ben's for its *salades saveurs*.[12]

As we consider movement from the other direction, from the domain of *haute cuisine* toward the industrial, we can discern the extent to which conditions have been created in the gastronomic field that permit those with a sufficient accumulation of symbolic capital the ability to convert it into economic capital. Since industrial firms have no other way to acquire symbolic capital other than to purchase it on the open market, it becomes a true 'seller's market' for the grand chef who, once installed at the apex of the profession by receipt of a third star in the *Guide Michelin*, is granted the magical power, Midas-like, to turn whatever he touches into gold. Everything is potential lucre, no matter how prosaic the object (aprons, cookbooks, pots and pans, bistros, commercial restaurants). A Bocuse, a Robuchon, a Ducasse (or once a Loiseau), and dozens of others, are able to either lease their names to other producers, attach their signatures directly to goods, or trade on their names themselves (by opening a much less expensive bistro next to their three-star restaurant, for example).

Once he has been granted a third Michelin star, there seems to be a shift in the discourse of the grand chef, from a language of 'purity' and 'excellence' and timelessness and priceless-ness, to the rhetoric of accessibility and democracy ('everyone should have the opportunity to savor the wonders of our kitchen'). So, for example, Alain Ducasse, who held three-star ratings in the Michelin guide for two of his restaurants (in 2009 he holds three), was featured in an article in the principal magazine representing industrial cuisine (on the occasion of the opening of his new chain of popular mass-market restaurants, 'Spoon') which was entitled: *I want to make accessible our culinary know-how*. Among other things, Ducasse noted that 'Freedom, diversity, and accessibility are the three rules of success in hotels and restaurants,' although his own accession to the top proceeded through institutions and practices that have little to do with any of the three rules (Thiaut, 1999: 53). Like a religious epiphany, those who have spent their careers sanctifying *haute cuisine* are suddenly converted to the religion of the market, a conversion made necessary by the high loan repayments for restaurant renovations that are almost obligatory in the quest for a third Michelin star.

This movement is also expressed by opening mass-market restaurants, as chefs with three Michelin stars now commonly open one or more 'annexes', bistros and other relatively inexpensive restaurants, sometimes right next door to their signature three-star restaurant (Pudlowski, 2000: 58–9). These establishments permit grand chefs to trade financially on the symbolic capital they have accumulated, by purchasing a restaurant designed for a higher volume of customers and a more popular clientele. When Paul Bocuse was hired by Disney to create an 'authentic' French restaurant at Epcot Center, the interchange went in both directions, for Bocuse returned to France with knowledge of the business potential of publicity and of expansion, both of which he claimed to have learned from Disney's 'master marketers' (Knight, 2004: 13).

Bocuse, who has become what *Le Chef* magazine (the principal journal of the profession) has called a living 'monument of French cuisine'; who has marketed a full complement of cookbooks, CDs, postcards, shopping bags, tableware, cookware; and who owns a gift shop devoted to himself and his image, invested heavily in mass-market restaurants upon his return from Disney (Fedele, 2003; Golan, 1995a). In financial terms this venture has proven more lucrative than his original restaurant near Lyon, with its seemingly permanent three-star rating. In 2003, revenue at his three-star restaurant was nearly six million euros (serving 98 tables a day, with the average diner spending 178 euros) while revenue that same year from his various brasseries totaled 22 million euros. It shouldn't be forgotten that his brasseries are sustained by the 'Bocuse' name, an appellation that would have little value without his three Michelin stars and other awards (like the *Meilleur Ouvrier de France*). In other words, not only is *haute cuisine* a site where symbolic capital is exchanged for economic capital, but each sustains the other in a mutually constituting and reciprocally confirming relationship.

While economic value has clearly become more and more central to the gastronomic field, the object of market exchange may not necessarily be the accumulation of economic capital, even in the last instance. A field may represent a market for whatever forms of capital social agents in that field happen to possess or bring to it, or otherwise be in a position to benefit from. Cultural fields exert a force upon those who enter them, and represent sites of contestation between those with a stake in preserving the existing arrangements and those predisposed to transform them. While *haute cuisine* may appear old, venerable, and a repository of traditional artisan values, 'a world apart' from the requirements of standardization and homogenization at the base of fast food, in recent decades the barriers that maintained it as a world apart and provided it with its definition have become much more porous. The symbolic and institutional firewall that once permitted *haute cuisine* to maintain an independence from pure commercial standards has become much more permeable in the last three decades. *Grand chefs*, like Bocuse and Ducasse and many others, are now able to break with tradition in pursuit of commercial rewards and public adulation because others have paved the way by crossing the firewall. For example, Michel Guérard, who had been associated with the culinary style known as *nouvelle cuisine*, appeared to have been the first to step over the wall separating *haute cuisine* and industrial cuisine when he signed a consulting contract with the Nestlé Corporation in 1976. Quickly habituated to the industrial logic, Guérard asserted with regard to his association with Nestlé, 'I have the feeling of being a fish in water' (Cordier, 1989: 36). Alain Ducasse, Paul Bocuse, and others would later plunge even more deeply into these waters, so that today a grand *chef de cuisine* is often, simultaneously, a *grand chef d'enterprise*.

An analytically fruitful way of representing such changes is to view them as an erosion of the historic and relative autonomy of the field. While the two poles of the gastronomic field in France have been expressed in the practices of *haute cuisine* and of industrial cuisine, it has been the former that has dominated both the social life of the field and its representation, both for the French and for the world. Its character emphasizes cuisine as an art, centered around the chef (artisan), whose knowledge is acquired in apprenticeship with a master, where there is value in the length of time devoted to culinary preparation, where raw materials are considered sublime, and where the nearly priceless creation is designed for a highly restricted (luxury) market. Industrial cuisine, on the other hand, prizes labor-saving technologies that facilitate short-time production, high volume (for a mass market), produced by de-skilled and polyvalent labor.

As I have tried to demonstrate in schematic form, these two regions of the field have become increasingly interpenetrated. Despite the apparent mutual contempt, even repulsion, expressed by the producers and consumers of *haute cuisine* toward industrial cuisine (contempt that often operates in the other direction as well through various kinds of reverse snobbery), at an institutional level they have become thoroughly interpenetrated through the exchange of symbolic and economic capital. The fabric of this arrangement requires that the economic capital of the *grand groupes industriels* remains somewhat hidden, so as not to reveal its seams, while the symbolic capital of the *grand chefs* is presented as the symbolic face of the field. The powerful cultural charm of French *haute cuisine* which, as we've seen, confers considerable symbolic capital to those at its apex and represents a key element of French national cultural identity, could be dissipated if its practices and its practitioners were perceived as being too close to the crass industrial/commercial logic of the economic field. The stakes are much higher now than they used to be, and so a symbolic façade is crucial in maintaining all appearances.

Acknowledgement

Special thanks are due Priscilla Ferguson for her thoughtful comments, criticisms, and encouragement.

Notes

1   In the larger study of the French gastronomic field from which this chapter derives, I am analysing the career trajectories and occupational histories of several hundred social actors from the field of gastronomic practices in France (*grand chefs*, with various levels of consecration; cooks in industrial food establishments; business executives from the industry *l'agro alimentaire*, etc.). Considerations of space make it impossible to present that data here in anything approaching a systematic way.

2   Represented by the expression '*La femme naît cuisinière, l'homme le devient*' ('The woman is born a cook, the man becomes one') noted in Jean Claude Ribaut, 'Cuisine au féminin' in *Le Monde*, 15–16 juin 2003: 18. According to Jack Goody, from as far back as the Ancient Egyptian era, male cooks had appropriated women's recipes for everyday cooking and transformed them into court cuisine, but French *haute cuisine* would have further reinforced this tendency because the rise of the chef profession in France was so closely bound up with nationalism, thereby raising the stakes involved and necessitating sharp social markers of differentiation. See Goody (1982: 101); and also Swinbank (2002: 469).

3   It was for this reason that the exposé written by a former Michelin inspector was treated as such a scandal when it was published (see Remy, 2004; Echikson, 1995).

4   It therefore makes perfect marketing sense for the principal published history of the

guide, *Trois étoiles au Michelin* to be subtitled *Une histoire de la haute gastronomie française* (Jean-Francois Mesplède, 1998).

5 In addition to more than half a million copies sold annually, the *Guide Michelin* receives some 25,000 letters per year from readers who send in their judgments of restaurants. They are never published in the *Guide* but are, reportedly, read by the inspection teams as part of the process of discovering new establishments and marking others for attention (Mesplède, 1998: 16).

6 The best-known of the various other culinary guides has been the *Guide Gault-Millau*, founded in 1969 by two food journalists as a more modern and less pretentious alternative to *Michelin*. *Gault-Millau* carries neither the same cult of mystery nor the aversion to commercial advertising that has buttressed the Michelin mystique, and it has never been as influential either (Terence, 1996: 114–24). While its symbolic power is substantial in sustaining the gastronomic field, in practical terms it is not tremendously significant. A marketing study commissioned by the trade magazine, *Le Chef*, reported that only 16% of restaurant customers had consulted a culinary guide in the previous six months, and of those (162 respondents) 50% had consulted the *Guide Michelin*, 23% had consulted *Gault-Millau*, while the various other guides consulted included the *Bottin Gourmand* (3%), *Guide du Routard* (9%), *Guide Pudlowski* (1%), *Guide des Relais et Châteaux* (3%), *Champerard* (1%), and *Guide Lebey* (1%) (Golan, 1995b: 52).

7 Portions of this section have been adapted from a previously published article. See Fantasia (2000).

8 Jose Bové is a sheep farmer and militant activist for the peasant's union, *Confederation Paysanne*. He famously demolished, with a tractor, a McDonald's outlet that was being constructed in Millau, a small city in the Aveyron region of France, as a protest against the use of hormone-treated beef. His arrest and subsequent trial became a *cause celebré* in France and Bové was soon propelled internationally as a figure of resistance to American domination of global food circuits and, specifically, the use of genetically modified crops and hormone-treated beef. He was recently elected a member of the European Parliament.

9 These did not include fast-food pastry and sandwich shops, and other adaptations of traditional foods to the fast-food formula, for which an even higher percentage were French owned. These data are available in 'La Restauration Rapide en France', *Revue Technique des Hotels et Restaurants*, No. 473, mars 1989: 98–107.

10 Data published in *NÉO Restauration*, No. 462, mars 2009: 31.Since 2002, the pace of new openings has cooled with roughly two new McDonald's outlets per month in France.

11 For example, Groupe Flo, a corporation owning several restaurant chains with close to 200 establishments, has purchased some of the most venerable historic bistros of Paris in recent years, including the Brasserie Lipp, Le Balzar, and La Coupole; and Fauchon, the Parisian purveyor of food delicacies was recently bought by a subsidiary of ACCOR.

12 'Les Industriels à l'Honneur', *Le Chef*, No. 38 décembre 1990 (no author listed).

4   Pierre Bourdieu's political sociology and public sociology

David Swartz

Pierre Bourdieu has inspired much work in the sociology of culture, education, theory, and stratification, but has received very little attention in political sociology and practically none in political science.[1] This chapter proposes a reading of Bourdieu as a political sociologist who offers both a sociology of politics and a politics of sociology. The first part will offer a brief overview of his analysis of power. The second part will examine how he thinks sociology can be used to speak politically. I will consider the kind of role he thinks should be played by the sociologist in the public arena. This role will be contrasted with several other views on the role of intellectuals in politics and some evaluation will be offered.

Bourdieu's political sociology

In earlier work I (Swartz, 2003a, 2003b) argued that Bourdieu can be read as a political sociologist. I (Swartz, 2006) have also argued that Bourdieu's work on politics has been neglected by North American political sociologists and political scientists in part because he did not write books or articles that fit directly within the disciplinary contours of the subfield of political sociology or the academic discipline of political science. Bourdieu did not devote much attention to those political units, such as parties, the state, lobbies, legislatures or constitutions, commonly treated as institutions by political scientists. Except for the act of delegating political power, Bourdieu did not devote much attention to political processes, such as decision making, social movement formation, coalition building, elections, or leadership selection and élite recruitment. Bourdieu's sociology attempts a broader sweep of political issues than those delineated by the boundaries of these academic disciplines. Indeed, I would argue that Bourdieu's sociology makes no distinction between the sociological approach to the study of the social world and the study of political power. For Bourdieu, the political dimension of social life goes to the very foundation of any collectivity, since he sees all instituted groups as emerging out of a symbolic struggle (struggle over representations) to impose selected representations as legitimate social identity. Any distribution of properties, such as age, gender, education or wealth, can serve as the basis of group divisions and therefore become the basis of political struggle (Bourdieu, 1981: 71). Such properties, or 'capitals', as Bourdieu calls them, require legitimation to function as power resources. His concepts of symbolic power, violence, and capital call attention to that power dimension where there are particular interests that go mis-recognized as representing universal interests. Symbolic power is a *world-making*[2] power for it indicates the capacity to impose the 'legitimate vision of the social world and of its divisions' (Bourdieu, 1987: 13; Bourdieu, 1989c). Bourdieu sees the very foundation of the social order as a struggle among various collectivities to impose as legitimate their particular identities and definitions of the social world. Symbolic power is a group-making power, for it is able to constitute social realities as legitimate entities. This occurs through struggle over the right to exercise that symbolic function. The task of sociology is to reveal the underlying character of those legitimation struggles. Viewed this way, all sociology for Bourdieu is, in fact, a sociology of politics.

Three dimensions of power in Bourdieu's sociology

Bourdieu analyzes power in three overlapping but analytically distinct ways: (1) power in valued resources (various types of social, cultural, and economic capital); (2) power in specific spheres of struggle (fields), and (3) power in legitimation (symbolic power, violence, and capital).

Power as a form of capital

In Bourdieu's sociology, power takes the form of valued resources, which Bourdieu calls *capitals*, that can be created, accumulated, exchanged, and consumed. Bourdieu (1989b: 375) conceptualizes resources as capital when they function as a 'social relation of power' by becoming objects of struggle as valued resources. His idea of cultural capital is most widely known but his work includes an array of capitals, such as social capital, economic capital, academic capital, and statist capital. Moreover, researchers inspired by Bourdieu's thinking have identified an ever-widening array of types of capital. These are unevenly distributed among social classes.

Power in fields of struggle

Capitals, as forms of power, exist not in isolation but are relational. They operate in what Bourdieu calls *fields*, which are arenas of struggle over capitals. Fields denote arenas of production, circulation, and appropriation of goods, services, knowledge, or status, and the competitive positions held by actors in their struggle to accumulate and monopolize these different kinds of capital. Fields may be thought of as structured spaces that are organized around specific types and combinations of capital.

   Field struggle, for Bourdieu, has two distinct dimensions. On the one hand, struggle occurs over the distribution of capitals within fields. This is a struggle to accumulate the more valued forms of capital or to convert one form into another more valued form. In this sense, capital is a stake in the struggle. On the other hand, struggle also occurs over the very definition of the most legitimate form of capital for a particular field. This is a struggle for symbolic power, a classification struggle, over the right to monopolize the legitimate definition of what is to be the most legitimate form of capital for a particular field. This can involve bringing in forms of capital from other fields.

Two particular power arenas that Bourdieu emphasizes in his sociology of modern societies are the *field of power* and the *political field*. The *field of power* is that arena of struggle among the different power fields (particularly the economic field and the cultural field in modern societies) for the right to dominate throughout the social order. It is the arena of struggle among the different forms of power (or capitals) for the power to be recognized as the most legitimate. The concept covers the dominant classes in modern stratified societies. Dominant classes are distinguished from other classes by their sheer volume of capital but are also themselves internally differentiated by cultural-oriented versus economic forms of capital. In his empirical analyses of the field of power in modern France, Bourdieu (1996b: 266–72) identifies different fields *within* the field of power, such as the artistic field, the administrative field, the university field, and the economic field.

Central to but not synonymous with the field of power is the *state*, which assumes the key role of regulating the struggle within the field of power. Extending Max Weber's definition of the state as that institution that claims monopoly over the legitimate use of violence, Bourdieu stresses the monopolizing role over symbolic as well as physical violence. For Bourdieu the state consists not only of bureaucratic agencies, authorities, ritual and ceremony, but also of official classifications that regulate group relations and are internalized as mental categories through schooling. The state regulates the classification struggle among social groups by giving some classifications and categories official legitimation while rejecting others. The state institutionalizes its own specific form of capital, *statist capital*, a kind of meta-capital that consecrates and renders official the most legitimate forms of power.[3] Thus, the state ultimately concentrates the power to designate the most legitimate forms of capital. The modern state regulates the 'rate of exchange' among the different forms of capital.

Power for Bourdieu also appears in a specific form of capital and in a specific sphere of activity that is commonly associated with politics. Bourdieu speaks of the *political field* and *political capital*. Political capital refers to a subtype of social capital that is the capacity to mobilize social support (Bourdieu and Wacquant, 1992: 119). The political field refers to the arena of struggle to capture positions of power using political capital (parties, occupations, media). It is structured around competition for control of the state apparatus. It roughly corresponds to Max Weber's (1978) third dimension of stratification: the sphere of politics.

Symbolic power, violence and capital

Bourdieu uses the conceptual language of *symbolic power*, *violence*, and *capital* to talk about a kind of power that legitimates the stratified social order. This is the most important contribution of Bourdieu to contemporary thinking about power and domination. Bourdieu sees power as a governing dimension of all social life, even where it is not explicitly pursued. He argues that power finds expression in the mundane activities of everyday life. It operates at a tacit, taken-for-granted level on both cognitive and bodily dimensions of human activity. Through the conceptual language of *symbolic power, violence,* and *capital* Bourdieu tries to answer the following question: how do stratified social systems of hierarchy and domination persist and reproduce intergenerationally without powerful resistance and without the conscious recognition of their members? The answer, he contends, is that the dominated internalize their conditions of domination as normal, inevitable, or natural, and thereby *misrecognize* the true nature of their social inequalities by accepting rather than resisting them.

The language of symbolic power and violence stresses that legitimate understandings of the social world are imposed by dominant groups and deeply internalized by subordinate groups in the form of practical taken-for-granted understandings. *Symbolic power* is the capacity to impose classifications and meanings as legitimate.[4] Symbolic power takes the form of embodied dispositions – what Bourdieu calls the *habitus* – that generate a 'practical sense' for organizing perceptions of and actions in the social world. The dispositions of habitus incorporate a sense of place in the stratified social order, an understanding of inclusion and exclusion in the various social hierarchies. Bourdieu puts power at the heart of the functioning and the structure of habitus, since habitus involves an unconscious calculation of what is possible, impossible, and probable for people in their specific locations in the stratified social order. Symbolic power creates a form of *violence* that finds expression in everyday classifications, labels, meanings, and categorizations that subtly implement a social as well as a symbolic logic of inclusion and exclusion.[5] Symbolic violence also finds expression through body language, comportment, self-presentation, bodily care and adornment. It has a corporal as well as a cognitive dimension. And *symbolic capital* designates the social authority to impose symbolic meanings and classifications as legitimate that individuals and groups can accumulate through public recognition of their capital holdings and positions occupied in social hierarchies. Symbolic capital is a form of credit and it takes symbolic capital accumulated from previous struggles to exercise symbolic power (Bourdieu, 1989c: 23).[6]

Two key properties of symbolic power are its *naturalization* and *misrecognition.* Bourdieu's symbolic power does not suggest 'consent' but 'practical adaptation' to existing hierarchies. The practical adaptation occurs pre-reflectively as if it were the 'thing to do', the 'natural' response in existing circumstances. The dominated misperceive the real origins and interests of symbolic power when they adopt the dominant view of the dominant and of themselves (Bourdieu, 2001a: 119). They therefore accept definitions of social reality that do not correspond to their best interests. Those *misrecognized* definitions go unchallenged as appearing natural and justified. Hence, they represent a form of violence. These properties of symbolic power help explain how inegalitarian social systems are able to self-perpetuate without powerful resistance and transformation.

Two criticisms

Power in the form of symbolic power and violence has not only been the most widely acknowledged contribution to contemporary thinking about power but also the object of sharp criticism. Just two frequent criticisms will be mentioned here. Bourdieu stresses that the state, through law, official classifications, and particularly education, institutes fundamental frames of reference, perception, understanding, and memory. It therefore monopolizes the means of symbolic violence as well as of physical violence. But in assigning to the modern state a monopolizing function of symbolic power and violence, Bourdieu underestimates the importance of other sources of symbolic power, such as religion, even in modern societies outside Europe.

Reproduction of social hierarchies is likely to involve much more than their misrecognition. The degree of acceptance and respect for existing hierarchies may be less deeply internalized in numerous instances than the idea of symbolic violence implies. There may be conscious recognition of inequality that leads to tacit forms of contestation or reluctance to resist for fear of reprisal (Scott, 1990).

Using sociology to speak politically

Bourdieu offers not only a sociology of politics but also a politics of sociology. There is a political project in his sociology that for the most part goes overlooked in its reception outside France. For Bourdieu, sociology is an intellectual project with a political objective to achieve certain effects. Doing sociology is doing politics in a different way. It is not just analysis of power relations but a form of political engagement. This section of the chapter will examine his normative vision for the political vocation of the sociologist.

Science: the great disenchanter

We have seen that Bourdieu assigns a central role to symbolic power in maintaining social order. Symbolic power points to those practical, taken-for-granted adaptations to existing hierarchies. Yet for Bourdieu it is in the very nature of science (the logic of science itself) to critically challenge taken-for-granted assumptions about the social world. The logic of science is an ongoing process of critical challenge of existing explanations, both lay and intellectual. By conceptualizing science as a rational process that questions fundamentally taken-for-granted assumptions and categories of the social world, Bourdieu attributes to the very logic of scientific discovery a debunking or disenchanting force against the taken-for-granted character of social worlds that 'conceal power relations' (Bourdieu, 1993e: 12). Science desacralizes the sacred (*Actes de la recherche* 1, January 1975). This disenchantment of the social order is profoundly political, for it strikes at the very efficacy of relations of domination.

In a 1970 interview, Bourdieu outlines the kind of political impact he believes science can have. Following the view of the French philosopher of science, Gaston

Bachelard (Bachelard, 1949, 1980, 1984; Tiles, 1984), that scientific discovery reveals the 'hidden', Bourdieu argues that by demasking taken-for-granted power relations 'genuine scientific research embodies a threat for the "social order"' (Bourdieu and Hahn, 1970: 15). Because symbolic power by its very nature is hidden from the everyday understandings of actors and goes mis-recognized as natural understandings invested by arbitrary power relations, its exposure strikes at the very core of its efficacy. Scientific research, therefore, 'inevitably exercises a political effect.' Since the power relations that sociology reveals owe part of their strength to the fact that they do not appear to be power relations, 'all sociological discourse has a political effect, even by default (ibid.: 19). Clearly, Bourdieu invests in his understanding of science a progressive political project that he tries to legitimate in the name of scientific authority.

There is, therefore, a political dimension to Bourdieu's conception of science and what sociology should do in the modern world. Bourdieu thinks of sociology as a weapon in the struggle for emancipation from symbolic domination. He thinks of the intellectual vocation as a social scientist in an activist sense. Acts of research, no matter how seemingly mundane, are acts of struggle, conquest, and victory over the taken-for-granted assumptions of social life: scientific research is a struggle against all forms of symbolic domination. By exposing through research the arbitrary and taken-for-granted mechanisms of social life that maintain power relations, the social scientist is able to challenge the legitimacy of the status quo. As existing power relations lose their taken-for-granted character, possibilities for alternative ways of constructing social relations open up. Thus for Bourdieu politics and science combine in the very objective of the social scientific vocation. 'Acts of research' – to borrow from the title of his journal – are for Bourdieu fundamentally 'political acts.'[7]

This view of science suggests a key role that sociologists can play in modern societies: 'The sociologist unveils and therefore intervenes in the force relations between groups and classes and he can even contribute to the modification of those relations.'[8] That a critical social science can potentially modify relations between social classes amounts to a strong claim for the power of sociological knowledge in modern stratified societies and for the vocation of the social scientist as intellectual. Indeed, a normative vision for the political effects of social scientific research characterizes Bourdieu's sociological project. This normative vision calls for protecting the autonomy of the scientific field from the distorting effects of politics while simultaneously orienting one's scientific research so that it will have the maximum effect in the public arena. It also calls for a reflexive practice of sociology, one that does not import the logic of political struggle into the scientific arena yet is able to produce symbolic effects that can shape political life.[9] A sociology of intellectuals informs Bourdieu's reflexive practice of the sociological craft and his political activity.

This reasoning points to an extraordinary idealism in Bourdieu's thinking about the role of the social scientist in the modern world. That Bourdieu believes that a critical and professional sociology can modify relations among the social classes amounts to a phenomenal claim for the power of sociological knowledge in modern stratified societies. It also points to a remarkable faith in the emancipatory effects of science, a view that came to be contested by postmodernism and the radical social constructionist view of science.

The theme that doing good social science means doing good politics resonates strongly throughout much of Bourdieu's work. He embraces the idea that defending the interests of science amounts to defending the universal interests of humanity. Critics like Michael Burawoy (2005b) are more skeptical. Burawoy suggests that Bourdieu's vision for an extraordinary role for his 'collective intellectual' in social transformation looks like what constitutes in Alvin Gouldner's (1979) terms a 'flawed universal class.' (Bourdieu was quite critical of Gouldner's new class theorizing (Swartz, 1998).) Perhaps, as Burawoy (2005b) suggests, Bourdieu's view here misrecognizes 'its own particularism as universalism.'

In the interview alluded to above, Bourdieu admits that even though sociology can weaken power relations by unveiling them, sociology can be accommodated and recuperated by dominant groups for their own interests. In revealing the hidden mechanisms of power, science may be of service to dominant groups in that it may lead to better and alternative modes of manipulation and social control. Those in dominant positions are better situated to benefit from the existing hierarchical order and thus meet the threat from science of having their privileged positions exposed. Their advantaged resources also give them opportunities to find alternative sources of legitimation for their privileged positions. But Bourdieu is banking on the other possibility, namely that when prevailing power mechanisms are exposed, they will lose their efficacy to the benefit of those subordinate individuals and groups who have access to and are able to use this knowledge. For Bourdieu, science is on the side of subordinate individuals and groups.

This points up a tension in Bourdieu's thinking about the nature of science, between science as description and science as political intervention. On the one hand, he recurrently warns social scientists against partisanship in the social struggles they study. Social conflicts are to be objects of study, not occasions for choosing sides. Bourdieu's field analytic perspective offers a more comprehensive view than any one of the parochial interests involved. Yet, no field analysis is ever complete. The view of the social scientist itself stems from a field position that limits attainment of a fully objective view – a criticism Bourdieu himself stresses in his call for a sociology of sociology as a necessary tool for assessing the limits of the scientific view. On the other hand, he believes that science necessarily sides with the interests of subordinate groups since by exposing the mechanisms of power, science renders them less effective for dominant groups. Yet, he admits that dominated groups often lack the cultural capital needed to grasp the findings of good, critical social scientific work. Moreover, it is not clear that scientists on the whole tend to support political opposition parties as Bourdieu's view hypothesizes. Indeed, there are likely to be important variations among types of scientist (e.g. pure versus applied research, government versus private industry funding) and from one country to another.

Bourdieu's line of argument points to the central role that he assigns to symbolic power and violence (legitimation) and its misrecognition in the maintenance of power relations. It also assigns a key debunking role to science. This role presupposes that science holds considerable and a different kind of authority in order to produce this kind of debunking political effect. This kind of scientific authority can come only from increasing the autonomy of the scientific field from outside interests. Indeed, the kinds of political effect he seeks would seem possible only so long as science enjoys a legitimacy superior to that of politics.[10] However, this points to a complex if not ultimately contradictory position in which Bourdieu finds himself. To achieve the desired political effects, belief in science as a form of disinterested knowledge and inquiry must exist. Yet, the thrust of Bourdieu's (1975) own work on the scientific field emphasizes the very political character of that social universe. And though intellectual politics are undoubtedly different from electoral politics, they nonetheless are politics.

A change in emphasis

Bourdieu's thinking about this tension evolved over time making it even more problematic. In a key 1990 text Bourdieu (2000e) reflects on the relationship between sociology and politics from a changing historical perspective. He recalls that sociology emerging in the nineteenth century was primarily concerned with social problems and reform. For a long time sociology and socialism were connected in the eyes of many. However, in order for sociology to gain legitimacy as a science, it had to develop its own norms of validation and define its own social scientific problems as an autonomous intellectual enterprise rather than simply taking up the prevailing social and political agendas of the day. Durkheim's (1966) *Rules of Sociological Method* and Weber's ideal of 'ethical neutrality' were important expressions of the development of sociology as an intellectually autonomous discipline worthy of scholarly recognition. However, in order to gain scientific respectability, sociologists had to expunge social reform and political dimensions from their work. The development of a professional sociology with scientific status came with a price, that of censoring from consideration politics. Bourdieu (2000b: 104) makes the following critical historical and personal observation:

> By a self-censorship that constituted a veritable self-mutilation, sociologists – and I who frequently denounced the temptation of becoming a social prophet or advocating a social philosophy was a prime example – self imposed refusal of all attempts to propose an *ideal and global* representation of the social world as if such would fall short of proper scientific morality and therefore discredit their author.

Observing that sociology had achieved scientific status and considerable autonomy from outside influence, an autonomy where much sociological work is oriented toward its own professional audience, Bourdieu became concerned that the arenas where political agendas are set up and maintained no longer receive any significant input from a critical scientific perspective. Moreover, in Bourdieu's (2000b: 104) view, scientific professionalization had the effect of relegating the political function sociology once assumed historically to 'the less scrupulous and less competent sociologists or to politicians and journalists.' Bourdieu grew increasingly concerned by the growing influence of the mass media and economic forces on intellectual life and the power of neoliberal thinking to dominate political discussion. These constraining forces called for more aggressive resistance. In his view the urgency of the contemporary situation no longer permits the strict science/politics separation that had been important for the development of sociology as a legitimate scientific practice. This separation, he (2000e: 105) concludes, is no longer necessary or tenable.

> I believe that nothing can justify that scientistic abdication, that ruins any political conviction, and that the time has come when scholars need to intervene in politics with their competence in order to impose utopias based in truth and rationality.

Weber's idea of 'ethical neutrality' that Bourdieu says represented a fundamental advance in the professional ideology of sociology to obtain scholarly legitimacy, including Bourdieu's own use of Weber's principle, seems to be no longer acceptable (Bourdieu, 2000e: 104). Sociologists must engage more directly the political arena.

Despite this shift in emphasis Bourdieu does not propose a return to the sociology of the nineteenth century where social reform and social science intermingled without clear distinction. The autonomy of science is to be protected from political and economic encroachments. Yet, he (Bourdieu, 2000b: 105) sees no 'antinomy between autonomy and engagement, between separation and collaboration.' However, the tension, if not contradiction, in his thinking does not go away and is accentuated by some of his public pronouncements and public interventions, particularly in his later life.[11] His ideal, as we will see in the next section, is of the intellectual who intervenes in politics, like the French literary figure, Emile Zola; as someone whose intervention is legitimated by his accomplishments in an autonomous area of expertise, art, philosophy and science. The authentic intellectual derives his intellectual authority entirely from his intellectual work, not from political activities or journalistic or media visibility, and intervenes politically as Zola did with an intellectual competence and authority. He cites Noam Chomsky and Andrey Sakharov as two contemporary illustrative examples. We need therefore to look more closely at the kind of political vocation he sees for the sociologist as an intellectual.

Intellectual roles in politics: Bourdieu's collective intellectual

Bourdieu's view of social science and the ensuing function of sociologists it entails suggests a model for intellectual political activism that can be contrasted with other prevailing views. While Bourdieu defends the autonomy of intellectual and cultural fields, particularly science, he is ultimately interested in the political effects of science rather than science for science's sake. He therefore rejects the *ivory-tower model* of the intellectual role. The sociologist is to engage the public sphere. On the other hand, Bourdieu is sharply critical of the sociologist as *technocratic* expert who sells his/her services to outside groups, such as the state, foundations, political parties, or corporations. To allow external groups to set the research agenda sacrifices intellectual and scientific autonomy.

While Bourdieu rejects the intellectual role of service to established powers, he also rejects intellectual subservience to parties and social movements attempting social transformation. He has been a sharp critic of the Granscian idea of the organic intellectual who links 'organically' to classes and social movements in order to bring about social transformation. Echoing concerns about intellectual autonomy voiced by the French literary scholar Julian Benda (1927), Bourdieu sees *organic intellectuals* as surrendering their autonomy. He also fears they will usurp leadership of these social groups.

Preserving more critical attachment than the organic intellectual, the *fellow-traveler intellectual* is the model made famous by Jean-Paul Sartre who for a period of time conceptualized his relationship to the French Communist Party in these terms. This does not entail membership or a close working relationship as the organic intellectual formula does, but an independent status that retains some critical distance though in public solidarity with the party. For Bourdieu, this stance nonetheless sacrifices too much critical independence and tends to blunt needed criticism of the party for political strategic reasons.

But maintaining an autonomous and critical posture does not mean that the intellectual is without interests and that he/she is able to transcend all parochial interests as the popular image of Mannheim's *free-floating intellectuals* suggests. Bourdieu's intellectuals function in fields of specific interests; they pursue their particular interests in the competition to advance their own positions within the scientific field and their interests in the struggle over the definition of what is legitimate science. However, in this struggle to advance the cause of science they also advance universal interest insofar as science debunks power relations and therefore opens up the possibility for thinking differently about existing social arrangements. Mannheim's view received little attention by Bourdieu. However, Sartre's view of the role of a *total intellectual* received much critical comment. Sartre epitomized on the political left (Raymond Aron on the politically center right in France) the intellectual activist who draws on his notoriety as an intellectual to speak out of conscience on all the issues of the day. Bourdieu was sharply critical because he thought this kind of public intellectual role failed to bring any grounded expertise to the public debate or sufficiently challenge the very terms of the debate.

In contrast to Sartre's generalist view of the intellectual's political vocation, Bourdieu's preferred view comes much closer to Michel Foucault's idea of the *specific intellectual* who intervenes in the public arena only on those issues that his specialized knowledge permits him to speak about with authority. It is the authority of specialized knowledge not individual conscience (Sartre's model) that guides where and how the intellectual will enter the public debate.

Like Foucault, Bourdieu thinks the proper role for the intellectual is to attack the foundations of symbolic power, to question the fundamental assumptions made when people think politically. Foucault (1997: 131) says that 'the role of an intellectual is not to tell others what they have to do. By what right would he do so?'

> The work of an intellectual is not to shape others' political will: it is, through the analyses that he carried out in his own field, to question over and over again what is postulated as self-evident, to disturb people's mental habits, the way they do and think things.

What is a sociologist as a 'specific intellectual' to do? The sociologist is to contribute to public debate in a way that is compatible with authority of the specific expertise the sociologist can legitimately claim. In Bourdieu's conceptual language, the sociologist must convert the symbolic capital obtained from recognition for his scientific contributions into political capital.

In an effort to respond to shortcomings of the Foucaultian model, such as the highly individualistic character of intellectual work, increasing intellectual specialization, and the overwhelming dominance of mass media in public debate, Bourdieu develops the idea of the *collective intellectual*. He proposes a model of collective work by intellectuals on a small number of common objectives. We find an early formulation of the idea of the collective intellectual in the late 1980s.[12] The 1992 postscript 'For the corporatism of the universal' to *The Rules of Art* (Bourdieu, 1996a: 399–448) appears as a kind of manifesto that outlines an activist strategy calling for the collective organization of intellectuals, a call that 'takes a normative position based on the conviction that it is possible to use knowledge of the logic of the functioning of the fields of cultural production to draw up a realistic programme for the collective action of intellectuals.' It defines an activist role for the scientific intellectual that Bourdieu sees going back to the example set by Emile Zola during the Dreyfus Affair and that Bourdieu would more and more employ for the remainder of his life.

One of the special types of expertise that the sociological perspective can bring to the public arena is the capacity to analyze the conditions making possible political discourse, even in those areas not explicitly viewed as political. Bourdieu's social constructionist perspective on political discourse asks critically what creates the terms of public debate and how it is framed. In other words, the critical intellectual work for the sociologist is essentially a symbolic work, one of deconstructing and thereby demystifying the jargon of domination (the doxa) of official political discourse. In the later years this emphasis led Bourdieu to focus more and more of his attention on the role of journalism and the neo-liberal assumptions present in much journalistic political debate (Bourdieu, 1998a). The model of the collective intellectual role and of the scientific intellectual who attends primarily to critical analysis of political discourse would also seem to lead naturally to concern with the media and we in fact see this shift in concern later in his career (Swartz, 2003a). In fact, when reflecting on the social movement of the mid-nineties, of which he was one of the leading intellectuals, Bourdieu (2002a: 465–9) rejects any sharp distinction between the role of the scholar and the role of the political activist and advocates 'scholarship with commitment.' He presents the relationship between the researcher and the social movement as one where the researcher helps by providing instruments of analysis, created out of the autonomous logic of the scientific field, to use against the symbolic effects created by experts working for those multinational organizations promoting globalization. He (Bourdieu, 2002b: 466) distinguishes this role of providing critical conceptual tools from that of ideological control or prophetic pronouncements that he finds to be key dangers for organic intellectuals.

Bourdieu's model of a collective intellectual became institutionalized to some extent during his lifetime as a loose array of networks and centers across several organizational settings primarily but not exclusively within the French academic research and cultural world. It included contacts with former students, researchers, publishers, and academic circles.[13] It represented a kind of 'anti-political politics' model[14] where Bourdieu as the intellectual did not assume an administrative position within government or function as a kind of 'counselor to the prince' or to any political party, but is a permanent anti-establishment critic of the establishment, whether it is left or right, against injustice. Indeed, Bourdieu proved to be a sharp critic of the French Socialists soon after they came into power in 1980. This model contrasts with the position taken by Anthony Giddens who became an adviser to the Tony Blair regime in the United Kingdom and to Václav Havel who became an elected official in the Czech Republic.

Bourdieu, by contrast, is both heir to and reacts against a long tradition of French intellectuals assuming prominent positions in public life. To be a prominent artist, writer or teacher, and on the political left (though there were some on the political right as well) meant almost by definition taking on a public role of signing petitions, participating in public demonstrations, writing op-ed pieces, appearing on TV (in recent years), and so on. Bourdieu was frequently critical of French intellectuals for this kind of intellectual/political activism that was based on individual conscience and desire for public notoriety, rather than on scholarly expertise. Indeed, Bourdieu's criticism of Sartre as a total intellectual and Bourdieu's espousal of a specific and collective intellectual reflect this position.

Yet Bourdieu most always designed his work to have a public effect. He oriented his work toward 'public' issues, such as colonization, class inequality, education, and housing (Bourdieu, 2002a; Swartz, 2003a). He saw himself as forging concepts and developing analyses that political activists could use in particular domains, such as education in particular. Seldom did Bourdieu work on policy issues. His two reports from the Collège de France to the Socialist government on educational reform are notable exceptions.[15] He spoke as a 'critical sociologist' being sharply critical of other approaches and sociologists and calling for the reflexive practice of sociology.

Implications for the study and practice of politics

Thus, we can see in Bourdieu's sociology analysis of three types of power: power vested in particular resources (capitals); power concentrated in specific spheres of struggle over forms of capital (fields of power), and power as practical acceptance of existing social hierarchies (symbolic power and violence). The implications for the analysis of politics are numerous. Bourdieu offers a conceptual language that encourages examination of inter-relationships across levels of analysis and ana-lytical units that usually are isolated for specialized focus. It suggests an intimate and complex relationship between symbolic and material factors in the operation of power. Public opinion (Champagne, 1979, 1990) and political participation (Gaxie, 1978) are areas where Bourdieu's thinking can be of help to students of politics. Recent applications of various components of Bourdieu's can be found in the analysis of the state (Loveman, 2005), the analysis of social movements (Bloemraad, 2001; Crossley, 2002; Goldberg, 2003), the analysis of social and citizenship boundaries (Brubaker, 1992; Lamont and Fournier, 1992), the analysis of political culture (Aronoff, 2000), the analysis of political transformation in the post-Communist era in Eastern Europe (Eyal, 2003, 2005), and the analysis of the mass media (Benson, 1999; Benson and Neveu, 2005) to name just a few.

Bourdieu's thinking can also be a source of inspiration for the practice of demo-cratic politics (Wacquant, 2005). He invites sociologists to employ social scientific inquiry as a means to debunk taken-for-granted assumptions that seem crucial for maintenance of the established powers. He envisions a political vocation for the critical sociologist that would be politically relevant, but would not compromise the science of asking critical questions. Yet there are limits to Bourdieu's vision that is rooted in an excessively strong view of the role of symbolic power in maintain-ing power relations, a view that seems at odds even with the more direct forms of political activism Bourdieu himself adopted in his later years. Indeed, Bourdieu's own efforts as a public sociologist stand in sharp contrast to aspects of his theory of symbolic power and violence. He saw his sociology as an effort to denaturalize and defatalize the social world, which he tried to communicate to people. But given the powerful force of habitus to operate beyond the reaches of conscious decision making, it is not clear how the debunking force of sociology could be effective against the unconscious force of habitus and the dynamics of misrecognition it reinforced. I have noted how Bourdieu's shift in thinking and political practice seems to acknowledge to some extent this limitation.

Bourdieu's view of science calls for a rupture with common-sense under-standings. While agents are not dumb – they follow a logic of practice – they misrecognize the true nature of common-sense meanings; namely, that they are vested with unequal power relations that establish arbitrary hierarchies between individuals and groups. Only science can reveal the conditions of misrecogni-tion. There is no significant provision in Bourdieu's thinking for recognition of the conditions of misrecognition outside of the insights of science. This allocates to the social scientist a formidable role in creating the cultural conditions for social transformation. This line of reasoning also implies that we must therefore defend the autonomy of science at all costs because by defending the corporate interests of science we also defend the universal interest of humanity by provid-ing a means for freeing people from the clutches of misrecognition. As Burawoy (2005b: 429) says, this is 'quite a leap from science to the public defense of humanity.'

Nonetheless, Bourdieu's perspective challenges the commonly held view that symbolic power is simply 'symbolic.' Symbolic meanings and classifications are a constitutive force in organizing power relations in stratified social orders. Moreover, the concept of symbolic violence is designed as a critical break with the view that power has become much more benign and less relevant in societies where the most authoritarian and crudest techniques of coercion have been replaced with persuasion, consent, choice, influence, and negotiation. It reminds us that power remains very much an organizing force in modern societies though its forms have changed.

Notes

1 Some notable exceptions include Calhoun, 2005; Grenfell, 2005; Lee, 1998; Steinmetz, 1999; Topper, 2001; and, of course, Wacquant (2004, 2005), who belonged to Bourdieu's research center at the Collège de France.
2 The term comes from Nelson Goodman (1978).
3 Bourdieu (1994: 4) writes that this special type of capital, a kind of *meta-capital*, emerges with the concentration of other types of capital and 'enables the state to exercise power over the different fields and over the different particular species of capital, and especially over the rates of conversion between them (and thereby over the relations of force between their holders).'
4 Symbolic power is 'the power to impose and to inculcate a vision of divisions, that is, the power to make visible and explicit social divisions that are implicit, [and] is political power *par excellence*' (Bourdieu, 1990c: 138).
5 Symbolic violence is 'a gentle violence, imperceptible and invisible even to its victims, exerted for the most part through the purely symbolic channels of communication and cognition (more precisely, misrecognition), recognition, or even feeling' (Bourdieu, 2001a: 1–2).
6 Wacquant (Bourdieu and Wacquant 1992: 119) says of symbolic capital that Bourdieu's 'whole work may be read as a hunt for its varied forms and effects.'
7 Accardo (1983), Grenfell (2005), Pels (1995), Robbins (1991) and Wacquant (1992) are others who have caught this activist sense of Bourdieu's conception of social scientific research.
8 Bourdieu and Hahn (1970: 20). See Swartz (1997: 247–69) for a discussion of how Bourdieu thinks that the sociologist, armed with the tools of critical science, can and should have a responsibility to play a key role in modern political life.
9 See Bourdieu and Wacquant (1992) and Swartz (1997) for a fuller discussion.
10 Bourdieu (1989a: 100) advances the following proposition to speak of the political effects of increased field autonomy:

> The greater the intellectuals' independence from mundane interests because of their specific expertise (e.g., the scientific authority of an Oppenheimer or the intellectual authority of a Sartre), the greater their inclination to <u>assert</u> this independence by criticizing the powers that be, the greater the symbolic *effectiveness of* whatever political positions they might take.

Thus membership in a relatively autonomous field of cultural production is crucial for, in Bourdieu's thinking, it seems to generate a propensity to contest the power of holders of economic and political capital and to do so with greater effectiveness.
11 See Poupeau and Discepolo (2004) and Swartz (2003) for accounts of his public political activities.

12 See Bourdieu (1989a), 'The Corporatism of the Universal: The Role of Intellectuals in the Modern World', and (2002c), 'Pour une Internationale des intellectuels'.
13 The *Raisons d'Agir* association is the most successful, continuing expression of Bourdieu's vision for the 'collective intellectual.' Dedicated to the goal of bringing social scientific research into the public arena for advancing the cause of the political left, affiliated members have published numerous books and reports and been moderately successful in entering public debates in France. In 2003 the association launched a new journal, *Savoir/Agir*, that is now in its seventh edition. See the *Raisons d'Agir* website for both a history and a current agenda of political actions since Bourdieu's death: http://www.raisonsdagir.org (accessed 4/3/2009). Nevertheless, Bourdieu's collective intellectual project has not yet found broader and robust institutionalization in the form of an international collective body of intellectuals who intervene regularly with a common political message on current political issues.
14 The term is suggested by Dick Pels (1995).
15 'Propositions pour un enseignement de l'avenir' (Bourdieu, 2002d) and 'Principes pour une réflexion sur les contenues d'enseignement' (Bourdieu, 2002e).

5 Dis-identification and class identity

Mike Savage, Elizabeth Silva and
Alan Warde

Bourdieu's contribution to stratification analysis is controversial. He offered a subtle and complex analysis in his essay 'What makes a social class?' (1987), the significance and coherence of which are lucidly teased out by Elliot Weininger (2005). The analysis entailed the isolation of different types of capital, and the possibilities for their combination, conversion and transmission as they operate across different fields. The essay explicitly rejected the possibility to read off class formation or class identification from distributions of capital. A somewhat different impression is given in *Distinction* (Bourdieu, 1984), where the notion of class habitus serves to underpin a fairly simple correspondence between class position and cultural practice and within which actors' reflections on their class identity have little part to play. The results of this disjuncture may be partly understood in the context of the relationship of Bourdieu and his school to mainstream European stratification theorists. The latter criticized Bourdieu for lack of theoretical and technical rigour and sought to exclude his approach from wider consideration. In turn, Bourdieu, ignored substantive sociological issues upon which that orthodoxy thrived. One such issue was class identity, a phenomenon which had always intrigued positivist approaches to class analysis, because of the lack of correspondence between 'objective' characteristics and 'subjective' perceptions of class location. Bourdieu, of course, considered one aspect of his general theoretical contribution to be the overcoming of such a distinction and hence probably never recognized it as a relevant problem. However, other scholars inspired by but not aligned with the Bourdieusian programme, of whom there were many in Britain, were concerned to examine the alignment between his work and mainstream class analysis and make connections between them (e.g. Skeggs, 1997; Devine, *et al.*, 2005; Savage, Warde and Devine, 2005; Le Roux, *et al.*, 2008). One topic for such attention became class identity, or more specifically 'dis-identification', which concept was used as an orientation to contemporary debates in Britain.

Prompted by high-profile claims that we now live in a 'classless society', yet mindful of great, and intensifying, social inequalities, sociologists in the past decade have explored the means by which people identify with, and more generally talk about social class (for examples see Savage, 2000; Devine, *et al.*, 2005). This body of work has generated a large measure of agreement about the paradoxical and ambivalent features of contemporary class awareness. At one level, the idea of class seems to be widely understood and is clearly recognized as an important feature of social inequality. Yet, at the same time, people are generally reluctant to identify themselves unambiguously as members of social classes and class identities do not necessarily seem highly meaningful to them. This seems different from the main emphases of the classical tradition of post-war British sociology and cultural studies, which insisted how distinctive class cultures were related to structural class inequalities and political mobilization (Marshall, *et al.*, 1988; Devine and Savage, 2005; Reay, 2005). This recent work, often indebted to the arguments of Pierre Bourdieu, focuses instead on evasions and 'dis-identifications' from class (Skeggs, 1997, 2004a; Bottero, 2005; Payne and Glew, 2005).

Taking stock of this recent revival of interest in class identities, we explore familiar questions using detailed survey and qualitative (interview and focus group) material generated as part of the 'Cultural Capital and Social Exclusion' (CCSE) project to offer an account of the nature of contemporary class awareness.[1] Do people in the UK feel that they belong to a social class, and if so, which one? To what extent are such identities meaningful, and do they incorporate class terminology into their talk, whether through survey responses, in qualitative interviews, or in focus groups?

In the first part of the chapter we examine key unresolved issues in arguments about 'dis-identification' from class. Secondly, we report on the evidence of class consciousness gathered from the survey material generated as part of the CCSE project which points to strikingly limited amounts of overt class identification. Thirdly, we examine the 'class talk' evident from both focus groups and interviews to review the forms and contexts in which the term *class* is explicitly used currently by people in the UK. Here we show that very few people willingly and unreservedly claimed direct class membership, especially of the middle class, except when this is defined fluidly, for instance as part of a 'mobility story'. In that sense we argue that 'dis-identification' is at least as pertinent in distancing people from middle-class identities as from stigmatized working-class ones. This ambivalence demonstrates how our research participants sought to distance themselves from direct class categorization, while personally often simultaneously being well aware of the existence of a 'politics of classification'.

Dis-identification?

Since the 1990s British sociologists have probed an intriguing paradox: that while social inequalities in life chances have intensified, there actually appears to be limited, and possibly declining, overt class consciousness and awareness (e.g. Bradley, 1996; Skeggs, 1997; Savage, 2000; Crompton, 2008). Some sociological theorists have argued that class awareness has declined as a result of globalization, the emergence of reflexive modernity, and the development of consumer cultures, especially through the way these encourage individualization (Giddens, 1991b; Bauman, 1998). More recently however, critics have emphasized that class identities have been re-made rather than eradicated, less along lines of collective and solidaristic sentiments and more through individualized emotional frames (Savage,

2000). Interview data have been mobilized to demonstrate how the minutiae of class hierarchies continue to inform the making of differences in daily life, much of which has been influenced by feminist concerns (Bradley, 1996; Lawler, 2000; Savage, *et al.*, 2001; Walkerdine, *et al.*, 2001; Payne and Glew, 2005). Similar findings have been elaborated on the basis of ethnographic evidence (Skeggs, 1997; Hey, 1997; Charlesworth, 2000; Evans, 2006), surveys (Savage, 2000; Heath, *et al.*, 2008), and historical and documentary analyses (Savage, 2005b, 2007; Lawler, 2008).

Arguments about 'dis-identification' stem from Beverly Skeggs's (1997) pivotal work, based on a longitudinal ethnography of young working-class women in the Midlands in the late 1980s and early 1990s. Skeggs argued that class is absolutely central to the lives of the young women. Yet, so powerful was class as a structuring feature, that the women themselves could not easily articulate an account of it. Instead, they were more vested in respectable and feminine identities which were more legitimate and socially acceptable. Elements of this approach which emphasize the mismatch between objective life chances and people's subjective awareness of class can be traced to Richard Sennett and Jonathan Cobb's *The Hidden Injuries of Class* (1993), and the approach now forms the current orthodoxy in the UK (for other similar statements, see Walkerdine, *et al.*, 2001; Hey, 1997; Reay, 1998b; Savage, 2000; Savage, *et al.*, 2001). It is also increasingly influential in other countries, for instance Chile (Mendez, 2008) and Denmark (Prieur, 2008).

However, the 'dis-identification' argument raises a series of important critical issues. We highlight four of them.

1   It can be used to justify 'false consciousness' models of identities, which allow researchers to read behind what people actually say in order to reveal a 'deeper' identity which is only accessible to the skilful researcher. The issue here is how one handles what is said by respondents. In her chapter on '(Dis)Identifications of Class', few of Skeggs's (1997) participants actually mention class at all, and the focus is on how notions of moral worth and value are talked about in more elliptical ways. Although this demonstrates very effectively the power of stigmatizing and moralizing forces, it is contestable whether class is the fundamental underpinning of their discomforts. Alternative concepts, such as status, might do the job equally well. Most importantly, and in keeping with feminist arguments, it may be preferable to avoid seeing 'dis-identification' as an absence of class identity and instead demonstrate the positive and performative ways in which class is actively effaced, exploring the precise terms in which class is dissimulated. Investigation requires probing to determine whether, when people discuss moral and political issues associated with inequality, they are actually using a form of class-based frame of reference, even if not overtly using class terminology.

2   It is not clear whether dis-identification is restricted to those holding working-class identities. Are the middle classes, who presumably feel less stigmatized, less likely to dis-identify from class? Or is there a more general process by

which everyone feels that they need to distance themselves from the more overt language of class? For example: 'Who would want to be seen as working class? (perhaps only academics are left)', Skeggs muses (1997: 95). However, not all of the working class 'dis-identify'. Survey evidence typically indicates that over half the population continue to see themselves as working class, there having been only a moderate decline in working-class identification since the 1960s (Evans, 1992) despite de-industrialization and the shrinking numbers of manual workers. As Mike Savage and colleagues (2001) argued, there is also a tendency for the contemporary middle classes to reject direct middle-class identification through focusing on their 'mobility stories'.

3   What is the relationship between class and other inequalities, notably gender? Possibly the working-class women studied by Skeggs are more likely to dis-identify with the working class than are working-class men? However, ethnographic evidence, for example that presented by Simon Charlesworth (2000), does not suggest that young working-class men are particularly proud of being working class. Nor does survey data necessarily suggest that on the whole women are less likely to identify as working class than men (see the discussion in Heath, *et al.*, 2008).

4   Finally, what is actually meant by class labels, notably middle class and working class, which have always been the two most popular ways of defining one's class identity? Savage, *et al.* (2001) argued that it is less important to focus on the precise class label used, and more on how people narrate class; the major difference being between those who were confident enough to use class labels reflexively and those who feel defensive and prefer to avoid being positioned in class terms. The latter are often concerned to emphasize that they are 'ordinary', which they do either by adopting a middle-class label (taken to mean average, typical or normal) or a working-class one (also taken to mean typical because 'most people work').

To explore these issues further we use results from the CCSE project whose mixed-method research design offered some considerable advantages (Silva, *et al.*, 2009). The project comprises survey data (from a nationally representative sample of 1,564 respondents in the UK, and an ethnic boost sample of 227 individuals). It also includes qualitative interviews with 44 householders (22 of whom also answered the questionnaire, making it possible to link their survey and interview accounts) and 11 members of the British 'élite'. It also contains data from 25 focus groups involving 143 participants. The survey focused on respondents' cultural taste, knowledge, and participation in the areas of visual art, reading, music, sport, television and film, and embodiment. While we do not report our detailed analyses of this material here (see the comprehensive account in Bennett, *et al.*, 2009), we should note that the study demonstrates that class does have a primary and powerful structuring effect on cultural tastes and participation. We therefore take it as given for the purposes of this paper that class is objectively very important in affecting cultural practices and life chances. Our focus in this chapter is on how the research material – survey responses, interviews and focus groups – convey popular understandings of class and class positions.

The limits of class identity: survey evidence

The survey contained two relevant questions about class identity: whether respondents thought of themselves as belonging to a social class, and whether or not they did, which it would be if they had to choose.[2] This last question mirrors similar questions asked on numerous other British surveys (for instance *British Social Attitudes* survey, see Heath, *et al.*, 2008) and allows us to make some comparisons with other survey analyses.

One intriguing finding (see Table 5.1) is that only 33 per cent of our sample thought of themselves as belonging to a social class, the lowest level ever found in a UK survey – considerably below the figure of 45 per cent which was found in the survey conducted at a similar time and reported by Anthony Heath and colleagues (2008). Why might our responses be lower? Perhaps the positioning of this question after a battery of questions about people's cultural interests somehow discouraged respondents from expressing the feeling that they belonged to a class, maybe because they had been made more aware of the power of cultural classifications and hence wanted to avoid – through refusing a class identity – the impression that they themselves were directly involved in processes of classification.

Responses to this question are structured partly in the manner anticipated by Skeggs (1997). Those who are most structurally disadvantaged – the young, the poorly educated and women – are the most likely not to report a class identity. The proportion of those who feel they belong to a class drops to 22 per cent amongst the 18–24 year olds, 29 per cent amongst women, and 28 per cent of those with no educational qualifications. Higher levels of class identification are exhibited by men (37 per cent), those over 65 years of age (37 per cent), the professional and executive class (38 per cent) and university graduates (39 per cent).

Whether or not they normally thought of themselves as belonging to a class, all respondents were asked in the follow-up question to say which class they thought they belonged to. An unusually high proportion, 8 per cent, refused a class identity even when prompted (the usual figure is below 5 per cent). The general patterns thereafter are similar to findings from other studies. Two-thirds identify themselves either as middle or working class, with those identifying as working class (41 per cent) easily outnumbering those who see themselves as middle class (27 per cent). If one puts together all the working-class labels (including lower working class, 3 per cent, upper working class, 9 per cent), then 53 per cent identify as working class, compared to 39 per cent who claim to be middle class (including 10 per cent lower middle class, and 2 per cent upper middle class). Hardly anyone thinks they are upper class. The extent to which middle-class labels remain relatively unpopular is striking: unlike most other nations, the British still do not adopt middle-class identity as their 'default' position (see the comparative discussion in Zunz, 2002).

Table 5.1 Identification and class identity

Categories		Belongs to a class %	Does not belong to class %	Total* numbers
Gender	Men	37	63	708
	Women	29	71	849
Age	18–24 year olds	22	79	144
	25–34	30	70	295
	35–44	34	66	314
	45–54	35	65	266
	55–64	33	67	238
	65–74	37	63	168
	75+	37	63	129
Occupational class	Professional and executive	38	62	360
	Intermediate class	32	68	446
	Working class	31	69	708
Educational level	No educational qualification	29	71	417
	'O' level	28	72	371
	'A' level	32	68	210
	Vocational	37	63	169
	University	39	61	356
Total		**32.5**	**67.5**	**1,557**

*Due to missing data not all subtotals will equal the overall total of 1557.

Class talk: the power of classification

Our qualitative data generally bear out the survey findings regarding the relatively muted character of direct class identification, but with some important caveats and qualifications. We found relatively little explicit reference to class in the interviews, but the notion was addressed more frequently and directly in the focus groups whose members had the chance to engage collectively with one another. This contrast reminds us that different methods themselves are conducive to producing different kinds of class account (see Silva, *et al.*, 2009). In only two out of 11 'élite' interviews and in 17 out of our 44 household interviews was 'class' mentioned at any point by the interviewee. For the élite interviews these two cases emerged spontaneously out of discussion. For the household interviews, references to class usually arose in response to a question at the end, where the interviewee was shown a card with different classes on it and asked to pick which, if any, applied to them (see question in note 2 at the end of this chapter), although this question was not systematically asked in every case. Only in 5 cases out of 44 did the interviewees introduce the term 'class' themselves in their discussion, where it invariably served as an adjectival qualifier. For instance, Maria, a teacher from a northern city, referred to her mother growing up in 'working-class inner city'. Jenny, a writer, talked about 'working-class' music. Vasudev, an owner of a small business, talked about his house being in 'not a very upper-class area'.

By contrast, the term *class* was explicitly used more frequently by participants in focus groups, where it featured in 13 out of the 25 groups. Only Amani, in the women professional focus group, explicitly denied class belonging: 'I do not fit into any class.' However, the idea that class is of limited importance was quite widespread. The 'business élites' group seemed to think that class has disappeared, and there were other instances of this opinion among 'professionals' and the 'Black middle class'. However, class – with a qualifier like 'working' or 'middle' – was used on many occasions (as an adjective) to explain differences in behaviour. It was often used after the fashion of lay sociology. In all bar two of the focus groups where the term was used, people demonstrated that they know how to use the concept of class to classify people or practices. That means that the term *class* is used to talk about others more than about self, more as an account of 'the world out there' than something which is directly relevant to the personal experience of any individual in the group.

CCSE has an unusual resource to employ since ten of the interviewees who were asked about class had also previously answered the survey, allowing identification of discrepancies between what was claimed in these two research encounters. Interestingly, two out of the ten actually changed their class identification at the interview (from middle to 'upper working' class in the case of Jim Shaw, a building consultant and from working class to 'lower middle class' in the case of secondary-school teacher Rita McKay).

When asked about his social class Jim Shaw, a retired, affluent contractor who had worked in the building trade changed his mind about whether he was middle class: 'I would say upper working class'. Discussing how he might feel in a potentially embarrassing social situation of a vignette, he emphasized that you 'take me as you get me and that's it.' 'I wouldn't say we like to be flash or anything like that, we just like to be normal'; '… we never go out of our way just to say to people look at us, we've plenty of money sort of thing you know.' Jim is one example indicating the muted appeal of middle-class identity partly due to its assumed association with snobbish characteristics. Even the well-off who could have chosen to pass themselves off as middle class if they had wanted to, found this a problem to negotiate.

This type of disavowal of being middle class, which is seen to embody a kind of conspicuous display and a contrived way of relating to others (on the historical precedents of which see Savage, 2005b), was even exhibited by a young couple who acknowledge their own social and cultural advantages. Secondary-school teacher Rita McKay is white, has a rural background and feels at home living in a secluded part of Scotland. She has middle-class professional parents. Her dream home would be bigger but similar to the current one. 'I think I ... certainly, you know, I have kind of middle-class values I think, and obviously sort of middle-class profession as well.' The qualifiers are informative. She ultimately refuses to classify herself straightforwardly as middle class, saying 'I think probably lower middle class'. The same applies to her husband, an agricultural supplies salesman, who prides himself on his cultured upbringing: 'I was brought up to polish my shoes, hence I have never owned a pair of trainers.' Yet he also classified himself as lower middle class, reflecting:

> 'I wouldn't say we were well off, we're both from families who own ground, more my side than the other, my father's a fairly large area, but up further north. I don't know maybe a bit of snobbery but salary as opposed to a weekly wage I think comes into it, that's from the old school. [...] Probably social circle, a lot of professional friends, whether it's you know services, school teacher friends, professional on the sales side of things. I'm as happy going to a black tie dinner as I am going to McDonald's and that side so ...'

The shifts in self-identification represented by Jim and Rita (and shared with her husband) support Savage, *et al.*'s (2001) suggestion that the distinction between middle class and working class may be less salient to people than sociologists might like to think and also implies strongly that research context makes a difference.

Of those ten interviewees, five reported in the survey that they normally thought of themselves as belonging to a social class. Three of these, Vasudev, a business owner, and James and Jenny, both educated professionals, went on to identify themselves as middle class. However, neither Vasudev nor James incorporated significant reference to class into the interviews about their daily lives and cultural consumption.

Nevertheless, even though our most privileged interviewees did not talk directly about being middle or upper class, this did not prevent some of them from showing distance from, even resentment towards, the working class. In some respects, a desire to evade classification is their overriding concern. Thus Jenny Hammett, who studied to be a librarian, and is creative writing tutor for university as well as a published writer, discussing her taste in music, says when explaining why she does not like jazz, country and western, electronic, heavy metal and urban music, that 'maybe it's more a kind of, I don't know about working class or background thing, I don't know. Having said that, my brothers liked country, my sister likes country.' Thinking aloud, seeking to understand the roots of her preferences, she comments that she is working class by origin, though she has identified herself as lower middle class in her survey responses. Yet she is culturally sophisticated. For a dream home she says she would like a minimalist style and cites projects from the television programme 'Grand Designs' (Silva and Wright, 2009). She is an omnivore (see Warde, *et al.*, 2007), knowledgeable and engaged with many forms of culture.

Similar tendencies are evident amongst other research participants who express dislike for 'working-class' practices but seek to avoid defining themselves as straightforwardly middle class. Fruit Bat, a young laboratory technician talks about 'reverse snobbery': 'I've heard people say that they don't want to go to opera for instance, or theatre because that's above them or you know that's for people with taste and they're not interested in it … which is a reverse of someone wanting to go but not being allowed.' His dream home would be a traditional old-fashioned manor house or castle where he could entertain large groups of people. When presented in interview with a list of classes to which he might belong he says:

> Oh, I hate classes. Well, I'm definitely not upper class. And I'm not really sure the difference between working and middle class any more because it seems a little bit blurred … I'd have to say middle. I think standards have changed so much, it's not a case of having to go down the pit for three days in a row, coming up, you know, back to your bare house and eating bread for tea.

Another instance is Cherie Campbell, a heritage worker who is happy to talk about the politics of snobbery, but did not normally think of herself as belonging to a class (she claimed to be middle class when pressed in the survey). In discussing her response to an attitude question in the survey proposing that the old snobbery associated with cultural taste had disappeared, she changed her mind in the interview in the light of her distaste for the then recent media naming and portraying of working class people as 'chavs':

> … because they've taken to wearing Burberry baseball caps, and this bling jewellery and the gold plated jewellery and all this kind of stuff, … you wouldn't say that about a coloured person or somebody on the basis of their sex but I mean just every time you pick up the paper they're saying nasty things about the chav style, and what they're really talking about is people, the way people dress in housing schemes and it's nasty.

These accounts indicate a concern to establish distance from the labels attached to classes when applied to self, even whilst recognizing their applicability to others. In addition they reveal a distinctive feature of contemporary class talk, discernable more generally in interviews and focus groups, which is a concern to resist middle-class identities. By contrast, and contrary to Skeggs (1997), who emphasizes the stigmatized nature of working-class identities, we detected a more vibrant and positive evaluation of the 'down-to-earth' values associated with the working class, based around a lack of pretension. Consider Joe Smith, an electrician: 'If anyone comes round, they take us as they find us.' For his dream home: 'It doesn't have to be a grand old house or nothing like that, just new, modern and posh!' His wife Edie comments: 'We're just working class, we're just your everyday, we haven't got loads of money, we haven't got, we don't, no airs and graces, just working class we are.' A similar form of working-class identity was also explicitly and readily embraced by Joe. The testimony of Jim Shaw (above) also reflects a positive evaluation of working-class virtues.

Resistance to middle-class identity when considered together with a second feature, an awareness of the politics of classification, offers a distinctive angle through which to understand 'dis-identification' from class. This may lead either to a reflexive concern to emphasize one's own mobility between classes, or, in some contexts, to pockets of political class consciousness.

One important device allowing people to refuse a direct class identity whilst recognizing how classes involve cultural classification, is the deployment of a mobility story. This allows them to acknowledge that they are now middle class, but as part of a story of how they had risen in the social ladder and, therefore, were not born into privilege. Ali's account, from the lesbian focus group, was probably the most explicit in adopting a middle-class identity, but this was premised on the fact that she had not been born into this class.

ALI: It's all kind of changed my own taste in a way, kind of thing. But I know that I'm quite middle class actually you know. I'm like from a working-class background but, you know ..., I go to university, you know, I listen to Radio 4, I like classical music and jazz blah, blah, blah ..., you know, I do karaoke as well but you know my ... they're tastes like ... when I'm myself my tastes are quite similar to tastes of my family or tastes I was brought up with. I don't feel snobby about other people's choices about that. I just know what I like for myself.

Thus, tellingly, Ali's recognition of her middle-class tastes was linked to an account of her social mobility, so becoming a marker of her achievements and individuality (see also Savage, *et al.*, 2001; Savage, 2007). We can also see her awareness of the power of cultural classification. Such recognition is evident amongst many of the ethnic minorities. Angela from the Black middle-class focus group is one example.

ANGELA: Yes, yeah, my parents were, without doubt, of working-class background and I went to a girls' grammar school in a very nice area of [City], and I went on to quite a nice sixth form and then I got into Oxford, so there was kind of quite a spread in terms of my life experiences based from [City] through to university and then entering the law and I guess that I've made my own personal decisions about what I, what I take on and what I don't. And I feel quite lucky in that I feel I understand um some middle class. I mean I know that I'm classed as middle class now because of my occupation, but certain things would have been lost on me, I think, if I hadn't had the experience that I have of the educational system.

A further example was evident in the account of Nimesh Gopal, a catering supervisor in the West Midlands, who saw that 'in terms of experience' he was 'made middle class'. 'I would say that I'm a middle class you see. Although I am working class but I have seen life when I was a shopkeeper and other things you see, so I would rather say middle class.' While the location of his home, the cultural capital he displayed, the self-classification of his wife and his job delivering meals on wheels to pensioners all pointed to an objective working-class location, he prefers to name an 'earned' middle-class identity for himself. Overall, no one expressed great pride in being middle class, nor any resultant sense of superiority.

Not all ethnic minority members felt confident enough to deploy the language of class. None of the four Asian focus groups use the term *class* at all, ethnicity being the primary and fundamental marker of identification. For them, class is clearly not a very significant consideration, or strong identity, at least in relation to issues of taste. Less highly educated and older ethnic minorities were more defensive. Stafford's case is revealing. He is Afro-Caribbean, works as an assembler and welder, is 62 years old and lives on his own in housing association property. The interviewer noted that the experience of being interviewed might have felt 'like a trial' to him. Two exchanges sum him up. Talking about TV viewing he says he does not like to go deeply into things. Talking about his style of dress he says that he prefers not to stand out. 'I'm not from here' is a notion figuring strongly in his account. In the survey he claimed not normally to see himself as a member of a class (though he chose a working-class identity when pressed) and he agreed that snobbery was a thing of the past, which he seemed to associate with his experience of work. He said, referring to employers or managers being less aloof and authoritarian: 'they are more approachable now'.

INTERVIEWER: … class distinctions … do you think they're less important now?
STAFFORD: It could be there, depends on where you go. But I think society lose a bit of that now because of the way people live you know.
INTERVIEWER: In what way? What do you mean 'the way people live'?
STAFFORD: Well you have a breakdown, from the hierarchies come down, you have a breakdown in society so – you find they are approachable easily now rather than before.
INTERVIEWER: so 'they' being people of higher, higher in the hierarchy or …?
STAFFORD: or could be, it could be other people you get more educated now so you can deliver yourself, so you can approach anybody, you don't care where they come from or who they are. You just say what you feel or what you like so you don't subordinate much now.

An overarching awareness of the politics of classification can lead to various kinds of response, ranging from a refusal of middle-class identity, to the deployment of mobility stories, and to various forms of defensiveness. However, in certain situations it can lead instead to a politicized response. This was especially marked in the three Welsh working-class focus groups. They were distinctive in the extent to which they see the social world and the operation of culture in class terms, allied also to a national sense of Welshness. They make quite extensive use of the concept of class, and are clearly aware that class plays a role in the making of personal and social boundaries, and partly as a consequence of the different cultural activities with which classes engage. They talk directly about the stigmatizing power of the middle classes, and the way that élites manipulate cultural and social participation (see also Warde, 2008b). Here is an example from the skilled manual workers focus group:

MODERATOR: I don't like talking about social class because it makes us sound like snobs but …
BJ: Yeah, but there is a class difference there. There is yes.
LIZ: Definitely.
BJ: I work for 'Odd-Bins' and I go to wine tastings and people ask me my opinion on wines. Yeah, I go to wine tastings and you meet some quite arty geeks there. And they are all like sniffing the wine.

A similar account was evident amongst the supervisors of manual workers:

DAI: But ignoring that, the people who go to the opera, they seem to understand where the play takes place. What those people are feeling. And that's not what we do. It's more a social type of thing again. It's been taught to them in their schools.
GLYN: Again you're talking about a class difference …
DAI: I wouldn't say class, I'd say *crachach*. [Authors' note: *crachach* means 'posh'.]
GLYN: No, no, it's a class difference. The people that go to this are people … [pause] Convent Garden, for instance, the majority of people that go there, well, they are not short of a few bob. And it's part of their social life. And the ordinary people, I say the ordinary people because whatever we might say about ourselves, working class, others think they are middle class, but a lot of us don't want to mix, not mix, but don't want to be looked down upon.

This group also had a distinctly class-based recognition of the power of culture, with a dispute about whether public support for the arts was concerned with subsidizing 'the middle class' (Dai's view) or 'the upper middle class' (Glyn's view). However, other disadvantaged groups in England, Scotland and Northern Ireland did not produce this kind of class awareness and resentment.[3] As the reference to *crachach* suggest, there seems to be a distinctively Welsh form of class awareness, one able to mobilize the resources of national identity to buttress class awareness.

It is clear from all these examples that, in talking about class, many research participants understand that a wider politics of classification exists. This may take the lay sociological form of understanding that certain class groups are predisposed to particular sorts of thing, a taste for particular sports or musical genres, for example. It may very occasionally (as with the Welsh working-class groups) lead to a politicized analysis in which the state is seen as supporting middle-class culture. Alternatively, it may provoke a reaction which is more an assertion of individual exceptionalism, that one's own particular biography confounds any specific class stereotyping. In other instances it leads to defensiveness. We would argue that this awareness of the recognition of the importance of classification processes is central to how individuals deploy idioms of class in their accounts and equally how they avoid the use of the term. Moreover, we found instances in which these very processes of classification affected the accounts generated in our research as the rules of interaction in focus groups, or in interviews, positioned individuals differently in the research relationship, affecting the topics of talk (see Silva and Wright, 2005).

Conclusions

Although our data have their limitations, we feel confident enough to draw three substantive conclusions. Firstly, claiming a class identity is a minority response if conceived in terms of membership of a class collectivity in the classical sociological sense, especially if the corollary is expressly class politics. Only the Welsh working class exhibited any political class consciousness. Most people, from all social groups, present ambivalent accounts of class position and location. However, lack of direct awareness and explicit acknowledgement of one's own class membership is mediated by a wider recognition of the cultural politics of class, in which they have a sense of the stakes – snobbishness, élitism, ordinariness, decency – which are implied in the mobilization of class idioms. This demonstrates, following Bourdieu and Skeggs, the importance of the issues posed by 'dis-identification' arguments. People generally recognize that they live in an unequal social world. This animates many people's sensitivity to a wider politics of positioning and classification in which they are keen to find reasons for being themselves outside or beyond social labels, whether by effacing them, parodying them (as in the *crachach* reference), providing mobility stories to explain how they are transitional between them, and so forth. Ambivalence is then not the product of confusion or ignorance, but actively and creatively produced. It is also a means of elaborating a distinctive social identity which recognizes the pervasiveness of inequality.

Second, whereas much of the literature focuses on working-class disidentification, we have evidence of similar processes amongst the middle classes. Those who have benefited most from the remaking of neo-liberal capitalism often seek to efface their own distinctive privileges. Many people continue to find it difficult to claim a middle-class identity, resisting being defined straightforwardly as 'middle class' in contrast with many other nations, where a middle-class identity is often chosen as relatively 'neutral' (Devine, 2005; Zunz, 2002). Working-class identification is actually more common among survey respondents, and some people continue to take pride in seeing themselves as working class.

Third, and most speculatively, perhaps a comprehensive analysis of contemporary class identities needs to go beyond the concept of dis-identification. Although this concept was vital in generating a more subtle account of class identities, it suffers from the potential problem of assuming a 'deficit' view of identity, where the lack of an obvious class identification is emphasized. Following feminist arguments about identity, it is more useful to focus on the mechanisms by which even ambivalent and hesitant identities are manufactured and defined. This, we suggest, supplies an agenda for the study of the 'politics of classification', of the way that people today are surrounded by innumerable modes of classification – social, cultural, moral, ethical – which create instabilities and anxieties at the same time as reproducing class terminology.

Finally, on a theoretical note, the phenomenon of dis-identification supplies a reason for agreeing with Bourdieu that orthodox approaches which distinguish sharply between objective and subjective class are likely to be ineffective, but that nevertheless, paying specific attention to how people understand the attributes of class positions and to how they talk about class, is a valuable focus for continuing sociological investigation. Class identity was difficult for Bourdieu theoretically because he could offer no immediate apparent connection between the combinations of different types and volume of capital of an agent and class identity, other than to appeal to its being intrinsic to class habitus. The view that the concept of habitus presents too passive or automatic an account of the self conscious actor has led many scholars, otherwise or formerly sympathetic to Bourdieu, to emphasize processes of classification (e.g. Lamont, Chapter 10 in this volume). This would appear compatible with a recognition that the distribution of capitals within populations provides a useful way to understand structural inequalities (Savage, 2005b; Warde and Savage, 2010) while still leaving implications for class identity somewhat opaque. One corrective may be to examine the historical record. The analysis by Heath and colleagues (2008) of *The British Social Attitude* survey data shows that since the 1960s, more than half the population have typically responded to questions asking them if they normally think they belong to a social class with a negative reply. Savage (2007), comparing the accounts of Mass-Observers in 1948 with those in the 1990s, argues that whereas in the earlier period the educated middle classes thought it was vulgar to talk about class and would tend to give terse and evasive responses to directives probing this issue, by the 1990s they were more likely to talk, sometimes at length, about their class experiences and identities. If the content of class talk is historically and institutionally dependent then we need both a theoretical framework which accounts for the specific power contexts in which culture operates as a mechanism for classification (cf. Bennett, Chapter 8 in this volume) and further empirical work to disentangle the significance of what is, and what is not said.

Acknowledgement

The authors would like to thank Tony Bennett, Annick Prieur and Gitte Sommer Harrits for comments on a previous version of this chapter.

Notes

1 The research team for the ESRC project Cultural Capital and Social Exclusion: A Critical Investigation (Award no R000239801) comprised Tony Bennett (Principal

Applicant), Mike Savage, Elizabeth Silva, Alan Warde (Co-Applicants), David Wright and Modesto Gayo-Cal (Research Fellows). The applicants were jointly responsible for the design of the national survey and the focus groups and household interviews that generated the quantitative and qualitative data for the project. Elizabeth Silva, assisted by David Wright, co-ordinated the analyses of the qualitative data from the focus groups and household interviews. Mike Savage and Alan Warde, assisted by Modesto Gayo-Cal, co-ordinated the analyses of the quantitative data produced by the survey. Tony Bennett was responsible for the overall direction and co-ordination of the project.

2 'Do you think of yourself as belonging to any particular social class?' Yes/No. 'If you had to choose one from the following, which social class would you say you belonged to?' Lower working, working, upper working, lower middle, middle, upper middle, upper, none of these.

3 We did not conduct focus groups with working-class participants in Scotland, which might also have produced similar findings. The working-class focus groups conducted in England were all from ethnic minority communities. The focus group with benefit claimants in Northern Ireland made no reference to issues of class at all.

6 From the theory of practice to the practice of theory

Working with Bourdieu in research in higher education choice

Diane Reay

The backdrop to this chapter is my own critique of the use of habitus within educational research (Reay, 2004), where I argue that it is used pervasively but mostly as intellectual display without doing much, if any, analytic work. Reinforcing this tendency to utilize habitus superficially, as a form of academic gravitas rather than an active analytic tool, are the ways in which it is regularly deployed independently of the concept of field. So this chapter is attempting to do a number of different things. It is examining the utility of the notion of *habitus* in empirical work, but also its limitations. However, beyond exploring habitus' analytic potential, the chapter is attempting to make connections between habitus as a conceptual tool and the possibilities it holds for contributing to theoretical explanations, not only of social reproduction, but also of social transformation.

In order to do this, the chapter draws on data from three ESRC projects I have been involved in. In the ESRC research on choice of higher education (HE) together with Stephen Ball and Miriam David, we looked at how HE choice is exercised in different ways for different groups of students utilizing Bourdieu's theoretical framework (Reay, *et al.*, 2005). In a second ESRC project, this time exploring white middle-class choice of inner-city comprehensives, Gill Crozier, David James and I attempted to make sense of the identities and identifications of white middle-class families who appear to be 'acting against self-interest' by sending their children to schools avoided by the majority of white middle classes (Reay, *et al.*, 2007). In a third ESRC project in collaboration with Gill Crozier and John Clayton we explored the experiences of working-class students across the higher education field, focusing on both their social and learner identities and how these were maintained or transformed by higher education (Reay, *et al.*, 2009a). In all three projects the concept we found most useful for thinking with was habitus.

Despite accusations of determinism, habitus is a dynamic concept, a rich interlacing of past and present, individual and collective. Habitus then can be understood as a compilation of collective and individual trajectories. Bourdieu conceives of habitus as a multi-layered concept, with more general notions of habitus at the level of society and more complex, differentiated notions at the level of the individual. A person's individual history is constitutive of habitus but so also is the whole collective history of family and class that the individual is a member of.

Thus for Bourdieu 'the subject is the individual trace of an entire collective history' (Bourdieu, 1990c: 91).

Thus a collectivist understanding of habitus is necessary in order to recognize that individuals contain within themselves their past and present position in the social structure 'at all times and in all places, in the forms of dispositions which are so many marks of social position' (ibid.: 82).

Habitus' duality as both collective and individualized offers theoretical potential, but also, as Cicourel (1993) points out, conceptual difficulties. Bourdieu often refers to class habitus and a number of researchers have also worked with the concept of class habitus (Bourdieu and Passeron, 1979; Bridge, 2001; Hartmann, 2000; James, 1995; Sawchuk, 2003). The largest and most comprehensive research study of class habitus is Bourdieu's own study of *Distinction* in French society (1984). Although the study draws on both quantitative and qualitative data, because habitus cannot be directly observed in empirical research and has to be apprehended interpretively, much of *Distinction* is devoted to a qualitative study of the myriad artistic/culinary preferences and practices which cluster in each sector of social space; that is, within each class and class fraction, in order to identify the specific habitus that underlies them (Weininger, 2004). However, as well as the utility of spatial notions of habitus, temporality is another productive aspect of habitus. Bourdieu actually writes that habitus 'refers to something historical, it is linked to individual history' (1993d: 86). Individual histories therefore are vital to understanding the concept of habitus. Habituses are permeable and responsive to what is going on around them. Current circumstances are not just there to be acted upon, but are internalized and become yet another layer to add to those from earlier socializations:

> Habitus as the product of social conditionings and thus of a history is endlessly transformed, either in a direction that reinforces it, when embodied structures of expectation encounter structures of objective chances in harmony with those expectations, or in a direction that transforms it and, for instance, raises or lowers the level of expectations and aspirations.
>
> (Bourdieu, 1990c: 116)

In fact, for someone who is regularly accused of determinism, Bourdieu uses the term *transformation* a lot. Schooling, in particular for working-class children, often provides a source of transformation:

> The habitus acquired in the family is at the basis of the structuring of school experiences ... the habitus transformed by the action of the school, itself diversified, is in turn at the basis of all subsequent experiences ... and so on, from restructuring to restructuring.
>
> (Bourdieu, 1972, cited in Bourdieu and Wacquant, 1992: 134)

Here Bourdieu clearly sees habitus as a product of early childhood experience and, in particular, of socialization within the family. Such a view provides the genesis for a conceptualization of familial habitus. And I would argue that a notion of familial habitus – the deeply ingrained system of perspectives, experiences and predispositions family members share (Reay, 1998a) – helps us to make better sense of gendered and intra-class as well as inter-class differences in both secondary school and HE choice practices.

'Too true to warrant discussion': the middle classes and university choice

An important aspect of familial habitus is the complicated compilation of values, attitudes and knowledge base that families possess in relation to the field of education. It is profoundly influenced by the educational experiences of parents.

Thus for a majority of the middle-class families in the research project on choice of higher education, university attendance was taken for granted. Pat Allatt (1996) writes about the 'taken for granted assumptions' embedded in middle-class family processes where the expectation of going to university does not need to be articulated. It is 'too true to warrant discussion' (Douglas, 1973: 3–4). We saw such assumptions over and over again in the middle-class transcripts. Familial habitus results in the tendency to acquire expectations that are adjusted to what is acceptable 'for people like us' (Bourdieu, 1984: 64–5). In relation to higher education, Bourdieu and Passeron argued that:

> Depending on whether access to higher education is collectively felt, even in a diffuse way, as an impossible, possible, probable, normal or banal future, everything in the conduct of the families and the children (particularly their conduct and performance at school) will vary, because behaviour tends to be governed by what is 'reasonable' to accept.
>
> (Bourdieu and Passeron, 1977: 226)

A significant majority of middle-class applicants in the study were engaging with higher education choice in contexts of certainty and entitlement. Established middle-class familial habituses generate the pursuit of advantage and the defence of distinction. And we can see this clearly in Mrs Cope's words. Her claim that choosing was an unscientific process emphasizes the importance of affective aspects of habitus.

> Choosing was a very unscientific process actually. My father went to Trinity, Cambridge to do law and he was always very keen to show her Cambridge and his old college, which he did when she was probably about thirteen. And she fell in love with it. And she decided that was where she wanted to go there and then.

But the quote also underlines how within established middle-class familial habituses, going to university is part of a normal biography, simply part of what people like us do, and often too obvious to articulate. Mrs Mattison provides another example of this apparent seamlessness:

DIANE: When did you first consider what Tim would do after finishing A levels?
MRS M: (laughs) Like when he was born. It's always been an expectation. I think it's always been implicit because the academic world is part of our life and very familiar to Tim. I just assumed he would go. I suppose it was just seen as natural.

Later, talking about the league tables she asserts that Tim did not need to refer to them because

> [i]n a sense he just knew which the best ones were. And it wasn't the league tables. It's just the sense of the university, the location, the history and just a kind of knowing that people just do know what's good.

Here we can see the reproductive strategies that privileged families produce without consultation or deliberation, which have 'the effect of contributing to the reproduction of existing positionings and the social order' (Bourdieu, 2000d: 146). As Bourdieu argues, those who have a feel for the game do not have to pose the objectives of their practice as ends, because they are absorbed in the doing, in the 'coming moment'. Habitus is evident in its very inexplicitness. We have a very clear articulation of established middle-class habitus and what Bourdieu calls 'the paradox of natural distinction' in which

> [o]ne of the privileges of the dominant, who move in their world as fish in water, resides in the fact that they need not engage in rational computation in order to reach the goals that best suit their interests. All they have to do is to follow their dispositions which, being adjusted to their positions, 'naturally' generate practices adjusted to the situation.
>
> (Bourdieu, 1990b: 108)

These examples of white middle-class choosing exemplify the pre-reflexive rather than the conscious, the practical rather than the discursive, the ways in which dispositions are 'objectively adapted to their outcomes without a conscious aiming at ends' (Bourdieu, 1990a: 53).

The established middle classes, and in particular private-school students, talked of going to university as 'automatic', 'taken for granted', 'always assumed'. The decision to go to university is a non-decision. It is rational and it is not; what Bourdieu calls 'intentionality without intention' (Bourdieu, 1990b: 108). Decision making comes into play in relation to which university, and often their understanding of the right sort of university for them, is ingrained, tacit, taken for granted. They do not even need to articulate the divide between old and new universities because going to a new university is just not what someone like them does. Rather, we see 'the self-assured relationship to the world' (Bourdieu, 1984: 56) of middle-class habitus reinforced and augmented by the élite institutional habituses of private and selective schooling, layering privilege upon privilege:

Well, just since I've been born, I suppose it's just been assumed I am going to university, because both my parents went to university, all their brothers and sisters went to university and my sister went to university and so I don't know if I've even stopped to think about it. I've always just thought I am going to go to university, and I don't know, I have kind of grown up with the idea that's what people do, most people do that. I mean, quitting school has never been an option for me. If I really wanted to I think my parents would probably support me, but I've just never even considered it as an option, I have always assumed I have been going to university and the choice has just been which university, rather than will I go at all, I suppose that's just the way my parents are, they just send us to university.

(Nick, white, middle-class student)

There is little sense in the middle-class students' words of habitus as 'the art of inventing' (Bourdieu, 1990a: 55). As Omar, a middle-class Iranian student, explains in relation to his private boys' school:

If you take a group of ten people and nine people have applied to these sorts of universities, like London ones, or you know, prestigious ones, and you don't really want to feel like – I am going to apply to this place just because I want to. And they will say – why are you doing that? Why don't you join the flow? This tends to happen ... You sort of find you've done it without realizing it.

Throughout the middle-class transcripts we see repeatedly how processes of class internalization become externalized, how individuals operate through an embodied 'sense' of how to behave rather than through conscious calculation.

'Fish out of water': working-class students choosing élite universities

But just as cultural capital works well as a concept that makes sense of middle-class ways of being and acting but is more problematic in understanding the working classes as anything other than deficient, so habitus as pre-reflexive and operating beneath the level of consciousness is not particularly helpful in understanding working-class applicants to university. For our working-class students, the pre-reflexive has had to become reflexive, and predispositions evolve into new dispositions.

In this quote Fiona hints at the unsuitability of her white working-class habitus for dealing with the process of HE choice:

All of us in my family are very short-term people, we don't think about the future that much until it arrives. Which is good to some degree but not really in situations like sorting out university because you don't sort of get what you need to get done.

Here Fiona is elaborating a working-class habitus. However, when I point out to

Fiona that she clearly did sort out university as she has been offered a place to read History of Art at Edinburgh, she tells me, 'I had to have a very clear plan of action and work everything out in advance – not very me really'. We could almost talk in terms of Fiona having an 'out-of-habitus' experience. But maybe it makes better sense to talk in terms of an 'out-of-field' experience. While our middle-class students were firmly located in familiar social fields, our working-class students were already in transition and dealing with the unfamiliar field of predominantly middle-class sixth forms. Schooling for these students is generating new disposi-tions, a turn towards what Bourdieu terms 'a cultured habitus' (Bourdieu, 1967: 344). In *Outline of a Theory of Practice*, Bourdieu writes that the principles embodied in habitus 'are placed beyond the grasp of consciousness and hence cannot be touched by voluntary deliberate transformation, cannot even be made explicit'. But while an understanding of middle-class habitus as 'beyond the grasp of consciousness' worked well in terms of our data, it made little sense for many of our working-class students struggling in unfamiliar fields. So Shaun who went to Sussex to study English said:

> Socially, or through my family, I don't know anybody who has completed university, you know, I don't know anybody well, who has completed uni-versity. My uncle, was the first person in my entire family, like, ever, to go to university and complete it, but he died in 1993, so I don't know, I didn't really have time to talk to him about it, or find out anything or get any encourage-ment, advice or anything like that from him. So I suppose that's maybe why I didn't know about the reputations of the universities or any sort of things like that. Apart from what I was told by the prospectuses, the brochures, computers, what my teachers told me, although they didn't really help much. I sort of had to get to grips with it and work it out as I went along, play it by ear.
>
> (Shaun, white working-class student)

Working-class students like Fiona and Shaun are characterized by conscious delib-eration and awareness; they – unlike their middle-class counterparts – are engaged in acts of invention or, more accurately, reinvention.

The limitations and possibilities of habitus

Bourdieu developed habitus in part as a means of countering the undue emphasis on consciousness in social science (Warde, 2004). As we have seen, the concept works particularly well in capturing 'the too obvious to articulate', those reproduc-tive moments when habitus and field are in harmony. However, Lois McNay (2001: 146) asserts 'there has been an increasing emphasis in Bourdieu's more recent work on moments of disalignment and tension between habitus and field, which may give rise to social change'. In *In Other Words*, Bourdieu writes about reflexivity emerg-ing 'in situations of crisis which disrupts the immediate adjustment of habitus to field (1990c: 108). In particular, in *The Weight of the World* (1999) there is a great deal of striving, resistance and action aimed at changing current circumstances, as many of the poor and dispossessed interviewed by Bourdieu and his colleagues, search around for ways of changing and transforming their lives. Bourdieu takes the example of upward social mobility, arguing that the movement of habitus across class fields can result in

> [a] habitus divided against itself, in constant negotiation with itself and its ambivalences, and therefore doomed to a kind of duplication, to a double perception of the self, to successive allegiances and multiple identities.
>
> (Bourdieu, 1999c: 511)

It is not a lack of action that is problematic in relation to habitus but rather, firstly, Bourdieu's over-emphasis on pre-reflective dimensions of action and, secondly, the negative connotations embedded in notions of 'a divided habitus' with its associations of instability and neuroses.

I want to deal with pre-reflexivity first. As Andrew Sayer (2005) convincingly argues, Bourdieu overplays the unconscious impulses and aspects of habitus, neglecting mundane everyday reflexivity; what Sayer terms 'our inner conversations' (see also Archer, 2003). In doing so, he marginalizes the life of the mind in others. In a similar vein, Brenda Farnell (2000) asserts that in Bourdieu's formulation of habitus, individuals' adjustments to the external world are all apparently unconscious, or less than conscious. Nick Crossley (1999: 658) makes an identical criticism that habitus as a concept levels out the distinction between reflection and the pre-reflective and that 'it needs to recuperate the reflective and creative aspects of practice'. As Noble and Watkins (2003: 529) argue, by dismissing conscious calculation, Bourdieu 'empties ordinary cognition of its conscious elements: in making the valuable argument that belief is corporeal, he overstates his case to argue that cognitive structures are not forms of consciousness but dispositions of the body'.

Implicit in the concept is that habitus operates at an unconscious level unless individuals confront events or new unfamiliar fields which cause self-questioning, whereupon habitus begins to operate at the level of consciousness and the person develops new facets of the self. Such disjunctures between habitus and field occur for Bourdieu when individuals with a well-developed habitus find themselves in different fields or different parts of the same social field. This was the case in the research project on working-class students attending university, particularly for working-class students attending élite universities. So Linsey ponders her 'culture clash' on first attending Southern University (Reay, *et al.*, 2009b): 'At first I never thought I would fit in, my background was so different. Everyone seemed cleverer, more attractive, more confident.'

However, she goes on to describe how the insights she developed about Southern led to feelings of belonging and growing confidence:

> I realized that Southern was full of people who are obsessive over little things which is quite fun and reassuring because it makes my obsessiveness seem normal ... Some people are obsessed with venus fly traps or a mathematical

equation or there are just lots of people who are a bit weird, they have their eccentricities. But the good thing is that everyone knows they've got a little something that's odd about them, that's a bit different, but everyone tolerates each other's differences because they all know that everyone is a bit odd.

(Linsey)

According to Bourdieu, 'consciousness and reflexivity are both cause and symptom of the failure of immediate adaptation to the situation' (1990b: 11), and this was evident in Linsey and other working-class students' adaptation to the élite context of Southern university.

However, as Sayer (2005) argues, and I think correctly, disjuncture and the resulting striving, resistance and/or new awareness (what Bourdieu (1990b) terms *socioanalysis*) can occur during the formation of habitus and indeed can be constitutive of the habitus. As Sayer points out in Chapter 7 of this volume, habitus need not be in harmony with the field or with wider discourses, even during individuals' formative years. Although the emphasis on 'protension' – 'the feel for the game' rather than calculation and strategizing is an important counter to rationalism, Bourdieu seems to leap straight from a rationalist interpretation to an anti-rationalist one. One key consequence, according to Sayer, is that Bourdieu's focus on the unconscious and the pre-reflexive does not allow for the development of the ethical dimensions of the habitus. Nick Crossley (2001: 138) makes a related point when he argues that habitus needs to include 'dialogues with oneself'. In *Sociology in Question*, Bourdieu writes that habitus includes ethical dispositions (1993e: 129) and argues that it is not just dispositions but convictions that constitute habitus, but because of his emphasis on protension, these aspects of habitus remain underdeveloped in his writings. Sayer's important work (2005) recuperating ethical dispositions or 'moral sentiments' for habitus enhances the possibilities for and of habitus and allows us not only a richer understanding of the strivings, struggles and disenchantments of those burdened by 'the Weight of the World' (1999). It also provides the potential for a broader conceptualization of habitus that makes space for 'cares, concerns and commitments', and weaves together conscious deliberation with unconscious dispositions so that we can attempt to grapple analytically with aspects of identity such as our personal and political commitments and values that current conceptualizations of habitus marginalize.

'Out of tune': facing unfamiliar fields

I want to focus now on disjunctures between habitus and field, the extent to which they lead to a questioning of already existing predispositions and generate potential for social transformation. One of the most persistent debates about habitus revolves around whether it is essentially static or capable of changing dynamically in different conditions and circumstances (Hillier and Rooksby, 2005). Bourdieu makes brief reference to situations of discordance between disposition and position, the mismatches and misfires, but accepts that habitus has degrees of integration and change in response to new experiences (Bourdieu, 2000d: 157 and 160–1), and I have tried to demonstrate aspects of this in relation to working-class students in élite HE contexts. However, in the recent research project on the white middle classes choosing inner-city comprehensives (Reay, *et al.*, 2007), facing an unfamiliar field was more likely to generate a protective reinforcement of white middle-class habitus and a mobilization of capitals in order to defend against the discomforts of the field rather than any long-lasting change in habitus. Despite high levels of anxiety, both parents and children rarely questioned their class and race privilege even in multi-ethnic working-class contexts where their privilege was very apparent:

> Mary and I went to see the head about it who was very defensive and thought we were complaining and we weren't we were just saying he needs help. I mean he was very bright and he wasn't getting enough stimulation and he was feeling 'extra' all the time if you know what I mean because he always knew the answers and the other kids didn't and so you know he felt excluded. And the school was fantastic he got extra lessons they celebrated his 'extraness' if you like within the class and got the other kids to celebrate it as well and so you know they cheered him on rather feeling he was different from them.
>
> (David Goldblum, father, London)

As is evident in David Goldblum's words, these white middle-class parents continued to operationalize their class advantages whilst, for the most part, apparently not recognizing the inequitable consequences of them. Only occasionally were there glimpses of the reflexive habitus.

Yet, as we have seen in the example of Linsey, this was clearly not the case for our working-class applicants to élite universities. In the ESRC projects on working-class students' experiences of choosing universities and later attending them, the disjunction between field and habitus means that nothing could be taken for granted. The conjunction of working-class habitus and the middle-class field of the sixth form and the élite university generated adaptation, critical assessment and added impetus to the refashioning they had already had to engage in, in order to become academically successful students. However, what both the working-class students and the middle-class families did share was an ambivalence and anxiety about the contexts in which they find themselves. Skeggs (2004b) argues that Bourdieu cannot account for the ambivalence that lies at the heart of being human. That is true in the normal course of events – for Bourdieu, when habitus and field are in agreement. Ambivalence arises, as Bourdieu himself demonstrates in *The Weight of the World*, when individuals find their dispositions no longer fit the economic and social fields they find themselves in.

However, while both the middle-class students in working-class contexts and the working-class students in middle-class contexts were managing high degrees of dissonance, they responded with very different degrees of receptivity, openness and acceptance in the field. I would argue that this is because 'the dialectical confrontation' (Bourdieu, 2005a: 47) which Bourdieu describes between habitus and field leads mostly for the middle classes in multi-ethnic working-class fields to a reinforcement of originary habitus; while for working-class students in the middle-class field of higher education, habitus is 'being restructured, transformed in its makeup by the pressure of the objectives structures' (ibid.: 47). Both the white middle-class families and the working-class students have incorporated the principles of vision and division constitutive of the dominant social order (Bourdieu, 2000d), and as a consequence the middle classes feel they have little if anything to learn from the working classes – unlike their attitudes to those of other ethnicities. There are issues here around the incentives of the field. It is only by seeing fields in terms of the extent to which they represent dominant and dominated spaces in relation to habitus that we can make sense of why rupture generated transformation in one case and not in the other. Most of the middle-class families with their dominant cultural capital who chose to send their children to working-class comprehensives could and did employ their cultural capital to ensure their children occupied dominant spaces within the top sets and gifted and talented programmes. Bourdieu's 'dialectical confrontation' resulted in a tendency for white middle-class habitus to transform the objective structures according to its own structure through strategies of advantage that ensured their children monopolized scarce educational resources. And for the most part, their children brought a familial habitus grounded in an intrinsic sense of class superiority which mitigated against any class mixing and protected their class interests, but was often no protection against ambivalence and anxiety.

Such white, middle-class attitudes are encapsulated in the following quote from a young white middle-class woman in the sample:

> I had everything that the working-class kids didn't have. You know everything that my mum and dad had given me and I was more intelligent than they were and there was more going for me than there was for them. And I think also because my mum and dad had achieved so much I think I probably felt quite second rate to them and being friends with these people made me feel like the one you know who was achieving you know and was superior to them.
>
> (Camilla)

This was not the case for working-class students applying to élite universities. They brought a sense of 'not quite fitting in' which generated dispositions of self-scrutiny and self-transformation, 'a constant fashioning and re-fashioning of the self' but one that still stubbornly retained key valued aspects of working-class self. Upward mobility was premised on self-fashioning and self-improvement. The exemplar par excellence of self-reflexivity is a self constantly monitoring and improving themselves (Featherstone, 1991; Giddens, 1991b), and this is what these working-class students were engaged in. As with the white middle classes in unfamiliar fields, there were high levels of ambivalence and anxiety but the incentives of the field generated new learning and social change to a far greater degree. However, while habitus was clearly being continually modified by individuals' encounters with the outside world (DiMaggio, 1979), there was none of the wholesale 'escaping of the habitus' that Friedmann (2005) writes about in relation to upward social mobility. Rather, there remained layers of embodied experience within habitus that were not easily amenable to self-fashioning (McNay, 1999). Far from 'disappearing into a new world' (Friedmann, 2005: 318) these students appeared determined to hold on to former aspects of self even as they gained new ones. So Jamie said:

> I guess I am an interesting mixture. Here I am just as swotty as everyone else but then in the vacations I go home, working on the building site, go out drinking with my mates, and I'm just as comfortable with both.

Both social mobility studies and those on the working classes tend to depict working-class cultures and the habituses they generate as either limited or lacking in some way (Charlesworth, 2000), almost as if, in being seen to lack value, they can be discarded without cost. As Savage, Bagnall and Longhurst (2005: 120–1) point out, 'the issue here is the perennial difficulty of understanding working-class habitus through the lens of intellectualized and culturally privileged academic research'. This continues to be a challenge in contemporary sociological work using Bourdieu's concepts as it was in his own research (Bourdieu, 1984; Bourdieu, *et al.*, 1999).

Conclusion

Wendy Bottero (2009) argues that habitus helps tackle the class paradox in which class shapes people's lives but does not translate into constantly claimed cultural identities. Through habitus we can recover social class as an identity implicit in social relations rather than in explicit self-identification or collective mobilizations. However, its middle-class bias remains. Bev Skeggs (2004b) challenges the usefulness of habitus as a conceptual tool, arguing that the more we use models of habitus, the more we as researchers perform middle-class politeness and will not be able to understand the different forms of (non) sociality that we are supposed to be able to analyse. And I would agree that notions of habitus as well as those of cultural capital can result in a predominantly middleclass-centric view of the world if they are not used sensitively. Despite Bourdieu's criticisms of privilege and élitism, and particularly the role of academics in perpetuating both, empirical work, including his own, that utilizes concepts of habitus and cultural capital often presents the middle classes as normative in ways that residualize the working classes, especially if they refuse the dominant principles of vision and division.

However, I would argue that habitus is still rich and generative as a conceptual tool as long as we ensure our data leads the analytic direction rather than allowing the conceptual framework to dominate. Moreover, it is in the ruptures, the disjunctures, the edges of coherence between habitus and field that the most interesting theory lies. There is the key issue of whether any new fields that individuals find themselves in lead to the questioning of already existing dispositions, the acquisition of new ones, and a degree of transformation. For our white middle classes in inner-city schooling it rarely did. Their dispositions of certainty, entitlement and social confidence, although tempered by anxiety, unease and ambivalence at the unfamiliarity they faced, meant they rarely questioned their class and race advantages even in multi-ethnic, predominantly working-class contexts where their privilege stood out. Although a number of the middle-class young people played at being 'the other', there was no serious attempt to become 'the other' and, only infrequently, to learn from 'the other'. For the middle classes, interactions tended to be governed by strategic advantage and the consolidation of their already existing cultural capital. However, this was not the case for the working-class students in élite universities. They brought to the field dispositions of uncertainty, heightened self-awareness and self consciousness, and highly developed practices of self-monitoring and self-vigilance. Although there were aspects of self in relation to familiar others that all the students were anxious to retain, there was also a great deal of intellectual and social growth in their attempts at 'conciliation of contraries' (Bourdieu, 2007: 103). It is not just the change in field that is crucial but rather a habitus characterized by dispositions that are open to change. As Sweetman (2003: 537) argues, reflexivity and flexibility may actually characterize the habitus of some individuals and 'for those who display a flexible or *reflexive* habitus, processes of refashioning – whether emancipatory or otherwise – may be second nature rather than difficult to achieve'.

In *The Weight of the World* we see habitus as internally contradictory and fragmented, and in Bourdieu's self-analysis (Bourdieu, 2007) he writes about his own experiences of a cloven habitus beset by tensions and contradictions. Yet while those in *The Weight of the World* often appear overwhelmed by the ravages of a divided habitus (McRobbie, 2002) his own experiences of living and working through a divided habitus have clearly been extremely creative and generative. Conversely, the extent to which 'the well-adjusted' habitus (Bourdieu, 2005a: 214) can also be an unreflexive habitus raises far-reaching concerns about propensities for conformity and the extent to which an unquestioning acceptance of the status quo is common among both the middle and working classes who remain in familiar fields. However, as we have seen in relation to the white middle classes in multi-ethnic urban comprehensives, new and unfamiliar fields do not necessary bring change and adaptation. While the possibilities for socio-awareness and social change lie in the jolts that unsettle habitus through either exposure to unfamiliar fields or turbulence in a familiar field, dispositions of openness and receptivity also appear to be key prerequisites for transformatory social and personal learning to take place, and this is as true for us academics, including Bourdieu, as it is for those we research.

7 Bourdieu, ethics and practice

Andrew Sayer

In adopting social science's spectator's view of society, together with its prioritizing of positive description and explanation and its wariness of normativity, it is easy to overlook the fact that life is normative; we are evaluative beings – beings whose relation to the world is one of concern. We not only act and make sense of things but continually evaluate how things we care about – including our own well-being – are faring, and often wonder what to do for the best. Perhaps most importantly, we continually assess how we and others are being treated; even though we may be predominantly self-absorbed, we often act towards others, or at least certain others, with regard to their well-being; for example, showing them respect (Filonowicz, 2008; Smith, 1984 [1759]). Social life would be unimaginable without at least some such behaviour. Moral – and immoral – sentiments such as compassion, shame, resentment at injustice, guilt and contempt can loom large in people's lives, and they are frequently prompted by inequalities and domination. But as I shall argue, these are not merely 'feelings' or 'affect', but assessments of the import of certain social circumstances. To ignore the *import* that things – particularly social interactions – may have for people is to produce a bland, alienated account of social life.

Bourdieu has greatly deepened our understanding of the soft forms of domination and oppression, naming and analysing processes that had hitherto eluded identification. In his more explicitly political speeches and other short articles, his anger at social injustice is clear (Bourdieu, 2008b). Yet, in his academic work, with one significant exception, individuals are represented not so much as having ethical and political concerns but as having a mastery of certain kinds of practical action which derive from living within the particular social relations and practices available to them in their part of the social field. They cope and compete, but one doesn't get much impression of their ethical and political assessments of their situation. The exception is *The Weight of the World* (*La Misère du Monde*) and it is significant because it consists mainly of people speaking for themselves rather than Bourdieu's renderings of their situation (Bourdieu, *et al.*, 1999). While he provides many resources for understanding aesthetic valuations in everyday experience, most famously in *Distinction* (Bourdieu, 1984), he says little about people's ethical values and valuations. At best these things might be deemed implicit. Although his concepts of habitus and the logic of practice have certain affinities with a broadly

Aristotelian approach to virtue ethics, he stops short of developing such a connection. His approach includes both features that could assist in the understanding of this crucial dimension of life, and features which obstruct it. I shall argue that to unlock the potential of the former, we must alter some of the latter.

I argue that the ethical dimension of social life needs to be taken more seriously in social science, but to understand this dimension we need: (1) a modified concept of habitus that allows room for individual reflexivity and includes ethical dispositions; (2) a focus on emotions as intelligent responses to objective circumstances and as indicators of well-being; (3) a broader understanding of normativity that avoids reducing it to either the pursuit of self-interest and various forms of capital or outworkings of the habitus; and (4) an acknowledgement of human vulnerability and our relationship to the world of concern. A more Aristotelian approach can help in several respects here.

The habitus, reflexivity, and ethical dispositions

Most critics of Bourdieu have targeted their fire on the concept of habitus, arguing that it is too deterministic and ignores individual reflexivity and the capacity to behave in ways that are not necessarily accommodative to the dominant social relations or discourses within which they are located (e.g. Archer, 2007). While I partly agree with the critics, I, like Nicos Mouzelis, wish to argue that we still need something like the concept of habitus, albeit a modified version of it (Sayer, 2005; Mouzelis, 2008).

The processes by which we develop a habitus range from a kind of osmosis or unconscious adaptation through to a more conscious process of learning how to do things so that we can do them without thinking. Bourdieu's accounts mostly suggest the former, yet his favourite example of the responses of the competent tennis player actually suggests the latter model. The player can do remarkably skilful things without thinking much about the details of what she is doing, through 'protension' rather than calculation. No two games are the same so it requires attentiveness, responsiveness, strategizing and creativity. Bourdieu often responds to critics by reminding them of the creative nature of the habitus, but he consistently understates the role of reflection and reason both in the acquisition of its constitutive dispositions and in their mobilization in particular contexts, and more generally in influencing action. The tennis player has to monitor her practice and concentrate in order to get her strokes right so that she can come to do them not only automatically but successfully, and in a particular game she can consciously choose different strategies. Bourdieu does occasionally acknowledge more conscious reasoning, but only to quickly discount it or reduce it to strategic calculation: 'It is, of course, never ruled out that the responses of the habitus may be accompanied by a strategic calculation tending to perform in a conscious mode the operation that the habitus performs quite differently' (Bourdieu, 1990b: 53; see also Bourdieu, 2000d).

Bourdieu helps counter the kind of sociology which gives an inflated role to norms, making it appear that actors just follow these, either because they have internalized them or because they fear the consequences of not following them. He argues that insofar as they internalize them, they do so through practice, through repeatedly having to act within specific kinds of social relation and context so that they acquire the appropriate dispositions, and a feel for the game. Norms may therefore be little more than abstract formalizations of valued dispositions that are largely acquired through practice, and may have little force in their own right.

Margaret Archer is highly critical of the concept of habitus, arguing that it ignores the way in which the constraining and enabling effects of social contexts on individuals are mediated by their own deliberations. Individuals' internal conversations mediate 'the role that objective structural or cultural powers play in influencing social action and are thus indispensable to explaining social outcomes' (Archer, 2007: 5). In other words, the effects of discourses and circumstances will depend on *how* they are interpreted, and this in turn depends upon how individuals relate them to their own subjectively defined concerns. Archer's empirical research on people's internal conversations provides plenty of evidence to support this (Archer, 2003, 2007). Although Bourdieu does not acknowledge it, the interviews in *The Weight of the World* show individuals discussing how, through their internal conversations, they have made sense of their experiences and responded to circumstances (Bourdieu, *et al.*, 1999). However, we need to steer a middle course here that still acknowledges the influence of the habitus. For example, the middle-class child may reflect on the things that are expected of her and on the things that her elders have done and come to see that she too can achieve them, but she is also likely to have a sense of entitlement acquired partly through osmosis, through simply being accustomed to having easy access to many of the goods society has to offer. It may simply not occur to her that she might become a cleaner, because such outcomes are not part of her practical experience.[1] Some social influences get beneath our radar, shaping our dispositions and responses without our even noticing them, while others are mediated in a more conscious way.

It is surprising that Bourdieu largely ignores the ethical dimension of the habitus – the fact that it includes ethical dispositions – or in philosophical terminology, virtues and vices – such as a disposition of respectfulness or selfishness. For example, through repetition of certain actions, and through the various kinds of encouragement or discouragement our actions prompt in others within those practices, we might develop a respectful disposition. Again, bearing in mind our comments about lay reflexivity, people may act ethically or unethically on the basis of conscious deliberation as well as spontaneously, without thinking; or sometimes semi-consciously, being just vaguely aware of what they're doing. We need to acknowledge the whole range. Ethical dispositions, once acquired, have some inertia, but their strength depends on the frequency with which they are activated, as well as on our reflexive monitoring of them. Change in such dispositions, so that individuals become more, less or differently ethical, tends to be gradual and again to require practice. For example, in the negative direction, people may find that engaging in minor immoral acts makes the transition to major ones less difficult, though they may realize, usually too late, that they have crossed a moral boundary (Glover, 2001: 35).[2]

An Aristotelian approach offers us an understanding of the ethical dimension which embraces both habituation and reflection. People develop embodied dispositions and characters through acting within particular kinds of social relation and context, which then recursively influence their actions: 'by being habituated to despise things that are fearful and to stand our ground against them we become brave, and it is when we have become so that we shall be most able to stand our ground against them' (Aristotle, *Nicomachean Ethics*, II.3). Aristotle therefore recognized the importance of moral education – whether through teaching or experience, good or bad – in forming such dispositions. While Bourdieu's sociological account of practice and the development of the habitus has many Aristotelian echoes, Aristotle left more room for reflexivity, responsibility and choice, for there can usually be different responses to any given context. Thus, there is nothing automatic about the development of virtues: people could act in a courageous or cowardly way in response to the same situation, 'for we are ourselves somehow part-causes of our states of character' (ibid.: III.6).[3] Individuals still have some responsibility for how they respond to a given situation. According to this view, virtue is therefore more than habit; although the courageous or generous person is one who has developed those dispositions through practice, they still choose to act courageously or generously where appropriate and know why it is appropriate (MacIntyre, 1998: 62). In our everyday lives we hold one another responsible for our actions, and assume that we have at least some room for choice. We rarely accept purely sociological explanations of the failure of others to honour promises and responsibilities: a student who blamed her failure to do her essay on the habitus would get short shrift, even from a tutor sympathetic to Bourdieu. This theory-practice contradiction, common not only in Bourdieu but in much other sociological writing, illustrates the absurdity of denying everyday lay reflexivity and the way it is presupposed in social interaction. However, we do not have to go to the other extreme of rejecting the concept of habitus, as Archer seeks to do.

Perhaps even Aristotle's account is a little too rationalistic, and underestimates the way in which we can *also* have 'unprincipled virtues'; that is, a tendency to act in a reasonable, moral, way, without basing our actions on conscious, rational deliberation and hence without being able to articulate why they are reasonable or moral. Nomy Arpaly (2003) provides some interesting reflections on this phenomenon. One of her examples is from Mark Twain's novel *Huckleberry Finn*, in which Huckleberry gets to know Jim, an escaped slave. As a product of his time – a time when slavery was not seen as unethical – Huckleberry sincerely believes that the morally proper thing to do is turn Jim over to the authorities. But while he intends to do this, when the opportunity arises, he finds he just cannot do it, and afterwards he feels bad about his moral failings in not turning him in. It seems that in getting to know Jim, he had come to respect him, and to realize that he is a fully fledged human being, so that at a semi-conscious level returning him to slavery didn't seem right. Arpaly argues that this divergence between action and conscious reasons ('*akrasia*', as philosophers term it) is not necessarily irrational but a form of rational behaviour which the actor had not been able to articulate and justify at a discursive level. As Bourdieu himself put it:

Agents may engage in reasonable forms of behaviour without being rational; they may engage in behaviors one can explain, as the classical philosophers would say, with the hypothesis of rationality, without their behaviour having reason as its principle.

(Bourdieu, 1994: 76)

Many of our actions are not based upon decisions resulting from systematic deliberation, such as working through a list of pros and cons for some action.[4] Sometimes we intermittently muse on a problem over a long period without clearly resolving it, and eventually 'find ourselves acting' in a way which decides the issue, perhaps ending a relationship, or volunteering to take on an onerous job. Such actions are not purely accidental and arbitrary; the semi-conscious or distracted musings may have changed the balance of our evaluations and priorities. Whether we later come to view them as rational or mistaken depends less on whether we arrived at them by a process of logical deliberation than on the appropriateness of the actions that followed. As Archer acknowledges, our internal conversations may vary from focused and coherent deliberation to fragmented and fleeting musings.

Embodied habits of thought and action can remain important even where we change our minds through deliberating on some issue. Thus if people come to see that something they have believed is wrong through encountering a convincing argument and decide that they should now act differently, this in itself is unlikely to be sufficient to change their ways of thinking and acting completely. For example, even if a white racist comes to renounce her racism on the basis of argument, she may still find herself unintentionally making racist assumptions in everyday life – assuming that the new doctor will be white, that a black child cannot be academically gifted, and so on. Having become consciously and sincerely anti-racist she may feel ashamed about the persistence of these unreformed reflexes, but it can take many years of practice and reflection to re-shape these completely. The process involves not just acknowledging errors of thought and action, but becoming a different person with different embodied habits of thought. Although these examples seem to fit with a Bourdieusian approach, they do involve at least some reflection and deliberation.

Iris Murdoch makes a convergent point, and one which again might incline us to modify, rather than reject, Bourdieu's approach (Murdoch, 1970). She argues that modern philosophy has mistakenly equated normativity with free choice and the empty free will that steps back from, or out of the flow of practice, suspending emotions, abstracting from concrete matters, and deciding how to act purely on the basis of general principles (see also Filonowicz, 2008). Rather, we should understand lay normativity as embedded in the flow of practice and concrete experience, in which we continually monitor and evaluate things, partly subconsciously through our emotional responses, and partly consciously through reflection, whether this involves ephemeral musings or focused deliberation. Although we do much on automatic, we do so with some degree of attentiveness, often noticing failures of things to work out as hoped, feeling good or bad about them in various ways, and it is through these repeated minor evaluations that we confirm or gradually shift our moral inclinations.

> If we ignore the prior work of attention and notice only the emptiness of the moment of choice we are likely to identify freedom with the outward move-ment [i.e. observable action] since there is nothing else to identify with. But if we consider what the work of attention is like, how continuously it goes on, and how imperceptibly it builds up structures of value round about us, we shall not be surprised that at crucial moments of choice most of the business of choosing is already over. This does not imply that we are not free, certainly not. But it implies that the exercise of our freedom is a small piecemeal busi-ness which goes on all the time and not a grandiose leaping about unimpeded at important moments. The moral life, on this view, is something that goes on continually, not something that is switched off in between the occurrence of explicit moral choices. What happens in between such choices is indeed what is crucial.
>
> (Murdoch, 1970: 36)

Hence:

> Moral change and moral achievements are slow; we are not free in the sense of being able suddenly to alter ourselves since we cannot suddenly alter what we can see and ergo what we desire and are compelled by. In a way, explicit choice seems now less important: less decisive (since much of 'decision' lies elsewhere) and less obviously something to be 'cultivated'.
>
> (Ibid.: 38)

Here, ethical being is rooted in ongoing, often mundane practice, and the feel for how the game is going, including reflections on how we and the things we care about are faring. I suggest that this interpretation should be acceptable to followers of both Bourdieu and Archer.

Given that ethical behaviour can either challenge or confirm existing social arrangements, we need also to address the relation between habitus and habitat and the possible sources of resistance. Bourdieu's accounts of the development of the habitus seem to imply that whatever the pressures and opportunities facing us in early life, we adapt to them, so that there is a near-perfect fit (or 'ontological complicity') between habitus and habitat. Apparently, dissonance can only arise either when we move to a different part of the social field with different influences that do not match those of our habitus, or else as a result of politicization from some external influence which enables us to think and act differently. But even in early life, we are not indifferent to the processes which shape us, for we can only be shaped in consistent ways if we have certain physiological and psychological capacities and limitations which enable such shaping. This is why socialization does not work on plants or tables; they do not have the powers and susceptibilities to respond to it. Although we are susceptible to a vast variety of different kinds of socialization, there are some things we may never get used to, like abuse, and having to endure them produces various kinds of resistance and pathology. Like so much sociology, Bourdieu's work leans towards sociological reductionism because it lacks an examined notion of human nature, so that, by default, it produces an unexamined notion of human nature as infinitely malleable.[5] (I shall return to this point later.) The mind-body already has particular aversions and inclinations, including a sense of lack or neediness, before it gets habituated to a position within the social field, *indeed these are a necessary condition of the efficacy of socialization: without them we would be indifferent to social pressures* (Dean, 2003). That socialization also generates new inclinations and aversions and modifies the innate ones is not in contradiction with this; rather, as Aristotle argued, new potentialities contingently develop out of innate ones, according to socialization.[6]

Since the concepts of ethical dispositions and moral sentiments or emotions can be related to that of habitus, the same kinds of qualification that we made regarding the latter apply to them. Just as the habitus need not be in harmony with the habitat or with wider discourses, even during individuals' formative years, so individuals' ethical dispositions need not be entirely consistent with the particular nexus of relations in which they are situated or with wider discursive norms. On the one side there can be a tension between the body/mind and the practices and conditions in which people find themselves; on the other side, discourses, being both fallible and related to a wider range of experience than that available to individuals at first hand, can engender dissonance too. Such differences can generate anomalous behaviour and resistance, whether deliberate or inadvertent. To explain how such tensions can arise, we need to proceed to other matters neglected by Bourdieu.

Emotions and the habitus

Given that Bourdieu emphasizes our embodied and partly subconscious practical orientation to the world, it is curious how little he wrote about emotional responses, especially given their influence on action and their connection to the habitus. Even though symbolic domination works partly by producing feelings of inferiority or superiority in people, and hence shame or pride and low or high self-esteem, and even though these are part of the experience of inequality and matter a great deal to people, affecting their psychological and physical health,[7] this emotional dimension is left largely unexplored and for the reader to imagine (Sayer, 2005). Unless we take emotions seriously, we will not understand ethical being and lay normativity in general.

Emotions are clearly embodied, but they should not be reduced to mere feeling or 'affect', and counterposed to reason; rather they are responses to and commentaries on our situations in relation to our concerns (Archer, 2000; Barbalet, 2001; Helm, 2001; Oakley, 1993). They are cognitive and evaluative, indeed essential elements of intelligence (Nussbaum, 2001: 3). They are strongly related to our nature as dependent and vulnerable beings. They are *about* something, particularly things which are important to our well-being and which we value and yet which are not fully within our control. Thus, the loss of a friend occasions a stronger emotional response than the loss of a pencil. Emotions are highly discriminating, evaluative commentaries on our well-being or ill-being in the physical world (for example, pleasure in warmth); in our practical dealings with the world (for example, the frustration of failing to execute some task successfully); and in the social-psychological world (for example, self-esteem or shame) (Archer, 2000; Nussbaum, 2001).[8] In virtue of these forms of intelligent response, we can speak of 'emotional reason'. Emotions also *motivate* us to act in certain ways. The coupling of cognitive and motivating properties implies that 'emotional reason' figures prominently in practical reason – in reasoning how to act.

The commentaries which emotions provide are *fallible* – but then so too are the commentaries of unemotional forms of reason – yet they are usually adequate enough to warrant being taken seriously. Life without emotions would be hard because without them we would lack a crucial indicator of how the things that matter to us are faring. The relation of particular emotions to specific referents or causes may sometimes be unclear, and the causes may themselves be complex and diffuse – we have all had the experience of being unsure just what has put us in a bad mood – but again that is a good reason for reflecting on precisely what they are about. Particular emotional responses tend to be influenced not only by current events but by the character of our habitus and personality; we may be optimistic and outgoing or pessimistic and reserved, confident or nervous, adaptable or inflexible.[9] These dispositions appear to be shaped particularly strongly in early life, according to the nature of parenting and position in the social field. Emotions are also culturally influenced. While emotions like anger, happiness, pride and shame appear to be common to all cultures, *what* they tend to be aroused by varies among cultures, and within them, according to social position. 'If emotions are evaluative appraisals, then cultural views about what is valuable can be expected to affect them directly' (Nussbaum, 2001: 157). Thus in a liberal culture, restrictions on individual liberty are more likely to cause anger than in a communitarian society, which values individual liberty less. Emotions do not escape discursive influences and may be intensified or calmed by them, according to the way in which discourses assess the relative *import* of things.

Emotional responses to the inequalities and struggles of the social field and how people negotiate them are to be taken seriously both because they matter to people, and because they generally reveal something about their situation and well-being; indeed, if the latter were not true the former would not be either (Sayer, 2005). At the extreme, emotions such as shame and pride may concern matters which people value more highly than their lives. While the rationalistic tendencies common in social science incline many to ignore emotions, to do so is extraordinarily irrational: 'simply, emotions matter because if we did not have them nothing else would matter. Creatures without emotion would have no reason for living, nor, for that matter, for committing suicide. Emotions are the stuff of life.' (Elster, quoted in Archer, 2000: 194). Why would people bother to conform or resist, compete and struggle, as Bourdieu notes, if their success or failure made no emotional difference to them? As an opponent of rationalistic approaches to social science, it is surprising that Bourdieu paid emotions so little attention.

We saw earlier that the habitus includes ethical and unethical dispositions. These both influence and are influenced and activated by (im)moral emotions or sentiments such as gratitude, benevolence, compassion, anger, resentment, bitterness, guilt and shame (Smith, 1984 [1759]).[10] It is these embodied dispositions that allow people often to produce moral responses spontaneously, without reflection; indeed, it is interesting that we would have doubts about the moral character of someone who couldn't respond morally to events without first deliberating on them. I would therefore concur with Martha Nussbaum:

> Instead of viewing morality as a system of principles to be grasped by the detached intellect, and emotions as motivations that either support or subvert our choice to act according to principle, we will have to consider emotions as part and parcel of the system of ethical reasoning.
>
> (Nussbaum, 2001: 1; see also Oakley, 1993)

Lay normativity, ethics and capitals

At one level, Bourdieu recognized the deeply evaluative character of social behaviour in terms of how people value themselves and members of other groups, and the practices and objects associated with them. However, his interests in this regard lay primarily in the valuation of these things in strategic, functional and aesthetic terms. This is partly a consequence of his Hobbesian, interest- and power-based model of social life, and his adoption of a 'hermeneutics of suspicion' that is reluctant to acknowledge disinterested action, including ethical responses. Any ideas that certain actions may be disinterested are quickly deflated by deriving them from their habitus and interests (e.g. Bourdieu, 1984). Furthermore, he is more interested in the fact that goods achieved through disinterested pursuit for their own good often have a higher market value than goods pursued for money or other external rewards, than in the fact that people do indeed often act not for advantage, but because they think that certain courses of action are right or good in themselves. It is a matter of fact of enormous normative importance that people can also value others and their conduct in terms of their goodness or propriety, often regardless of their self-interest, and sometimes in ways that do not match the inclinations of their habitus. Thus, it is a significant feature of struggles concerning inequalities that there are usually some egalitarians amongst the dominant groups who actually seek to reduce the power of their own group because they recognize it as unjust. This recognition need not come merely from political discourse, but from having experienced some other, perhaps smaller, form of injustice themselves, which has heightened their sensitivity to injustice, or simply through being able to sympathize with others who have suffered injustice. The moral sentiment of resentment at injustice is not reducible to a matter of self-interest, but can be felt on behalf of others. As Adam Smith noted, our capacity for fellow-feeling – for understanding something of what others are experiencing, even without their telling us – is crucial to our capacity for ethical action and for the reproduction of social order (Smith, 1984 [1759]). Although individuals may, depending on their social position, act in largely self-absorbed ways for much of the time, they also usually tend to respect, help or be friendly to certain others some of the time, and to take pleasure in observing others behaving in such ways, even with third persons rather than themselves (Filonowicz, 2008).

We need to beware of a scientistic and macho variant of the scholastic fallacy, in which explaining social action purely in terms of power, habitus and self-interest is seen as scientific or hard-headed, while explaining it in terms of morality, emotion, attachments or indeed love is seen as unscientific and sentimental (Smart, 2007). Both are important; indeed, some forms of power operate by taking advantage of people's moral commitments. For example, one of the reasons care-workers are poorly paid is that employers can take advantage of their reluctance to put their clients at risk by going on strike; if they didn't have that moral concern and commitment they wouldn't be so easily dominated. We must avoid a common kind of adolescent iconoclasm, according to which the most cynical explanations of social action must always be the best.

If we are to understand lay normativity and lay ethical being, we therefore need to get beyond the overwhelmingly self-interested and strategic model of action that is implicit in Bourdieu's concepts of habitus and capitals. The concept of capitals reduces the use-values of things or the internal goods of practices to their exchange-value or external goods. These distinctions are fundamental to any understanding of normativity (Sayer, 1999, 2005). Thus, practices like musicianship or medicine have their own internal goods and satisfactions, their own internal standards of what constitutes good work, and these are what many practitioners primarily strive to achieve; but they are quite different from the external goods, like money, praise or prestige, which they contingently bring. Where actors put the pursuit of external goods before internal goods, the latter tend to get corrupted (MacIntyre, 1985).

As I have argued elsewhere, the struggles or competitions of the social field are not merely for power and advantage but are also about how to live; they are partly driven by the search for the good (Sayer, 2005). Thus socialists and feminists seek not to invert hierarchies so they can be at the top and dominate others, but to end domination. Green politics is oriented towards saving the planet, for which gaining power is a means to an end, not the end. That there are often other, sometimes discrepant, motives present in such movements does not mean the 'principled motives' are absent. Social scientists often like to be sceptical of claims like these, though they do not generally apply that scepticism to their own motives. Followers of Bourdieu admire his work because they believe it to be good according to the internal standards of the practice of social theory, not simply because their habitus disposes them to like it or because following his work augments their cultural capital (Sayer, 1999). They may develop a feel for the game of those internal standards, but it includes knowing why they're important, not merely being able to recognize them. In everyday cultural politics, people sometimes seek to distinguish the good from the merely posh (i.e. that which is merely associated with the dominant classes) and the bad from the common (that which is associated with the subordinate classes), rather than conflating the two. Challenges to the alleged

superiority of 'received pronunciation' – that is, the preferred accent of the dominant classes – are an example of this (Sayer, 2005).

Our attachments and commitments to particular people, practices and things
figure prominently among our concerns and our emotional state depends heavily on their condition; while we can generally give reasons for valuing them, our
investment in them is also emotional. They become constitutive of our character,
so that we define ourselves by reference to them (I am the father of …, the partner
of …, the friend of …, an academic, a socialist, etc.). Attachments and commitments develop slowly, through a process of interaction and engagement that again
lies between the extremes of osmosis through immersion in repeated practice and
reflection removed from practice. They become part of our habitus. We do not
simply decide one day that we are a political activist or a musician, but gradually
become them through ongoing engagement in politics or music making. Sometimes
we get into these things largely unintentionally in the first instance. However, we
tend to reflect on our engagement, though not necessarily in a particularly systematic or concentrated way, and adjust our relation to such practices. We may come
to find that they suit us well and matter to us, but we can also be disillusioned and
realize that a practice is 'not for us', that it is not what we had expected, or that it
is somehow objectionable. People can therefore engage in 'strong evaluation', as
Charles Taylor terms it, where they reflect on the worth of their various ends and
reassess them (Taylor, 1985); should they spend more time with their family?; is
getting promoted at work worth the effort?; is football taking too much of their
life? Bourdieu's account of investments and *illusio* emphasizes the embodied and
unreflective elements of the process of forming attachments and commitments, and
considers the practices to which the latter relate as competitive games in which
we engage unreflectively (Bourdieu, 1998b, 2000d). Yet many of the practices
or relationships to which we become committed are not competitive. Without an
acknowledgement of people's reflections on and strong evaluations of internal
goods, the account represents a demeaning, deflationary account of what matters
to people and how they make judgements about their commitments. One might
say that this view of practical action is a consequence of a kind of inverted scholastic fallacy in which academics imagine that only they are capable of reflection,
deliberation and disinterested judgement.

Human vulnerability and concern: why are we evaluative beings?

Further obstacles to understanding the ethical dimension of everyday life lie deeper
still in Bourdieu's work – and in much other social theory – in the implicit model
of human social being. Philosophers and sociologists are often wary of committing
themselves to any conception of human nature, because they see humans as beings
who in some sense are freed from nature by their capacity for reason and cultural
variation (which of course itself says something about human nature!). While it
is true that what we become depends partly on how we understand ourselves, and
different cultures provide us with different ways of making sense of this, and hence

allow different forms of self-making, we must beware of the dangers of disciplinary imperialism in attempts to claim human being for philosophy, anthropology or sociology and to resist any concessions to biology and psychology. As we saw earlier, attempts to avoid a conception of human nature result in an unexamined model of people as infinitely malleable. To be capable of socialization or acculturation, we must have the capacities, susceptibilities and drives that enable them to work on us; the influences of culture have to have some practical adequacy in the way that they engage and co-opt our neediness, and colonize and reshape it.

In everyday life, normativity in the form of ethical concerns is related to (ideas of) well-being. Bourdieu is clearly deeply concerned about social suffering, but his model of human being gives us little idea of why people can suffer, hence why they are concerned about their position and the way they are treated. The dispositions of the habitus do not seem to be related to pain or suffering, or indeed to well-being.

Yet well-being and suffering are not merely subjective or purely socially constructed; neither individual nor collective wishful thinking is likely to have much success in enabling us to flourish. To understand normativity it is vital to address the fact that we are sentient beings who can flourish or suffer – beings who can develop a wide range of capacities but also have many susceptibilities or vulnerabilities. As animals, we live in a state of neediness, in which lack and dissatisfactions of various forms continually produce the desire to overcome them. As social beings, we are in need of others for our physiological and psychological well-being. As beings who easily form attachments and commitments, our well-being becomes connected to theirs, and we become concerned about them. As cultural beings, our emotional responses are influenced by cultural conceptions of what is of value, though not just any construction or construal works, for not just any vulnerability or capacity affecting our well-being can be denied or invented; cultural mediation is not the same as cultural determinism. In consequence of our capacities, vulnerabilities, dependence on others and neediness, *our fundamental relation to the world is one of concern*, not mere adjustment and accommodation, as Bourdieu's work and so much sociology tends to assume. We are necessarily *evaluative beings* (Archer, 2000); our responses can range from resistance through indifference to enjoyment and investment. It is this vulnerability to suffering and capacity for flourishing that gives experience its normative character, and from which 'the force of the ought' as regards ethical matters derives. Although a complete definition of well-being or flourishing would be impossible, because it is always possible that we could develop new forms of flourishing, or come to realize that we have been mistaken about some aspects of it, the very fact of our survival indicates that we at least know something about it. And the fact that we can also be mistaken about what constitutes flourishing indicates that it is at least partly independent of our judgements. (If well-being were no more than whatever we 'constructed' it as, we could never be mistaken about it.)

Bourdieu brilliantly exposed 'the soft forms of domination' present in social life, but without a clear acknowledgement of our capacity for flourishing and suffering and their specific forms such as fulfilment, love, humiliation and disrespect; his *critique* of symbolic domination was only implicit, for it could not say why there was anything wrong with it. As Habermas said of Foucault, his work is 'crypto-normative', presenting insights into social processes that are likely to trigger emotions of anger, indignation at injustice and compassion in the reader but evading identifications of why things were bad. When we suffer – for example, when we are stigmatized by others – we are, as a matter of fact, in a certain state of being, but also a bad one; someone who didn't understand that suffering was bad, would simply not understand the concept of suffering. The term provides an evaluative description; if we try to re-describe suffering in a way that omits the evaluation, we will *mis-describe* it. An important range of concepts – thick ethical terms, as philosophers call them – concerned with our well-being, such as care, kindness, friendliness, respect, selfishness, cruelty, racism, elude the fact-value dichotomy. Avoiding these terms out of the desire not to make 'value-judgements' not only impoverishes our descriptions, but dulls our sense of why domination and other forms of avoidable suffering are bad.

Like many others, in his academic – though not in his political – writing, Bourdieu preferred not to comment on the very thing that matters most to us – well-being – as if it were merely a matter of convention and competitive struggle, and the few scattered remarks about ethics in his work generally have a deflationary tone, as if ethics were inherently misleading and dubious rather than vital for social order and well-being. Unless we explore various forms of suffering and flourishing and acknowledge the role of emotions in indicating them, ethics becomes disconnected from its reference point and key indicator and is left merely to reside in 'values', as mere subjective judgements having no external warrant.

It is crucial here to appreciate the difference between a merely *conventional* conception of morality (that is, one in which morality is no more than a set of conventions for co-ordinating conduct), and a *harm-based* conception of morality, in which it is about avoiding harm and promoting flourishing. As Shaun Nichols shows, research on how people make ethical judgements shows them to be generally capable of distinguishing the two. He reports an interesting study by Nucci of Amish children in the United States in which it was found that 100 per cent of them

> said that if God had made no rule against working on Sunday, it would not be wrong to work on Sunday. However, more than 80 per cent of these subjects said that even if God had made no rule about hitting, it would still be wrong to hit.
>
> (Nichols, 2004: 6)

Other studies of children have shown them to be able to distinguish the moral from the merely conventional by their third birthday (ibid.: 78). Interestingly, studies of psychopaths have shown them to be incapable of distinguishing the moral from the conventional, since they think of all wrongdoing in terms of the transgression of norms. By contrast, non-psychopathic criminals are able to appreciate that their actions were wrong not merely because they transgressed norms or conventions, but because they harmed others (ibid.: 76). How interesting, too, that some sociologists should support the idea that actions are only wrong because they are socially defined as wrong![11] Sociologists may sometimes cite actors' moral terms in inverted commas to indicate that they are not endorsing the judgements those terms imply, but it is a mistake to allow this methodological device to become an ontological assumption that they are just conventions rather than judgements about suffering or well-being.

Conclusion

In considering the moral dimension of everyday life there is much of value to draw upon in Bourdieu's work, though, as I have sought to show, at least in outline, we have to modify and add to his basic concepts and approach. This involves firstly acknowledging that the dispositions of the habitus include ethical ones, or virtues and vices, and taking lay reflexivity and judgement seriously, as judgements, and not merely as functions of social position (in effect, responding to others' claims by saying, 'they would say that wouldn't they, given their position'). Secondly, it involves taking emotions and emotional reason seriously as informative of people's situations and concerns. Thirdly, it means taking disinterested judgement – including ethical and political concerns – seriously, instead of seeing them as either competitive and strategic or a function of the habitus. Fourthly, and more generally, we need to acknowledge the fact that our relation to the world is one of concern for well-being, whether our own or that of others and things to which we have become committed. Bourdieu repeatedly insists on the difference between the practical sense or reason we use in everyday life and the contemplative or scholastic knowledge of academic spectators (Bourdieu, 1988, 1998b, 2000d). While philosophers do indeed have a tendency to reduce practical reason to a product of contemplative reason, they do at least acknowledge that ethical ideas are a major part of practical reason, whereas Bourdieu says little about them. I am well aware that a much lengthier defence of the position I have put forward is needed, but I hope to have at least opened up some worthwhile directions for later, fuller consideration.

Notes

1 She might get a temporary summer job as a cleaner while a student, but in the knowledge that it is exceptional and temporary.
2 This tendency is taken advantage of in military training: for example, novice soldiers are made to alter their ethical disposition towards violence through bayonet practice.
3 Actually I think Aristotle overestimated the extent to which people are likely to respond to the same situation in different ways, but he is surely right to refuse a wholly deterministic account.
4 As Arpaly (2003) notes, even when we do deliberate on something, such as where to go for our holidays, we don't necessarily decide to deliberate on it on the basis of some prior deliberation; it may just 'occur' to us to do so.
5 Sociological reductionism is also a form of sociological imperialism for it expands the putative domain of the discipline at the expense of other disciplines' claims. On one of the rare occasions Bourdieu mentions biological nature he notes, 'One of the tasks of sociology is to determine how the social world constitutes the biological libido, an

undifferentiated impulse, as a specific libido' (Bourdieu, 1998b: 78). A notion like this of what makes us do anything is indeed required, but we need to avoid a sociological imperialism which imagines that the social world can 'constitute'– or better, shape – this libido, drive or neediness in just any way, without constraint.

6 'Again, of all the things that come to us by nature we first acquire the potentiality and later exhibit the activity (this being plain in the case of the senses; for it was not by often seeing or hearing that we got these senses, but on the contrary that we had them before we used them, and did not come to have them by using them); but the virtues we get first by exercising them' (Aristotle, *Nicomachean Ethics*, II.i).

7 See Wilkinson (2007) on health inequalities.

8 This anti-subjectivist, anti-idealist claim that emotions have referents is borne out by social psychological research on aggression reported by Scott (1990: 186), which shows that victims' anger towards agents of injustice is not reduced where they displace it onto others or give vent to it in 'safe', legitimate activities such as sports (the 'safety-valve theory'). Experiences of injustice may also make people more disposed to aggression against innocent others, but such displacements have been found not to resolve the problem and the anger remains. Such emotions are clearly not undirected, non-specific urges lacking referents and capable of remedy through just any means.

9 My thanks to Linda Woodhead for comments on general emotional stances or dispositions.

10 In a rare reference to the ethical dimension of the habitus, Bourdieu argues that the word 'ethos' better refers to these dispositions, than 'ethic', which suggests coherent, explicit principles (Bourdieu, 1993e).

11 This subjectivist view of values goes back 2,300 years to Epicurus, and is reproduced in Durkheim's claim that 'actions are evil because they are socially prohibited, rather than socially prohibited because they are evil.' (Bauman, 1989: 173).

8   Culture, power, knowledge

Between Foucault and Bourdieu

Tony Bennett

What are the contrasting implications of the work of Bourdieu and Foucault for the place of culture within an analytics of power? Is anything to be gained by drawing elements from both to enrich our understanding of the ways in which culture – whose definition I shall postpone for the moment – operates as a part of the mechanisms through which power is exercised? These are the two main questions that guide my discussion in this chapter. While they are difficult enough in themselves, answering them is not made any easier by two silences. The first is that, in contrast to Bourdieu – for whom the concept of culture was a matter of central concern – Foucault has little to say about it. He did, of course, write about aesthetic matters,[1] and his account of an 'aesthetics of existence' (Foucault, 1989) finds a place for aesthetic practices as a counter to governmental power.[2] But there is no extended discussion of the concept of culture in his work which places the couplet knowledge/power, rather than that of culture/power, at the centre of attention. The second silence is that while – as associates and, occasionally, political allies – Bourdieu and Foucault did not discuss each other's work publicly when they were both alive, Bourdieu commented on Foucault's work, sometimes quite extensively, after Foucault's death in 1984. We do, then, know what Bourdieu took to be the shortcomings of Foucault's work, but do not know where Foucault might have taken Bourdieu to task. While usefully drawing attention to this discrepancy, Stefan Callewaert (2006) compounds its effects in siding unequivocally with Bourdieu by pigeon-holing Foucault among the philosophers whose dominance of the French academic field Bourdieu contested in the name of the empirical social sciences.[3]

This is not a course I want to follow. But nor am I inclined to side unequivocally with Foucault against Bourdieu, albeit that some aspects of my discussion will tend in this direction. For I shall suggest that a governmentality approach to the relations between 'culture' and the social affords a means of probing some of the shortcomings associated with Bourdieu's key concepts of field, cultural capital and habitus. However, I no more want to jettison these concepts entirely than I want to place Foucault on a theoretical and methodological pedestal. My concern, rather, is to identify where Bourdieu's and Foucault's insights might be mobilized in a complementary fashion.

I look first at Bourdieu's suggestion that Foucault's concept of the 'field of strategic possibilities' is similar to his own account of the 'space of possibles', only then to be chastised as idealist for its failure to anchor the organization of discursive possibilities in an objective social structure. I show why this is an illegitimate comparison which fails to appreciate why the regularities and dispersions Foucault attributes to the organization of discourse cannot be assimilated to Bourdieu's accounts of the relational struggles between agents within fields. I also argue that Foucault's construal of the relations between technologies of the self and technologies of power provides a more satisfactory account of the connections between the organization of social relationships and the cultural aspects of personhood than Bourdieu's concept of habitus. I then turn to the different accounts offered within Bourdieusian and Foucauldian frameworks of the roles that varied forms of cultural knowledge and expertise play in relation to the operation of power at the conjunctions of cultural and social practices. I also examine how the two approaches might nonetheless be combined. My closing arguments consider how viewing Bourdieu's concerns through the Foucauldian analytic of governmentality highlights the historical specificity of the concerns addressed by cultural capital theory.

Field: discourse

One of Bourdieu's most extended discussions of Foucault's work occurs in his 'Principles for a sociology of cultural works'. Originally presented at Princeton University in 1968 and later republished in *The Field of Cultural Production* (1993c), the essay lays out the principles of field analysis and their implications for the analysis of literary and artistic practices by means of two counterfoils. The first, largely Marxist in inspiration and represented by, amongst others, Georg Lukács, Lucien Goldmann and Theodor Adorno, he characterises as being committed to an 'external mode of analysis' that seeks to explain literary and artistic works by interpreting them as expressing the world views of particular social classes. The chief limitation of this approach, Bourdieu argues, consists in its '*short circuit effect*' (Bourdieu, 1993c: 181): that is, its reduction of such works to determinations lying outside the literary and artistic fields in the conditions of existence of particular social classes.

It was against the logic of this 'short circuit effect', Bourdieu tells us, that he developed his theory of the field to account for the role of those mediating factors bearing specifically on the organization of literary and artistic practices through which economic and social forces must pass in order to connect with those practices. This involves taking account of the activities of a wider set of agents than writers or artists who, in world-view analysis, constitute the main conduits through which the impress of social forces flows in order to acquire expression in literary or artistic forms. Instead, Bourdieu argues, analysis must also encompass the activities of reviewers, institutions of legitimation, the relations between different schools and movements, the organization of literary and artistic markets, etc., in order to understand the relational organization of the fields of literary and artistic production. This relational organization of fields bears on the positions of different agents (the consecrated artist versus the *artiste maudit*, for example) and their interests relative to each other, as well as on the intertextual relations between different genres arising from their different positions relative to the historicities of specific fields (the divisions between canonical genres and those championed by *avant gardes*, for example). These two sets of relations make up the 'space of possibles' which, even if they cannot consciously formulate them, implicitly inform the calculations of all the agents in a field if they are to 'be in the game'. Class or other aspects of social position do not affect literary or artistic forms directly; their influence is refracted through the intermediary role of this 'space of possibles'.

Bourdieu discusses Foucault as an example of internalist forms of cultural analysis which, while recognising the significance of those relational properties that are purely intertextual, fails to connect these to the relational positioning of different agents within specific cultural fields, and thereby fails to relate those fields to economic and social forces that are external to them. Nonetheless, Bourdieu sees some parallels between his own concept of the 'space of possibles' and Foucault's use of 'the name "field of strategic possibilities" to refer to the "regulated system of differences and dispersions" within which each individual work defines itself' (Bourdieu, 1993c: 179). The difference – and it is the difference, Bourdieu contends, between Foucault's 'orthodox structuralism' and his own 'genetic structuralism' – is that Foucault 'transfers into the "paradise of ideas" … the oppositions and antagonisms which are rooted in the relations between the producers and the consumers of cultural works' (ibid.). Like the Russian Formalists' concept of the literary system, Foucault's *épistème* treats the cultural order as 'an autonomous and transcendent system' (ibid.). Although setting up a structure similar to that of the 'space of possibles', Foucault, cast in the role of an idealist, 'finds it necessary to exclude the social space of which that space is the expression' (ibid.: 182).

The text that informs Bourdieu's discussion here is Foucault's: 'On the archaeology of the sciences: response to the Epistemology Circle' (Foucault, 2000 [1968]) which Bourdieu refers to as 'without doubt the clearest expression of the theoretical presuppositions of Foucault's work' (Bourdieu, 1993c: 294). Yet this text will scarcely withstand either the burden or the interpretation that Bourdieu places on it. The passage Bourdieu cites is from a passage in which Foucault summarises the principles for the analysis of discursive formations that he later developed at greater length in *The Archaeology of Knowledge* (Foucault, 1972). These principles are of interest here precisely because they point to the need for analysis to encompass the operations of statements whose regularities and dispersions precisely do *not* conform to – and cannot be contained within – the divisions between fields which Bourdieu's work proposes (Foucault, 2000: 320–1). Moreover, at the point in his discussion where he outlines the significance of intertextual relations in the analysis of discourse, Foucault's formulations call into question the principles of grouping texts into sets and attributing them to an originating source from which – in the logic of Bourdieu's field analysis – they derive a certain unity as the expression of the writer's or artist's habitus. The habitus, understood as a set of durable dispositions derived from the writer's or artist's position in the economic and social fields, serves, in however mediated a fashion, as the main route through which economic and social relationships impinge on the organization of literary and artistic forms. This is not, to be sure, the same thing as world-view analysis. Nonetheless, the logic of connection is similar to the degree that the work's form is judged to be the expression of the writer's or artist's habitus as shaped by the dual (and sometimes contradictory) pressures arising from their general position in the economic and social fields and their specific position in the literary or artistic fields.

It is not whether Foucault's concept of discursive formation is more or less productive than Bourdieu's construction of the relations between field, habitus, and work that concerns me here. My point is rather that these differences and their analytical consequences need to be properly registered if the issues at stake between the two sets of concepts are to be adequately engaged with. The kinds of regularities and irregularities in the field of discourse that Foucault proposes are not ones that can be retrieved to the logic of treating authors as subjects who can be placed behind the texts bearing their name as agents whose activities are understood in terms of their relational struggle for profits – whether economic or symbolic, or in whatever combination – vis-à-vis other agents. The same is true of the terms for historical analysis that Foucault proposes in enunciating the principle of discontinuity to disrupt the notions of continuity, tradition, evolution, development, and so on, which inform Bourdieu's understanding of the cumulative historicity of literary, artistic and scientific fields (Bennett, 2005). And, of course, in his subsequent elaboration of the principles governing the operation of *dispositifs* as heterogeneous assemblages of texts, statements, institutional practices, administrative procedures, etc., Foucault's commitment to open-ended processes went well beyond the more-bounded models of his earlier work (Frow, 2010).

Bourdieu's discussion, in brief, makes too much of the apparent similarity between Foucault's 'field of strategic possibilities' and his own 'space of possibles' and too little of the respects in which Foucault's discussion challenges the assumptions underlying his own concepts of field and habitus. But Bourdieu's choice of this particular text is also curious given the date of its initial publication: 1968. For by the time of Bourdieu's Princeton text, 1986, two years after Foucault's death, Foucault's interests had taken significantly new directions with, for example, his work on the history of sexuality and on governmentality. These aspects of Foucault's work have a direct bearing on the questions Bourdieu addressed in formulating his principles for a sociology of cultural works. The work on sexuality and Foucault's closely allied formulations concerning the relations between technologies of the self and technologies of power opened up questions concerning the mechanisms through which different forms of personhood are shaped that differ significantly from the conception of the relations between social and psychological life implied by Bourdieu's conception of the habitus. Indeed, as Nikolas Rose (1996) has noted, they dispute the possibility that the architecture of the person might be construed in terms of the universal socio-psychological mechanisms invoked by the concept of habitus. Rather, they stress the historically pluralized spaces and practices of self formation that are produced by the ways in which different epistemological and moral authorities format the person, laying out the self in the form of the divisions, crevasses, and surfaces that are needed for their own actions on it.

The work on governmentality (Foucault, 1991) similarly presents a powerful challenge to the ground that Bourdieu takes for granted in formulating the concerns and procedures of cultural sociology. This is so, first, in the respect that it displaces the social and the economy from the place that they occupy in Bourdieu's sociology as structures which affect the intellectual, cultural and scientific fields in ways that are not reciprocated by those fields. For in Foucault's analysis, the concepts of the social and the economy have no universal currency or validity of this kind. They are not aspects of the practices of all kinds of society, nor are they fields with an inherent tendency or dynamic of their own, but are rather the effects of the new ways of managing population associated with the emergence of governmental power.[4] Second, however, the optic of governmentality also displaces the centrality that Bourdieu accords to class, particularly in his account of the social processes of distinction. For it is an optic that focuses on the role that cultural practices play in practices of governance, particularly in organizing asymmetrical relations between those who govern and those who are governed in ways which, while they might involve relations of class, are not reducible to them.

Moreover, these questions are pursued in relation to a quite different conceptual schema from that organising Bourdieu's accounts of the fields of cultural production and consumption. For Foucault's silence on the question of culture is by no means accidental. Rather, it registers his scepticism regarding the possibility of developing a general account of the relations between culture – understood, in the Bourdieusian sense, as the realm of the symbolic – and the social. It also registers his diffidence in relation to Durkheim's account of the role of collective representations in social life which constitutes the deep background to Bourdieu's work. There can, then, be no Foucauldian entry into the problematic of culture that does not, at the same time, disperse its impossible unity into a set of differentiated and discrete issues. The closest point of entry is via the means it offers for examining the roles played by varied forms of cultural knowledge and expertise in organising a dispersed and differentiated set of power relations which act on the social in varied ways. To probe the relationship between them more closely, therefore, I now look at the area in which Bourdieu's and Foucault's perspectives most closely intersect while remaining significantly different: that is, in the roles they accord the operation of cultural knowledges in the organization of distinctive forms of power.

Space of possibles: field of strategic possibilities

In discussing the properties of fields of cultural production, Bourdieu argues that analysis must encompass not only

> the direct producers of the work in its materiality (artist, writer, etc.), but also the ensemble of agents which participate in the production of the value of art in general and in the distinctive value of this or that work of art.
>
> (Bourdieu, 1996a: 229)

The list of institutions and agents he draws up is a long one: critics, art historians, curators, publishers, dealers, academies, salons, juries, gallery directors; bodies like the *Direction des Musées Nationaux* and their role in regulating art markets;

and the institutions which train both art producers and consumers 'capable of recognising the work of art as such' (ibid.: 229). The perspectives from which he approaches the roles of these agents are, first, that of the degree to which they act to secure the autonomy of the cultural field in question or, to the contrary, bring it under the sway of heteronomous forces from the fields of power and the economy; and second, their role, within and across fields, in organising the relations between restricted and extended forms of cultural production.

Similarly, when considering practices of cultural consumption, Bourdieu's attention focuses on the activities of a range of mediating agencies involved in shaping tastes via their action on the habitus. These agencies range from the institutions of consecration and legitimation which organize aesthetic hierarchies and cultivate particular aesthetic capacities, those of the 'pure gaze' for example; through the role of the new cultural intermediaries (television producers, designers, cinema and jazz commentators) who mould the tastes of the new *petite bourgeoisie*; and the newspapers, magazines and advertisements which shape the working-class taste for the necessary (Bourdieu, 1984).

The procedures Bourdieu uses for analysing the properties of the fields of cultural production and those of cultural consumption are thus – as, indeed, they must be – isomorphic. Consumption reproduces the divisions that are produced between different forms of cultural production as different agents within each field vie for dominance in their struggles to assert the principles of autonomy or heteronomy. If this is a characteristic of each field, it also governs the relations between them in organising the different degrees of prestige and legitimacy that are accorded different fields of cultural production and consumption relative to one another. There is, then, a consistency informing the *modus operandi* of cultural agents, and the forms of cultural knowledge and expertise they mobilise, which derives, ultimately, from the objective structure of social space that arises from the distribution of different capitals. It is this structure which orders the relations of competitive striving for material and symbolic profits that govern the actions of all agents both within and between fields.[5] It is always and only in relation to the outcomes of such competitive strivings that the role and effectivity of specific cultural knowledges is assessed within a Bourdieusian framework. The manner of their operation is given in advance by the conception of an underlying social structure of class positions, defined along Weberian lines in terms of their unequal life chances, whose properties and effects are dynamically reproduced through the unequal distribution and symbolic legitimation of different capitals.

Yet, if we go back to Foucault's concept of a 'field of strategic possibilities', he was very clear that the analysis of the knowledge–power relations associated with specific discursive formations could not be bound into the kind of unity of action and effect deriving from a pre-given structure of this kind. Contrary to the logic of Bourdieu's 'space of possibles', the field of strategic possibilities does not relate to discursive options and the forms of action which they auspice that are rooted in the unity of a period or that of a society, but rather concerns the formation and dispersal of options across and beyond such pre-given unities. As such, the field of strategic possibilities does not concern the position-taking of actors relative to one another within the same social space but rather the role of discursive options in mapping out and laying open nature, the economy, or the social – or whatever the object of intervention might be – to specific kinds of action.

Yet Bourdieu is right to argue that in this particular essay Foucault's elaboration of discourse remains abstract in the sense that it is couched more or less exclusively at the level of ideas. Quite some time before he died, however, Foucault's elaboration of the respects in which discourses are always inscribed within particular *dispositifs*, and the connections between these aspects of Foucault's work and the Deleuzian literature on assemblages which fold discourse and 'the real' into the same single-planar level of analysis, had clarified that what was aspired to (however imperfectly realized) were ways of analysing the actions of discourses as parts of socio-material apparatuses or machineries whose capacities are woven into the constitution of the fields of action they engage with. The subsequent publication of his Collège de France lectures makes it clear that such fields of action are to be understood as historically distinctive 'transactional realities' that are produced through the operations of particular regimes of truth in ordering the objects of their attention and intervention (Foucault, 2008: 19, 297).

It is, then, this perspective – that of the relations between particular cultural knowledges and apparatuses, and their role in producing the 'transactional realities' through which they engage with and act on the social or the economy – that provides a Foucauldian alternative to Bourdieu's account of the role played by cultural knowledges in relation to processes of consecration and legitimation. While Foucault gave little explicit attention to the organization and operation of cultural knowledges, there is now a considerable body of work which has applied Foucault's perception of the centrality of particular regimes of truth to the exercise of governmental power to the forms of power produced and exercised by the deployment of particular cultural knowledges in specific cultural apparatuses. Much of this work was originally, as Clive Barnett (1999) has noted, focused unduly on the knowledge–power–government relations associated with the relatively sequestered spaces of nineteenth-century cultural institutions (the relations between art history or anthropology and museums, for example (Bennett, 1998) or between aesthetics, literary pedagogy and public schooling (Hunter, 1988)). While these initially provided the model for culture–power–government relations associated with cinema and the early history of broadcasting (Ouellette and Hay, 2008), there is now also a good deal of work focused on the role of cultural governance in relation to the regulation of populations across dispersed, non-territorialized and sometimes transnational spaces through networks of communication (see, for example, Goswami, 2004) in which, as Barnett puts it, 'action at a distance' becomes literal as well as metaphorical (Barnett, 1999: 384–6).

A number of general features stand out from this literature, differentiating the attention it pays to the social role of varied forms of cultural expertise from that accorded them in Bourdieu's field theory. First, what matters about the actions of such agents does not concern the role they play in relational struggles within or across fields, but how they connect with the social via the varied transactional realities which lay out the conduct of individuals or of specific social groups for varied kinds of action and intervention. Foucault proposed the public and the milieu as two historically fabricated surfaces through which governmental action was able to connect with and act on the ways of life, feelings, perceptions, and conditions of existence of populations in this way (Foucault, 2008: 20–2, 75). But regional cultural ecologies (Poulot, 2005), the synchronous totalities of 'other cultures'(Wilder, 2005), the co-ordinates of evolutionary time (Bennett, 2004), and the 'indigenous domains' forming the interfaces between settler and indigenous populations (Rowse, 1998) have also been proposed as different kinds of trans-actional realities which guide the actions of cultural apparatuses toward different aspects of social conduct while also providing different instruments for connecting with such conduct with a view to modifying it.

It is clear, second, that it is not possible, within this framework, to pose the question of culture's relationship to the social in a manner which grants a prior significance to one social relationship (class) by according it a structuring rule in the relations of competitive striving that govern the organization of fields, with the consequence that the roles of other relationships (gender, ethnicity) have then to be addressed through the 'add-on' logic of the sociological supplement. The ways in which different cultural knowledges act on the social is ordered via the 'trans-actional realities' that are produced by the operations of specific cultural knowledges and cultural apparatuses considered in their relations to social knowledges and apparatuses which also lay out and format the social for varied kinds of action (Law and Urry, 2004). Whether or not class is produced as a significant component of such transactional realities is a contingent matter depending on the organization of the relationships of government in question. For, in the perspective of governmen-tality theory, the relations that carry the greatest theoretical and ontological force are those between governors and governed, and these are historically specific and mutable depending on the configuration of the discursive and institutional practices which organize them. These relations have historically operated asymmetrically across class, gender, racial, and generational lines, and across the relations between colonizers and colonized, with historically circumstantial different degrees of emphasis. As such – as relations of government which organize the flow of dif-ferential forms of action in relation to different sections of the population – relations of equivalence or difference between such groups arise from their different relations to processes of governing rather than from their primary (class) or secondary (all other relations) roles in relation to an underlying structure generating inequalities of profit and honour. Within nineteenth-century formulations of liberal government, for example, women, children, lower-caste Indians, and primitives are posited as equivalents owing to their lack of a reflexive architecture of the self required for self-government (Valverde, 1996). The logic of social exclusion developed, as Foucault notes, as an adjunct to neo-liberal forms of governance establishes equiva-lences between varied social groups on a similar basis (Foucault, 2008: 203–7).

There is, finally, no space in Foucault's theoretical apparatus for the concept of the habitus which, in Bourdieu's account, connects the cultural dispositions of social agents to the determining ground of the structure of social relations in ways which allow those agents – as situated rather than transcendental subjects – to reflexively monitor and recondition the conditions that condition them (Bourdieu, 1990c: 12–14). This space, in which the cultural aspects of personhood are connected to social relations of power, is occupied quite differently within Foucault's formulations of the relations between technologies of power ('which determine the conduct of individuals and subject them to certain ends or domination' (Foucault, 1988: 18)) and technologies of the self ('which permit individuals to effect by their own means or with the help of others a certain number of operations on their own bodies, souls, thought, conduct and way of being so as to transform themselves in order to attain a certain state of happiness, purity, wisdom, perfection, or immortality' (ibid.: 18)). There is, though, some overlap between the two positions here: Bourdieu, too, speaks of the role of institutions of training in forming the habitus. Where they differ is in regard to whether these various ways of working on the self need add up to a unity and, if so, how that unity is to be accounted for. For Bourdieu, the habitus is characterized by a tendential unity rooted in class position to which – with some exceptions – the actions of all apparatuses shaping the various attributes of personhood are subservient. While Foucault acknowledges the relationship between technologies of the self and 'technologies of production' which require the 'modification of individual conduct – not only skills but also attitudes' (Foucault, 1988: 18), no priority or necessary connection is asserted between such aspects of person formation and those relating to the organization of the body, the soul, madness, sexuality, and so on. This is not to say that Foucault's position can be assimilated to the logic of Bourdieu's exception of the divided habitus for those who straddle different fields.[6] The point is rather that, for Foucault, there is no habitus to be divided; the apparatuses of person formation are more plural and dispersed, connecting with individuals in different ways through different compartments or registers of existence.

Distinction: governance

There are, then, significant differences between Bourdieu's and Foucault's perspectives on the relations between cultural agents, knowledges and expertise and the organization of social relations of power. This is not to deny that there are areas in which the two perspectives can be usefully combined. However, this is only possible if Bourdieu's field theory is 'loosened up' a little so as to rescue it from the forms of sociologism which characterized Bourdieu's insistence that the relationalities of fields must be rooted in an underlying social structure. John Martin (2003) has noted the tensions that are produced between Bourdieu's commitment to the principles of structural analysis and the purely positional concerns of field theory which, far from limiting positional possibilities within the constraints of a structure, stresses the multiplicity of the scales along which actions might be positioned relative to one another.

   It is, in this light, possible to explore how the activities of a range of cultural agents and knowledges operate as significant aspects of the processes through which social distinctions are produced and marked while at the same time being implicated in the processes through which the social is laid out for governmental action of different kinds in ways that may or may not be connected to the dynamics of class differentiation. Dominique Poulot (2005), for example, has noted the disparity between the statuses that are accorded the different knowledges associated with France's major national museums. While art history spills out from the exhibitionary domain to play a major role, alongside literary studies, in the institutions of scholarship (the school and the university) through which hierarchies of knowledge are produced, legitimated and connected to inter-generational processes for the transmission of cultural capital, this has not been true of either archaeology or ethnology. He makes this point, however, in order to register the pivotal role of archaeology in organizing a national polity in relation to the agendas of republican governance and, in the case of ethnology, its role in developing the templates for distinctive kinds of colonial and regional governance. The controversies that racked the relationships between the evolutionary and the diffusionist schools in British archaeology and anthropology in the inter-war years were similarly significantly implicated in questions of class politics, but ones centred more on the relative values of subordinate and dominant classes with respect to their ability to provide valid norms for conduct than with regard to the dynamics of distinction (Stout, 2008).

I have drawn on these examples from outside the literary and artistic fields that Bourdieu focused on to highlight the limitation that an exclusive focus on these places on the analysis of cultural knowledges and apparatuses. Of course, the relations between these aesthetic disciplines and other cultural knowledges can be analysed as hierarchically organized fields. James Clifford's (1988) account of the art/culture system does just this in ways that other cultural analysts have found helpful in identifying how art museums distinguish themselves, and their publics, from anthropology or natural history museums, for example (Bal, 1992). This is not to say, though, that the practices of aesthetic institutions should only be analysed in terms of their place and role relative to relationships of distinction. They are also implicated in the processes of inducting and organizing different publics into different ways of governing themselves as parts of different technologies for the production of civic capacities. Bourdieu's account of the historical organization of the pure gaze of aesthetic disinterestedness thus needs to be complemented by an account of the role of art museums in organizing different forms of 'civic seeing' which deploy works of art as resources for civic self-fashioning on the part of museum visitors in ways that cannot simply be mapped onto class divisions (Bennett, 2006).

Jacques Rancière's account of the 'aesthetic regime of the arts' is helpful here in suggesting that the processes of autonomization which, from the eighteenth century onward, separated art from its singular association with sovereign power, have generated multiple ways through which literary and artistic works connect with social relations and processes (Rancière, 2004b). While their role in processes of distinction is undoubtedly an important aspect of their contemporary social inscription, there are equally significant limits to this.[7] It is clear, for example, that the deployment of works of art has been crucially bound up with the post-Kantian system of 'character' as a means for training and exercising the will in order to bring the other aspects of the self under its control, but in ways that do not interfere with the freedom of the person. From this perspective, that of the governance of the person, the role assigned the state was that of making art widely available not as a matter of democratic entitlement, but as a means of extending the influence of élite forms of civic self-fashioning to broader populations (Bennett, 2008/9).

A good example of similar double-edged social inscriptions of cultural knowledges is afforded by makeover and reality TV programmes. The role of makeover programmes, or, as they are sometimes known, 'aspirational reality TV', has been tellingly analysed as conferring considerable power on a new group of cultural intermediaries – the 'tastemakers' who are now key components of television's personality system – to mediate new styles of décor to television audiences, but only by subordinating their tastes to those of the new cultural intermediaries (Philips, 2005). Laurie Ouellette and James Hay (2008) concur with this assessment of the role played by such programmes in establishing new styles of class distinction. However, they also interpret the development of lifestyle programmes in the United States as a part of a 'reinvention' of the relations between television and governance arising from the confluence between the post-1970s development of satellite and cable television on the one hand and the agendas of neoliberalism on the other. This confluence, they suggest, has displaced earlier governmental forms of television that aimed to promote a liberal, 'civilizing' education via broadcasting improving programmes to (formally) undifferentiated publics by substituting strategies aimed at cultivating new forms of self-governance and identity management on the part of collectivities identified in terms of lifestyle clusters. While arguing that such programmes organize class divisions based on principles of taste, they are equally concerned with their role in the development of differentiated formats for working on the self to produce distinctive forms of self-help and responsibility on the part of the socially excluded in the context of a diminished role for the welfare state: programmes like *Judge Judy* and *Brat Camp*, for example. It is not, in other words, the *modus operandi* of such genres in organizing differentiated dispositions relative to different class habitus but their role in distributing different cultural technologies of the self relative to the fault-lines between groups judged to possess different capacities for self-governance that matters here.

However, there is a broader question at stake concerning the roles the two approaches attribute to different forms of cultural knowledge and expertise in the mechanisms of social and cultural change. In Bourdieu's case, these consist in their roles relative to the relations of competitive striving which account for the dynamics of change within and across fields. By contrast, to view culture from Foucault's perspective of the transactional realities in which it is implicated is, to borrow Foucault's formulation regarding the state, to view it as 'nothing else but the mobile effect of a regime of multiple governmentalities' (Foucault, 2008: 77). The role of culture in processes of social change in this conception arises from the collisions between the different governmental rationalities in which cultural knowledges are implicated. Rather than deriving solely from the struggles between different forms of capital, change flows from the dispersed and countervailing sources of cultural expertise which constantly generate sources of resistance – counter conducts – to one another.

Cultural capital: governmentality

To recap, I have argued that Bourdieu's concepts of field and habitus and Foucault's concepts of governmentality and technologies of the self provide different, but not absolutely incommensurable, analytical grids for examining the relations between 'culture' and the social. The same forms of cultural knowledge and expertise often operate within both relations of distinction and relations of governance at one and the same time. While such relations are analytically distinct, there is often a good deal of empirical overlap between them so that particular practices can be seen to operate in both theoretical registers simultaneously. Take the now considerable post-Bourdieu literature on the cultural omnivore. The terms of the omnivore/univore distinction posed by Richard Peterson (2005) are now often, and rightly, qualified in favour of a range of different kinds and degree of hybrid taste formations, particular ones spanning the high/popular culture divide. These hybrid taste formations are usually associated with the occupancy of managerial and professional class positions, and are distinguished from more singular and restricted ones associated with working-class tastes. The social logic of distinction that is involved here is one in which higher class position is performed less through the command of legitimate culture than through the display of the versatility, sometimes cosmopolitan in form, needed to handle a variety of cultural repertoires across class and other boundaries. Yet the empirical data for such studies would equally well support the interpretation that such hybrid tastes manifest the key requirement of the subject of liberal government as articulated in the aesthetic sphere: that is, the ability to reflexively adapt aesthetic judgements to changing forms and circumstances in contrast to the over-dependence on prescribed rules and regulations that characterizes more restricted tastes (White, 2005). There is, indeed, particularly where the figure of the omnivore shades into that of the cultural cosmopolite, more than a little cross-over between the discourse of omnivorousness and the functioning of tolerance as a form of governmentality in which reflexive boundary crossing, and a receptivity to cultural difference, function as the unmarked position of a governing liberal discourse (Brown, 2006).

To simply leave the matter there, however, is not entirely satisfactory. To say that there are circumstances in which the two analytical perspectives overlap does not address what are to be the theoretical terms of their convergence. I therefore want to conclude by outlining the respects in which the perspective of governmentality affords a critical perspective on Bourdieusian cultural capital theory which suggest some limits – historical and political – to its scope. This will also help correct the second of the two silences I noted at the outset. For while Foucault never commented directly on Bourdieu, his comments on the relations between human capital theory and neoliberalism give some sense of where he might have parted company with Bourdieu. This is not to equate cultural capital and human capital theory – Bourdieu explicitly criticized the latter's association with rational choice theory – but merely to acknowledge the significant areas of overlap between them (Lin, 2001: 14–17). For it is these that concern me here.

Foucault's point of entry into human capital theory concerns its role, relative to classical economic theory, in moving the analysis of labour beyond its reduction to the quantitative variable of time to understand its operation as a set of capacities, construed as a form of capital that makes future income possible, that are inseparable from the qualities of the persons who possess them. In place of the classical conception of labour as the partner of an exchange, this substitutes the conception of the worker as an ability machine – or, as Foucault (2008: 225) puts it, a 'capital-ability' machine – that produces an income stream. The effect of this, Foucault argues, is to produce *homo œconimicus* in the form of an 'entrepreneur of himself, being for himself his own capital, being for himself his own producer, being for himself the source of [his] earnings' (ibid.: 226). This is not, Foucault stresses, a universal form of the worker; it is rather a neoliberal construction of the worker that gives a new form to the social, subordinating it to the economy by fashioning its actors on the model of the enterprise. It is in what Foucault goes on to say about how this makes the life of the individual into a 'sort of permanent and multiple enterprise' (ibid.: 241) that the connections between this construction of *homo œconomicus* and cultural capital theory become clear in view of the concern this generates with the nature, quantity and quality of investments in the 'capital-abilities' of the worker:

> Time spent, care given, as well as the parents' education – because we know quite precisely that for an equal time spent with their children, more educated parents will form a higher human capital than parents with less education – in short, the set of cultural stimuli received by the child, will all contribute to the formation of those elements that can make up a human capital.
>
> (Foucault, 2008: 229)

My point here is that cultural capital theory emerges in association with the development of a field of government whose interest in calibrating the quantity and quality of (differential) investments in the capital resources of future income earners reflected a refashioning of the social under the impact of neoliberal governmental rationalities. Bourdieu's personal intellectual and political opposition to the agendas of neoliberalism is well known. His position in relation to the educational and cultural policy agendas that his work was connected to were also (in)famously polemical. Committed to the cause of making legitimate forms of high culture universally available both for their own sake and as the forms of cultural capital investment with the best prospect of producing long-term income returns, he strongly opposed policies designed to build up smaller holdings of cultural capital by facilitating wider participation on the part of the subordinate classes in more popular cultural forms (Loosely, 2004). There is, nonetheless, a close fit and historical filiation between cultural capital theory and the development of governmental statistical apparatuses concerned with regulating, monitoring and, through a variety of policy measures in both the education and cultural fields, adjusting the levels and forms of investment in the 'capital-abilities' of income earners. Bourdieu's concept of cultural capital, it should be recalled, had its origins in studies which derived their conceptual impetus and funding from the intersecting concerns of education and cultural policy bureaus (Robbins, 2005). These are, moreover, apparatuses which work via the logic of the 'sociological supplement', adding new variables (emotional, national, and sub-cultural capital) that might contribute to improving and redistributing cultural capital as a capacity to be calibrated against a projected earnings stream.

What follows from suggesting that cultural capital theory can be situated historically in the space of a specific form of cultural governmentality in this way? At least two things. First, it suggests the need to place closer and more circumscribed limits on the historical and territorial purchase of cultural capital theory, better seen as the effect of the calculations and conducts of agents operating within a historically specific form of capitalism rather than being a characteristic of a generalized form of capitalism *tout court*. The modelling of human conduct through the lens of cultural capital theory thus proves, on this interpretation, to be far from the effect of an underlying economic structure in the manner that Bourdieu proposes. Rather, it emerges from a particular governmental ordering of economic life and its relations to other spheres of existence. Second, it suggests something of the political limits of cultural capital theory which can perhaps best be understood as an outcome of the kind of processes Foucault referred to as the 'governmentalization of the state' (Foucault, 1991) through which non-state forms of governmental intervention into the conduct of conduct are taken over by the state and subjected to processes of 'statification'. For, as Jonathan Rose (2002) has shown, there is, in Britain, a long history of inquiry into the correlations between cultural tastes, knowledge and preferences on the one hand and class, gender, and educational background on the other conducted by a range of voluntary or quasi-state organizations – the Sheffield Educational Settlement, the Workers Educational Association, and Mass Observation, for example. These were labour or socialist in aspiration and deeply committed to the cause of working-class (self) improvement as, in a Kantian sense, a politics of 'freedom through culture'. These earlier initiatives have now been entirely subsumed within/replaced by cultural participation surveys administered by arts and cultural bureaucracies in which cultural capital theory and social science expertise are drawn on to assist in the development of government policies intended to produce more equal forms of cultural participation to offset the divisive effects of social exclusion. It is, then, in these terms that we might use Foucauldian categories to place Bourdieu's work in a particular governmental space as an alternative to the ways of placing intellectual practices that inform Bourdieu's analyses of the organization of the academic field.

Notes

1 He did so, however, mainly in his early work (see the essays collected in Foucault, 2000) and did not return to give these questions any sustained attention in his work on governmentality or biopower.
2 First published in 1984, the interview in which Foucault develops this concept invokes the concept of an aesthetics of existence, with reference to his work on the history of sexuality and its lessons for ways of styling the self and conducting everyday practice, which would provide an alternative to the moral regulation of conduct. It is thus

concerned more with how aesthetics has construed the work of art as a template for the practice of freedom, than it is with a cultural sociology or a sociology of aesthetic works.

3   See Bourdieu's discussions of Foucault in *Homo Academicus* (Bourdieu, 1988) and *Pascalian Meditations* (Bourdieu, 2000d: 36).

4   See Foucault's criticisms of the methodological principles on which the analysis of universals rests and his advocacy of an historical method which re-situates universals as historically specific 'transactional realities' produced by specific governmental practices (Foucault, 2008: 2–19).

5   Jean Louis Fabiani (2001) notes the difficulties this occasions in Bourdieu's account of intertextualities which, since the relations between works must echo those between their producers, are denied any autonomy or effectivity of their own: texts are the creatures of the positional strategies of their authors.

6   See Bourdieu (2004) and Bennett (2007) for a critical discussion of the logic of the exceptions Bourdieu permits to his construction of the habitus as unified.

7   I part company here with Rancière's own rancorous assessment of Bourdieu (Rancière, 2004a).

9   The price of the people

Sociology, performance and reflexivity[1]

Antoine Hennion

The chapter of Bourdieu's (1979) *La Distinction* entitled 'Habitus and the space of life styles' is headed by two pages offering a series of interior photographs, each showing family members in the living room, the dining room or the kitchen. Many contrasts spring to the eye. Dress, furniture, gesture, occupation – all serve to reveal the occupants of these spaces. They cannot hide anything from the lens of the photographer; they are at home and they are their homes, as revealed by stereotypes of the family hearth. Formica chairs, modern contours, wallpapers with designs of large flowers, meals in the kitchen, pin-stripe suits, check shirts or tablecloths, necklaces – not counting facial features, which as the title of another series of photos tells us, immediately suggest a 'physique of the workplace'. The simple act of putting these on paper is in fact an amazing operation. These distinctions invade the pictures, being incorporated in hands, hairstyles, the bend of a back. They are objectivized in saucepans, curtains, shoes. Nothing is outside their scope. We see only them. The spontaneous reading we have of them indicates this clearly – lifestyles are in fact social classifications inscribed into our bodies and our belongings. Bourdieu is right.

What, however, have we learnt by looking at these photos? Nothing. Not only do we know nothing more, but this double page would carry no conviction if we did not already know it all before reading about it, if knowing it already were not part of the evidence. Formica in the kitchen and sweaty undershirts are working class. A suit and tie, polished shoes and tea in the living room are bourgeois. Some readers may believe they are cleverer than others because they can show that such and such a trait has been too hastily slotted into its category, but they have lost the battle before it is begun. By being content to retouch the painting they are offered, they tamely accept the frame around it. For the important thing is not to discuss whether these assignations are true or false, but rather to go one step further back and see that we make them spontaneously, whether or not we are shown them. It is to the exact extent that we are capable of instantly recognizing the oppositions presented and situating them socially that we *de facto* recognize their theoretical value. This serves to reinforce the validity of the author's theses.

What is this curious mechanism that transforms what in Bourdieu's own terms is merely our 'practical knowledge' into a theoretical finding, now attributed to him? The revelation that should convince us and make us believe in his theory is not lodged in the information that is added – it is not merely possible but indispensable that we know it all from the start in order for the revelation to be effective. Nor is there any new finding about their interrelationships – we need to know how to assign distinguishing social factors to goods and to people in order for the revelation to occur. We need to be classifiers ourselves in order to understand that we are being shown classification procedures. If, then, no knowledge is added, whence does the demonstration receive its power? It does from our recognition. Behind the use of photos – and also statistics, paintings, 'slices of life', interviews, newspaper cuttings – behind all the artifices the sociologist employs to present his scenario, lies our recognition. It reflects off the objects that have been shown to us and reflects back to the author who showed them to us. Nothing more is needed for the theoretical metamorphosis to take place. There is a change in the status of our knowledge, and a change of attribution, which makes the sociologist the happy father of an item of knowledge that pre-existed him.

But no less than this will do, either. We would like to show, by drawing on another depiction of the popular – that of the producer of popular music – that this work of staging makes all the difference, that it is another effect of his own direction that makes it seem that there was none, to efface himself before what he shows us. How can things be shown? By analyzing the staging of the evidence, we are doing its archaeology, since we are rendering visible the theoretical theatricality behind the demonstration.

Prologue: theory as stage direction

The first thing to do when directing is to draw a curtain. To withdraw several objects and people from view, to establish a certain rapport between them, to make them suddenly appear on the stage. The plotting involved is a veritable metaphor for causality. It brings out the contours of the situation in turn, slowly revealing what the whole pleasure has consisted in veiling then unveiling. Curtain, applause.

The sequence of non-recognition/recognition is part of the work of direction. This sequence, in which the theatrical plot is knitted together then unraveled, is also what theatre can teach us about theory. We do not see anything unless there is someone to show it to us. In other words, in order to obtain an effect of revelation, preliminary work must be done on the reader's knowledge. Texts never cease interpreting; that is to say, revealing what others hid. But in order to do this, they need to show that what they show was hidden. It is striking to see how much the big all-encompassing theoretical schemas, in pace with their own development, spend ever more time and energy establishing the state of non-knowledge that preceded them. Displacing the object of their work towards a justification of their own operation, they soon become interested only in proving to others that they are ignorant. Thus they become vast theories of non-recognition: of alienation, unconscious repression, more recently even of culture itself, this being based on 'things hidden' and then revealed by René Girard. In this sense, between Marx and Freud, between an Ideology that hides objective relations and the Unconscious that reveals the desire of the subject, Bourdieu does in fact operate a synthesis.

For him, non-recognition is not an obstacle to overcome, it becomes the theory itself. At the brink of tautology, it takes another step towards a perfect identity between the stage direction and the play, between the form and the background of theoretical work. The operation of non-recognition that founds the theory also becomes its only object.

Just like the playwright, the academic can always lift up the curtain that he himself has dropped, and put his effect of revelation onto the stage. As in the theatre, it is a question of making the spectator come half way, so that s/he is made to fill out the situations presented to her/him with things that s/he knows. The space of the stage, cut off from the world, only regains its meaning because, guided by the director, the spectator re-establishes one by one the connections between the stage and the world, between the characters s/he is looking at and those that s/he usually sees. Hence the simultaneous awareness of ignorance past and revelation present: the cutting-up involved in the direction gives birth to both at the same time, out of the silent non-differentiation of practical knowledge. This is what demonstration is.

From the reader's point of view, if we can jettison the fiction of a purely critical reading (the only reading that the reader is supposed to make of an academic text), then we observe rather that she has all the reactions of the spectator. Sometimes she is carried away, sometimes withdrawn, always moving. She is mobilized by the work that the direction performs on her. She moves. The reader does not have the objective fixity of a logical and universal receptor bringing nothing to the text being read. On the contrary, she only understands it if she brings all that she knows into it (Eco, 1979). The image of movement, which is indispensable if the reader is to re-establish links between the text and the world, is imposed as soon as one starts to talk about reading, about 'the footsteps of men through their own texts' (De Certeau, 1984 [1980]: 287). In this game between reader and writer, wherein each one strives to make the other 'follow' him/her, 'go in his/her direction', to not let go or get left behind, you cannot talk about the question of conviction by referring to the text alone. If you do not look at the reader's own knowledge, his/her act of recognition cannot be explained.

So we need to look at various stagings, which are variable according to their public. The popular is not the same if the director is a political man speaking to his electorate, a sociologist addressing her learned readership or a producer of popular music for the popular public themselves. In order to pursue this line,[2] we propose here to look at some consequences of work we have done on the production of popular songs and on the profession of artistic director (Hennion, 1981, 1989), by contrasting the presentation of the people by the sociologist and by the successful producer. The people are not something which is given, they are constructed. The producer is there to remind us what this construction costs, in work, in know-how, in money and in relationships, since success for him is contingent on all these resources. It is the blinding clarity of the family photos that will then become suspect. We need to bring out the work of direction involved in producing such evidence.

Act 1: The producer of popular music as a mediator of the popular

The hypothesis of theoretical theatricality – we only see what is shown us – re-establishes in the foreground, for all knowledge:

- the operation of non-recognition that founds it;
- the role of the mediator, who comes along as a screen between the public and its knowledge, which, presented this way, is thus revealed;
- and finally, the active role of the public itself, which gives its meaning to the representation by filling out the figures.

This hypothesis also enables us to do away with any a priori distinction between the credibility that we give to scientific work and to any other work of stage-management. There are no differences of nature, but means and effects to compare. As much as physics is completely invisible to us without the measuring instruments and the constructions of the scientist, so in the theatre do we pass through the intermediary of a director[3] to see the relations that we constantly maintain with others. In the same way, in the political arena, it is impossible, despite all dreams of democratic openness, to draw a line between the heavy machinery of parties and elections and the expression of our interests or of the general will. The representatives of the people are first and foremost 'representators'. What relationship is there between Marx's people and those of the medical hygienists (see Latour and Woolgar, 1979)? Between those of advertising agencies or opinion polls and Dostoievsky's? Change the characters, the *décor*, the plot and the reader, and then nothing is left of such a 'common' people (except the fact that the concept is often staged!) – and with reason, for it is never the same people who recognize themselves in the rubric.

We can go further with the idea of direction. We already know that we need to criticize the academic for her arbitrary cut-off points; the film director for his abuse of close-ups or zoom shots; the politician for the strings that make her our 'representator', and ourselves her puppets. But this critique is ambiguous. It relates to means, not to effects. It regrets that the act of stage-managing cannot render itself more invisible, rather than trying to render the power of stage-management visible. Instead of ceding to nostalgia for an invisible act of direction that could give us an unmediated reality, the work of the artistic director shows us that, on the contrary, the recurrence of intermediaries is interminable. One intermediary always hides another. Abstractions such as the people, art, the public, the common interest indicate doors opened by an intermediary to a string of mediations that can only be dealt with by going through the 'realization' of other intermediaries. What is the people of the popular music producer? To the degree that the people of the politician or the sociologist are solidly framed by the working definition they give us, the people of popular music prove evasive and dream-like, refractory to statistics, unpredictable. This is because we are not acting in the same play. The mediations of the artistic director mean nothing to us. We only hold one reference point intelligible in our language in common with him – the number of records sold. This indicator suffices to prove one thing: the mediation of the artistic director is effective, 'his' people exist, they buy what has been 'produced' for them, as it is said in Hollywood, rather more than they vote, organize classes or resign themselves as other demonstrators of the people (politicians or academics) might wish they would do.

How, then, can we analyze the work of direction? The producer himself (himself, not herself: it is not by chance that 99 per cent of producers are males), resistant to any attempt at objectivation, gives us right from the start of the game a magical identity: 'I am the public.' This is an affirmation that meets strong resistance in us. The sociologist of culture immediately denounces this abuse of power, and re-establishes the real determinants of market success: domination, alienation, standardization. And what if the producer's formula shocked us less by its complacency than by its crudity? What if, on the contrary, he were saying up front what others do, but dare not say? Speaking for the people, they continually put their words in the mouths of the people, of *avant-garde* artists or elected representatives, statisticians or philosophers. All projects using the concept of 'the people' begin by trampling on its corpse. Authors never claim credit for this stage management, which is often expensive – in questionnaires or in massacres, in number of pages or in public property. Only the dictator has the same realism as our producer in affirming, like him: 'I am the people.' The duplicity does not lie where we normally see it. Let us give the producer back his modesty in order to understand his work.

And let us surmount a second obstacle, that of psychology. If you do not want my social classes or my economy of tastes, I have what you need on another shelf – the subject, the imaginary, projections, identification. The artistic director identifies himself with the public, the artist projects her/his desire onto him. This has a nice result, in effect, when the public follows the reverse procedure. However, it is what needs to be explained, not what explains success.

The job of the artistic director is to search for young artists and to organize the career of those he has 'discovered'. He finds the personality, the repertoire that suits them, their style of arrangements, sound, images of the milieu they will appeal to – up to the point where the public recognizes its own. From the moment of first contact, the act of management begins. Take a young singer, full of hopes and doubts. The entire world is against him/her: an infinite series of skills, relationships, networks needs to be conquered. Closed doors, encouragement that leads nowhere, satisfaction quickly drowned in a flood of repetitive problems. And then, after being a supporting act, after a cabaret or a test somewhere, someone comes to see her, someone whose reputation she recognizes … It is the artistic director of some company, or an independent or freelance producer. Immediately, he is the one in front of the singer, suddenly hiding behind him this public which the singer dreams of but cannot succeed in seeing. 'Listen to me rather than the others.'

The role of the intermediary and the slow process of revelation that follows this substitution (if the singer accepts the scenario that the producer paints for her) are contained in the first meeting between the two. These now need to be realized. By standing in her/his way, the intermediary has captured the attention of the singer.[4]

He has put the obstacle of his body between the singer and the public's desire, and this obstacle concentrates on him all the forces that were going in every direction, as long as they did not run up against the localized resistance of a flesh-and-blood listener. The public was only a virtual image, and it was enough for the producer to act as a screen for him to take its place. The tacit contract that the two have agreed to in order to search for glory is a sign of this substitution. It is matched by another contract, this one very real and legal, which can only serve, however, to regulate the future division of a success that does not yet exist.

Henceforth, the candidate for popular success will no longer dream of an abstract non-critical public, to be shaped according to her/his constraints and setbacks. S/he has a concrete listener in front of her/him. An obstinate listener, whom s/he has to please, who lets nothing pass him by.[5] For the complacency of the imagination – that can see everything as if it has already happened – the producer substitutes in the singer the tyranny of the work of seduction. Soon, the former no longer has to say anything. It is enough for him to show a bit of reserve here, to let his enthusiasm flag there, for the singer to anticipate his reactions and to redouble her efforts to please. The mediation works. It has 'taken'. We can see that at the price of transforming her/himself, from the inside, s/he will renounce any small protective measures, one by one, and stand naked before the other's desire.

Dispossession, manipulation? On the contrary, the most intense interior work: the incorporation of the public – even if the public is only one man so far – realized by mediator interposed. The young singer gets to know intimately her own little quirks, fixations that she alone has and are insignificant for others, and to know those impasses or resignations in the face of the 'we will see' that conjures up images of the chopping block. A psychological, moralizing vocabulary? Of course it is. It is not a question of changing the theory according to needs, but of showing under what conditions the setting-up of certain relationships renders active categories that are normally inert. What goes before this running-up against the obstacle of the intermediary is a development, a more and more impassioned mobilization of the will to please, now entirely channeled into anticipating the reactions of the artistic director.

Here, of course, the producer plays the role of the public. This is a paradoxical role, since it permits him reciprocally to transform the candidate into an actor – that is, to make her/him enter into her/his own role. But their relationship does not reduce to this role-playing psychology, which could never explain its own effectiveness. Now that things have started up, the singer begins circulating along a network whose resources s/he will integrate, mediation by mediation. The framework offered by the artistic director for the game of apprentice-star is not a closed universe, a stable world wherein each is the mirror of the other. It is a scene that develops by bringing within the reach of the actor a progressive series of means, techniques, relationships, experiences that s/he can incorporate one at a time. Only the audience and the singer, in their final meeting, read the scene as a mere isolated universe, cut off from reality by collective fusion. The mediators who keep things going know that the scene only works because there are a thousand adjustments that hold it in place. What the scene less clearly indicates (since its task is to stop them, to fix them in place) is the recurrence and the reciprocity of the relations of the intermediaries. Reciprocity first of all. It is clear that if the artistic director places himself between the artist and the public so that these two blind lovers can see through him to each other, the young singer is the obstacle the producer runs up against in his desire to attain the public. He achieves his success by working on the resistance of the artist. His experience has proved over and over again that he can predict a potential public. However, he cannot really see it without going through the process of recomposing it from the beginning in miniature, inside a new artist.

The same thing goes for the recurrence of the intermediaries. The intermediary pulls everything back to the relationship that she mediates between two elements. In effect, if we displace the focus of our attention from the intermediary to one of the poles that she holds together, we can no longer see anything unless shown us by the new intermediaries. On the artist's side there are lyricists, arrangers, sound engineers, a new person each time some new element needs to be dealt with: music, orchestra, sound or words, staging … On the public's side, the recurrence of intermediaries is no less open – whether you are talking about the media or the stage itself. The knowledge that the producer provides is not some magical intuition of the public. It is the possibility of using, according to need, channels that already exist: techniques whose effects are known, professional guarantees, a network of relationships, a technical circuit, a mass of *savoir-faire*, publics already constructed. They string together concrete mediations. Wherever one is, as soon as it is a question of realizing the singer's 'public' the intermediaries set up a screen. The 'public' – or the 'people' – is a simple abstraction, which serves to summarize all the mediations that have taken place once the producer and the singer have seen how to make them. This is the cost of the act of stage-managing, the cost of this 'sense of the popular', which serves to oppose the opacity of its hazardous constructions to the realist transparence of the sociologist's pictures.

Act 2: Bourdieu produces the popular

Pierre Bourdieu's characters are resolutely tragic heroes. Prisoners of destiny in the form of perpetual chiasmus, they reproduce and distinguish between themselves because they do not recognize that they reproduce and distinguish between themselves. The rhetorical aspect of Bourdieu's theses has often been alluded to, as well as the immobility in which his model freezes people and society. This second remark is perhaps less accurate than the image of perpetual motion, which forbids any stopping on objects. These are continually re-appropriated and redistributed by the social work of reproduction in distinction. The first remark remains ambiguous: if there is rhetoric, it is because the text makes the laws of persuasion its very own.

Bringing the rhetoric out explicitly is merely doing justice to procedures used by all. To denounce rhetoric is simply to refuse to admit the necessity of theoretical theatricality in order to return to the naive view of a pure scientific text which exposes truth to a universal reader. Quite the contrary: the visibility of Bourdieu's rhetorical procedures is not normal in sociological discourse. Chiasmus and tautology are at once his style and his thesis, the form and the content of his writings, and they have made significant contributions to his success. Indeed, they have characterized his academic production. This visibility makes it clear to us what the good questions to ask him are: if there is to be rhetoric, who is trying to convince whom? What does the author want to get from the reader, and vice versa?

Like any academic, Bourdieu knows that he has to build a science that is at once independent of its author (in order to carry conviction), and attributed to its author (in order to get some advantage from it).[6] Thus he produces a sociology without a sociologist. Directed by an iron hand, the play proceeds without the slightest hitch, and the author merely scrawls his modest signature on stage sets that he has not painted. He has 'only' revealed them to us. Bourdieu not only aims – like anyone else – to unveil the actors' misrecognition of their own roles: he also places it at the heart of his plot. He transforms non-recognition into a circular principle which is at once the cause and the consequence of the actors' behavior. This non-recognition, which is shown to be everywhere, only works its revelatory effect on us at the price of another symmetrical non-recognition, hidden throughout – that of the production work the sociologist does for the benefit of his readers.

This production work, which is particularly systematic in Bourdieu, has as its principal goal the task of discreetly hiding with the left hand what the right hand will then be able to apparently reveal. Bourdieu – to borrow the style of his play – dissimulates the dissimulation which alone renders his revelation possible. This is a difficult act of dissimulation, which, even if it is not denounced as such, often sees its efforts fail because a good part of the public obstinately continues to see what it is not supposed to see. The rabbit peeks out of the hat. Try as Bourdieu might to charge that his zealous critics are mere philistines, there is always one fool who will remark that he already knew what is being revealed. There are continual remarks about the 'self-evident' character of Bourdieu's results. An example is the article by André Bruguière in the *Nouvel Observateur* when *La Distinction* came out:[7] an irritating piece of sarcasm that Bourdieu had so much the more difficulty getting rid of since it was cast in the most basic terms. The spectator's belly laugh at the magician's undisciplined rabbit destroys her spot more radically than a reasoned critique already in accord on the main points and prepared to ignore annoying distractions.

At this point, we can go in one of two directions. The first leads us towards a denunciation of the exorbitant power that the sociologist arrogates to himself. Thus the neophyte's extravagance is criticized by a philosophy that has learned its lesson of reserve over the millennia. This is the path taken by Jacques Rancière (1983) in his *Le Philosophe et ses Pauvres*, in which Bourdieu appears as the sociologist-king who has overthrown the philosopher-king. The sociologist is a competitor to the philosopher, but an unfair competitor, who does not pay any attention to the red lights. It must be shown that he has cheated. Along the way, this critique sweeps away the sociologist's pretensions to not be in competition with philosophy but to be playing another game, that of science. All the sociologist has to back this pretension is his 'statistics and enquiries', whereas 'the former accentuate an economic domination that should be dissimulated, the latter come back to the question of what the subject, who should be being surprised, is trying to say' (Collectif Révoltes logiques, 1984: 31). Here the philosopher leaves the metaphor of theatre, which has only served to denounce an artifice of the sociologist, in order to repatriate the debate to the civil state. It is not a question of production, but of power.

The other path consists of following the metaphor of the theatre until it leads us to some new finding. It is no longer a question of disqualifying Bourdieu because his production is stage-managed, but of showing how analyzing his text as stage management permits us to understand how it works on the reader. The critique of Bourdieu changes completely. It is no longer a question of contesting the sociologist's right to stage-manage the world – in particular by (at the last moment) taking this image seriously in order to attribute real power to her, when after all it is merely a question of the modest and ephemeral empire of the acrobat, which is forgotten as soon as we leave the theatre. It is now a question of criticizing her production work.

A first remark: when he claims the scientific character of his work, Bourdieu applies his own analyses only to his position, not to his results. His critical reflexivity aims at increasing their scientific character by purifying them of any dross due to his own interests as an academic (Bourdieu, 1990a). For the rest, he adopts the common hypothesis of a universal science – science itself need not be subject to scientific analysis.[8] Everyone else fails to recognize; dissimulates; stage-manages – but he tells the truth, reveals the 'structure of objective positions' (Bourdieu, 1979: 11), there where social groups continually, from their own viewpoints, mistake their partial view of things for this objective structure. To retranslate this into the language of theatre, this means to say that he is not a modernist director. He wants us to look at his play, not at the work of direction, so that we are caught up in his plot. We should not worry our heads trying to work out how he did it. Like a realist author, he claims to show us reality as it is – this from the man who is so good at denouncing the stage-management present behind the 'realism' of others. And here we are criticizing him in a very Bourdieu-like fashion, since we are trying to find in his position what his point of view dissimulates from us. If we accept the hypothesis of stage-management, it gives us the means to re-incorporate science, and to recognize that for it too – and this does not diminish in the slightest degree its specificity or its force – there is no revelation without dissimulation, no knowledge without ignorance.

Hence the real critique: at the cost of which dissimulation does Bourdieu's revelation gain its power? On what knowledge of the reader, on the knowledge of which reader, is the revelation based? Let us go over the prefabrication of roles that allows us to attain the 'evidence' of a page of photographs or a demonstration. There needs to be a complete critical kit for analyzing the definition of people and *décor*, the choice of a vocabulary, the adoption of a point of view in the most physical sense of the term.

But even if we do not achieve such a scientific work, the very existence of a direction reminds us that the sociologist needs a screen to show the public its own knowledge, and so provides us with an answer that is at once more simple and more radical. What Bourdieu dissimulates is the popular. To do so, he draws precisely on the denegation of the popular that he is revealing inside his readers – and then obtains the effect of recognition. The tautology of the model of distinction and reproduction is not that of a social system that functions by not being recognized and is rendered unrecognizable by its functioning, but that of the position of mediator that Bourdieu assumes. His text draws a curtain between the reader and her/his own vision of what the social consists of, so as to strengthen her/him in an ignorance which is then superbly rationalized. Bourdieu's imposing stage sets – which allow him to produce the people in figures, tables, in words and pictures – do not leave any place for the intervention of the people in his analyses. They do not leave room for any mediation other than the one that he has chosen for them. The people are not there because they do not figure in the work of production. It is not a question of showing the popular to the elect, but of transforming into a universal knowledge the hypersensitivity of certain layers of the middle class to the subtle play of social differentiation.

This is an admirable demonstration of the capacity of the sociologist to construct a reader for herself by drawing on a communal reconstruction of society. But if ever there were one, this is a partial point of view, which offers victory to the victors. It right away reduces others to the reconstruction that some people – as it happens, Bourdieu's readers – make of them. 'The people' is nothing else than the image of the people that these middle-class readers have, know they have, and deny – being at last so seduced when Bourdieu shows them back this repressed image. By an effect of interlocking consecration – such as those whose mechanism he has many times displayed – his readers are transformed into universal readers and into masters of the world in the same operation that transforms Bourdieu's production into universal knowledge and himself into master of sociology.

Epilogue: the price of the people

Whoever the elect are, one cannot do without intermediaries. Unlike the self-evident people that Bourdieu shows us, the unfindable people created by the myth of the authenticity of popular culture are also entirely supported by the rejection of the intermediary. An external observer would like to finally see the people, without passing through anyone or anything. She bumps into one after another of the obstacles that her procedure throws up in front of her. Recuperation, ideology, manipulation, dominated identities – the more she wants to abstract (i.e. make an abstraction of) away what prevents her from grasping the 'true' popular, the more her discourse gets caught up in the infinite denegation of a series of obstacles, until it gets lost from sight. When those in the political *avant-garde* wanted to refuse the cost of the construction of the popular by political professionals, their dreams of revolutionary masses got no further than their stereotypical small groups. Seekers of people, our fingers burnt by political experience, let us refrain from transplanting this experience onto the terrain of culture. In the guise of the popular, we only reconstruct a blurry picture of ourselves.

Notes

1 A first draft of this paper was written as a critical review of the book [La Distinction]: *Esthétique populaire ou théâtralité théorique?* (pp. 249–65) in 1985. It seemed relevant not to update the bibliographical references of this early version, except in the case of later translations into English.

2 And so to continue the debate begun, for example, in Collectif Révoltes logiques (1984).

3 The French word here is '*réalisateur*', and Hennion (1989) points to the use of this word as equating the director with someone who 'makes real'. (Translator note.)

4 On '*intéressement*' see Callon, *et al.* (1984).

5 A detailed analysis of the relationship can be found in Hennion (1989).

6 See, among texts contemporary of Bourdieu's, Callon and Law (1982) and Latour and Bastide (1984).

7 André Bruguière (19 May 1980) [Article], *Nouvel Observateur* 810: 160–6.

8 Bruno Latour (1983) criticizes this dissymmetry.

10 Looking back at Bourdieu[1]

Michèle Lamont

The co-editors of this volume have asked me to discuss the influence of Pierre Bourdieu on my intellectual trajectory, in an autobiographical mode. I have been quite reluctant to do so because writing such a piece requires a degree of reflexivity that I may have yet to achieve. Moreover, as a mid-career sociologist (or at least one who recently turned 50), I also hesitate to approach my own work as an object of commentary for fear of hubris. I have taken on the challenge, if only to clarify for myself the last 25 years.

My approach to Bourdieu's *œuvre* has been to view it as a point of departure, as a means for generating new questions, mainly through an empirical confrontation between it and other realities – such as American class cultures. Most of my writings have critically engaged Bourdieu, and this, starting in the early eighties, before the tradition of *Distinction* in English, and at a time when American sociologists still for the most part 'applied' and 'extended' Bourdieu's work to the United States, or engaged it through celebratory or expository exegesis. The growth and success of cultural sociology on this side of the Atlantic since the mid-eighties has paralleled and been fed by the diffusion of Bourdieu's corpus. I have benefited from this diffusion, to the extent that the new research questions I identified often had Bourdieu's work in the background. In this sense, I have piggybacked on his work, with the ambition of opening new vistas. Without denying the enormous significance of his work, I have found the exploration of new terrains more satisfying (because less predictable) than applying an extant (and highly consolidated) theoretical approach, however elegant, seductive, multi-leveled, subtle and complex that approach may be. The place of Bourdieu in the small pantheon of individuals who have determined the shape of the social sciences at the beginning of the twenty-first century is beyond question. And, as demonstrated by the many divergent voices assembled in this volume, we are still debating, following Claude Lévi-Strauss's formula, for what purpose he is 'good to think with'. My response is probably more pluralistic than most.

This chapter, then, describes my multiple engagements with Bourdieu's work by means of narrating my intellectual trajectory as it intersected with his *œuvre*. This approach helps to convey why his work was viewed as important in the early 1980s; the context in which it was imported to the United States; the discussions that surrounded it (connecting micro-interactions with broader processes of knowledge diffusion), and some of the transmutations to which it was subjected.[2]

First encounters

Before encountering Bourdieu, I was a neo-Marxist. My first serious piece of scholarship (never published) concerned the contradictory relationship (of relative autonomy and determination) between subject and object in the theories of knowledge and class consciousness of V. I. Lenin. The context was the debates opposing humanist and structuralist theorizing that animated neo-Marxists and critical theory circles during much of the 1970s, and that pitted (typically) Jurgen Habermas, Henri Lefebvre and Rosa Luxemburg against Louis Althusser, Nicos Poulantzas, and V. I. Lenin. I was on the side of those who gave more power to agency over structure. I discovered a first paper by Bourdieu shortly before leaving Canada to pursue my graduate studies in France in 1978. It was his (1972) critique of survey research titled 'Les Doxosophes'. This piece could only be described as mind-blowing: by analyzing survey researchers as agents involved in the construction and delimitation of social reality – as producers of a doxa – Bourdieu made the production of ideology something that could be circumscribed and studied in empirical terms. While this approach may seem commonsensical to many sociologists today, Bourdieu's focus on knowledge production practices was most refreshing when read against the background of a neo-Marxist tradition that ignored many of the micro-level relationships within which social agents operate in a field of cultural production. Moreover, Bourdieu provided an entirely novel approach to research that eschewed both naïve positivism and disembedded theorization, one that combined purposeful *'construction d'objet'* (or theoretically motivated research design) with empirically grounded research, as developed in *The Craft of Sociology* (Bourdieu, Chamboredon and Passeron, 1990). This was in stark contrast to the atheoretical approaches to survey research that prevailed at the time.

Within a few months after my arrival in Paris, I had revelled in the work of Michel Foucault (especially *The Order of Things*) and that of Michel de Certeau (*The Practice of Everyday Life* – then unknown in North America). But most importantly, *Distinction* was just coming out, and what an event that was. This book contained many 'revelations' (self-evident to many cultural sociologists today, but still novel then) – for instance, that the class struggle manifests itself through daily interaction and through a symbolic violence pitting those who master legitimate culture against those who don't; that other kinds of capital besides economic capital matter; or that aestheticism is made possible by one's distance toward material necessity. The concept of habitus made a particularly strong impression as it appeared as a brilliant transmutation of the concept of practice, building on Karl Marx's theses on Feuerbach, while bridging the micro- and the macro-levels of analysis. I soon started attending Bourdieu's seminar at the *École des hautes études en science sociales* and he offered to direct my studies.

Given my interest and background in the sociology of knowledge, Bourdieu suggested that I interview intellectuals for a dissertation that would make a contribution to the sociology of philosophers. Persuaded by the idea, and also influenced by his unmatchable charisma and solicitousness, I jumped at the opportunity, and started interviewing many influential intellectuals ranging from Michel Serres to Jean Baudrillard. I wrote a paper on Jacques Derrida, which became my first prominent publication: 'How to Become a Dominant French Philosophe: The case of Jacques Derrida' (published in *American Journal of Sociology* in 1987). This article took Bourdieu's writing on intellectual legitimacy (on Sartre for instance) as a point of departure (Bourdieu, 1969). Both building on and departing from Bourdieu, I proposed a systematic analysis of the intellectual, institutional, cultural and social conditions that led to the consecration of an interpretive theory (Derrida's work) for different publics (philosophers and comparative literature scholars) in two national contexts (France and the United States). Showing that Derrida was valued for entirely different sets of reasons in these different contexts, I emphasized the fit between context and cultural object and the adaptability of the cultural object as conditions for its diffusion and consecration. This interest in understanding valuation processes is one of the principal threads that has traversed all of my work to date, whether I have studied how upper-middle-class and working-class people define a worthy person, how academics go about evaluating the work of their peers, or, more recently, how members of stigmatized groups give value to their collective identities. This focus on valuation processes was suggested to me in part by Bourdieu's writings on competing instances of consecration in the artistic, literary, and scientific fields, although I developed it in a very different direction (see Lamont and Zuckerman, forthcoming). I could describe my research agenda through alternative, less Bourdieu-dependent frames, but I privilege this angle here given the mission of this edited volume.

During these Paris years, I progressively moved away from Bourdieu because, to put matters bluntly, he did not know how to mentor young women, wavering between too great proximity and distance.[3] In the highly gendered (although not gender-aware) Parisian intellectual milieu of the early eighties, he was much more at ease with young brilliant men, onto whom he could project his younger self (I thought). Moreover, his research center had notoriously treacherous interpersonal dynamics which seemed far too complicated for the 21-year-old woman that I was. Under the guidance of other generous mentors such as Pierre Ansart, I completed a dissertation on the rapid growth of the social sciences and the decline of the humanities in Québec between 1960 and 1980, analyzing the dynamics between the cultural and state-dominated poles of these academic fields. This dissertation, to which Bourdieu responded with great enthusiasm, developed a sociology of the academic field that resonated with themes central to *Homo Academicus*, which came out a few years later.

After the publication of *Distinction*, Bourdieu consolidated his theoretical apparatus (with *Le sens pratique*, published in 1980) and started applying his concept of field to a wide range of arenas (artistic, cultural, literary, academic, scientific, governmental, etc.). This period coincided with his election at the Collège de France (in 1981) and the institutionalization of his influence. What I came to perceive to be at times the over-mechanistic and highly predictable character of these applications lessened the appeal of Bourdieu's sociology for me; the generative and open-ended quality of his analysis remained what made it most attractive in my eyes. My departure from Paris turned out to be well timed as I was already in the process of developing a heterodox orientation toward Bourdieu's corpus just when orthodoxy was becoming more normative in Bourdieusian Parisian circles.

Passage to the United States

After completing my graduate work in 1983, I obtained a post-doctoral fellowship that brought me to Stanford University. There I quickly familiarized myself with American sociology, learned to write in English, and immersed myself in the art of engineering research designs and crafting empirically sound papers that could survive the close examination of American peer reviewers.[4] Most importantly, I was exposed to the inspiring and phenomenologically informed work of John Meyer, and also to a formidable woman, Ann Swidler, who was then working on her now famous 'Culture in Action' paper (Swidler, 1986). Conversations with her and others (Wendy Griswold was visiting for a year) oriented my involvement with the burgeoning field of the American sociology of culture. Although I did not know it then, I now realize how much these scholars helped shaped my intellectual tastes and proclivities – my understanding of what good sociology looked like – including my views on the similarities and differences between French and American sociology, which unavoidably affected my relationship to Bourdieu's work.

At this time I also had several exchanges with Paul DiMaggio, then a fellow at the Center for Advanced Studies in the Behavioral Sciences. Paul had already published a few Bourdieu-inspired articles, most notably, his wonderful piece on how the Boston upper class used high culture to create itself as a class and define its group boundaries (DiMaggio, 1982a). He also had a few articles that built on Bourdieu and mobilized American survey data on participation in high culture (1977, 1982b). Conversations with him fed my thinking about how Bourdieu's work could apply to the United States. I quickly became more critical of Bourdieu's approach than Paul was at the time.[5] Indeed, life in Palo Alto offered a splendid laboratory to think about *Distinction* in a comparative context – to consider the ways in which it could and could not account for the reality I was discovering. I observed that the Stanford upper-middle-class graduate students who were my friends had little in common with the offspring of the French 'dominant class' I had experienced in Paris and that Bourdieu described in *Distinction*. These students were not as concerned with demonstrating familiarity with high culture as Bourdieu would have predicted and they were proud of being able to repair their bicycles (the French dominant class looked down at practical tasks, Bourdieu told us). They did not care about using the appropriate forks and knives, and functioned in what I later described as a 'loosely bounded culture' where cultural practices are not clearly hierarchizing (Lamont, 1989), where distinction does not operate in terms of who is in and out, and where many are tolerant of or indifferent toward those who are different from them. My cross-national experience led me to question

Bourdieu's writings and to formulate criticisms that inspired the development of the 'omnivorousness thesis' (on this connection, see Peterson, 2005).

Tackling Bourdieu

Together with Annette Lareau, also a post-doc at Stanford at the time, I started working on an agenda-setting paper on cultural capital. Annette had recently completed a Bourdieu-inspired dissertation on how middle- and working-class parents interact with schools, which led to her award-winning book, *Home Advantage* (1989). Although she was and remains more exclusively focused on class reproduction and less critical of Bourdieu than I (see also Lareau, 2003), we agreed to write on the ways in which one should adapt Bourdieu's work to account for the articulation between culture and the reproduction of inequality in the United States.[6] After a close examination of Bourdieu's writing on cultural capital, our paper concluded that it was often under-theorized and contained methodological flaws and conceptual gaps. We also developed many themes that have been empirically studied and widely discussed since: for instance, whereas Bourdieu presumed that a legitimate culture existed, we suggested that there is cross-national variability in the permeability of class boundaries and the degree of consensus and stability of the legitimate culture. We also suggested the multiplicity of forms of cultural capital and the potential autonomy of lower-class culture; and the idea that forms of capital are like a hand of cards that can be played when needed (Annette's representation of habitus). We also argued that instead of defining cultural capital as familiarity with high culture and what is valued by the school system, one should examine through interviews and observation what counts as high-status cultural signals for particular social actors (this became my agenda which I shared with others).[7]

This article, which came out in 1988 under the title 'Cultural Capital: Allusions, Gaps, and Glissandos in the Recent Literature' (Lamont and Lareau, 1988) was warmly received in part because it parsed out the often contradictory meanings Bourdieu assigned to the concept of cultural capital at a time when many social scientists were trying to make sense of his work. Moreover, ours was also the first paper to attempt to 'decouple cultural capital from the French context in which it was originally conceived to take into consideration the distinctive features of American culture' (ibid.: 153). An accompanying piece, a little-known paper I wrote titled 'The Power-Culture Link in Comparative Perspective' published in 1989, located Bourdieu in relation to other authors such as Foucault and charted many of the questions that came to be at the center of my comparative research on France and the United States from the late 1980s on. Here I developed the idea of studying classification systems comparatively and from the ground up. I was particularly concerned with variations in the degree of consensus surrounding cultural hierarchies (or their loose-boundedness, as revealed by the degree of tolerance for cultural differences and of hierarchizing of cultural tastes).

I was fortunate that I arrived in the United States before the translation of *Distinction*. I was already familiar with Bourdieu's work at a time when American social scientists were for the most part only beginning to become acquainted with it (with the exception of sociologists of education and a few cultural sociologists and cultural anthropologists). Having been offered by Anthony Giddens a Polity Press contract to write a book on Bourdieu, I had read almost all of his work and had drafted chapters, yet by 1986 I decided to abandon this project after becoming aware of the impossibility of writing a critical book on Bourdieu's work that would meet with his approval. Bourdieu had invited me to help diffuse his work in the United States, just as he did with Loïc Wacquant a few years later – and this collaboration resulted in the influential and canonical *Invitation to Reflexive Sociology*, published in 1992. Interested in shaping its reception, he eagerly collaborated with the Polity Press project until I showed him a draft chapter that described his intellectual and institutional conditions of possibility, using the same theoretical model I had used in my Derrida paper. I believed that, perhaps paradoxically – given his commitment to reflexive sociology[8] – he was displeased by the objectifying character of my analysis and this was an additional reason for abandoning the project. Thus I changed course: my new familiarity with the entire Bourdieu corpus put me in a position where I could both explain his complex writings and critique it empirically. Partly inspired by Bellah, *et al.*'s *Habits of the Heart* (1984), I built on this knowledge to develop a research project that would allow me to consider empirically some of my main criticisms.

My first book, *Money, Morals, and Manners: The Culture of the French and the American Upper-Middle Class* (1992) critiqued Bourdieu on a number of fronts, but also used his work as a point of departure to ask novel questions. This book took on explicitly and systematically the question of whether *Distinction* applied to the United States – not that Bourdieu claimed it would, but many scholars thought it did. It drew on 160 in-depth interviews conducted with professionals, managers, and entrepreneurs living in Indianapolis, New York, Clermont-Ferrand and Paris to identify high-status signals prevalent in the upper-middle class, and to compare patterns of valued status signals across societies, between cultural centers and periphery, and between social and cultural specialists and for-profit workers. It also offered an explanation for these patterns that considered the supply side of culture (available cultural repertoires) and the proximate and remote context in which people lived. I determined that high culture was less central a high-status signal than Bourdieu's focus on 'legitimate culture' suggested;[9] that it was a predominant type of high-status signal only in Paris, and that across places professionals and managers were also concerned in various proportions with socio-economic status and morality as types of high-status signal.[10] The book tackled several additional empirical problems not connected to *Distinction*: for instance, the permeability of group boundaries, and the relationship between symbolic and social boundaries (describing the symbolic as a necessary but insufficient condition for the social). I argued that differentiation does not necessarily translate into exclusion as Bourdieu suggested and I questioned his assumption about the zero-sum character of social positioning implicit in his concept of field. Building on and criticizing Swidler (1986), I explained boundary patterns not only by available cultural repertoires, but also by the conditions that increased the likelihood that one would use some repertoires rather than others. Most importantly, *contra* Bourdieu, instead of predefining what counts as a high-status signal, I used the interview as a laboratory to ask respondents to engage in boundary work within the context of the interview by, describing whom they liked and disliked, and whom they perceived to be similar and different from themselves. Against an essentialist fallacy often encountered in American interpretations of Bourdieu, my analysis showed that although the members of the American upper-middle class do not generally appreciate high culture, they nevertheless share cultural scripts concerning what is a worthy person that are partly defined in opposition to scripts perceived to be valued in other groups.

As this book came out in 1992, I also published *Cultivating Differences: Symbolic Boundaries and the Making of Inequality*, which I co-edited with Marcel Fournier, a former student of Bourdieu who has since become a renowned expert on Marcel Mauss and Émile Durkheim. We were fortunate enough to be able to attract a strong cast of authors, all sociologists working on social closure and symbolic classification and who were influenced by theorists ranging from Émile Durkheim and Max Weber to Mary Douglas and, of course, Bourdieu. The volume fed the agenda of the growing field of the sociology of culture by attacking a number of related questions (about class cultures, ethno-racial and gender boundaries, high culture, classification systems, etc.). It also helped diffuse Bourdieu's work beyond cultural sociology to neighboring subfields and brought many new questions to the attention of the broader field of sociology.[11]

The timing was propitious: the late 1980s and 1990s were a period of exceptional growth for cultural sociology in the United States. The Culture Section of the American Sociological Association (ASA) was founded in 1986, under the leadership of Vera Zolberg, Gary Alan Fine, Richard (Pete) Peterson, and many others (I was also involved and chaired the section a few years after its founding). The section quickly grew to include more than 1,000 members and is now the largest section of the ASA. The work of Bourdieu did a lot to stimulate this interest and has had a lasting influence. According to a colleague who served on the section's competition for the best book in the sociology of culture in 2008, Bourdieu's work remains at the center of a significant majority of the books submitted for this competition. This increased influence has occurred at the expense of symbolic interactionism, which it partly absorbed: today, newly minted sociologists studying meaning-making in micro-interactions are probably more likely to declare themselves cultural sociologists than symbolic interactionists and concepts such as frame and script are as central to the literature as are the concepts of narrative and repertoire (Lamont and Small, 2008). Cultural sociology also grew at the expense of cultural studies, which has flourished in literary studies, American studies, communications, and cultural anthropology, but less in sociology. While widely considered an isolated and marginal specialty of sociology in the early 1980s – at the time of the publication of Howard Becker's *Art Worlds* (one of the milestones of the subfield) – the sociology of culture had become 'mainstream' by the mid-1990s, with many of the top departments hiring in the field (Lamont, 2004). The growing popularity of multi-method approaches, including in the training of graduate students, contributed to this sea change and to the decline of the polarization between quantitative and qualitative research, a decline also facilitated by the diffusion of Bourdieu's work.[12] Cultural sociology remains one of the fastest-growing areas of the American Sociological Association, attracting a larger number of graduate students than any other section.[13] Its influence is spreading across a range of specialties, as demonstrated, for instance, by a 2008 issue of the *Annals of the Academy of Social and Political Science* which reviewed how culture was conceptualized and studied across a number of substantive areas (e.g. Charles, 2008). Economic sociology; the sociology of organizations; the sociology of education; the sociology of social movements; comparative historical sociology; urban sociology; poverty, race, immigration and gender studies; and even network analysis can be said to have taken or being in the process of taking a 'cultural turn'.

Away from Bourdieu and back

After the publication of *Money, Morals, and Manners*, I became less interested in engaging Bourdieu than in studying boundary work per se (as noted by Sallaz and Zavisca, 2007). I started considering the properties of boundaries, the mechanisms that influenced their porousness, and other topics, and was for a few years involved in a 'symbolic boundaries' network organized by the Culture Section of the American Sociological Association. This group, which met annually for a few years and organized various events (including a 2003 electronic conference), brought together approximately thirty scholars interested in a range of boundary-related topics.[14] This new interest led to 'The Study of Boundaries in the Social Sciences', a 2002 article co-authored with Virág Molnár which remains one of the most popular (or downloaded!) papers published in *Annual Review of Sociology*. This article helped consolidate an agenda for the study of group boundaries that went beyond Bourdieu's writings on classification struggles toward a broader sociology connecting with the tradition of Benedict Anderson (1983) in the study of imagined communities, Frederic Barth (1969) in ethnic and racial studies, the more recent writings of Richard Jenkins on identity (1996), and many others. The idea was to consider more systematically boundary processes across various fields of study and draw comparison so that, for instance, what we know about ethnic boundaries would feed our understanding of organizational boundaries, and vice versa. The goal was also to draw from this comparison a better understanding of the properties of boundaries and of the mechanisms that produce and change them. This broader synthetic project is being pursued today in various literatures by a number of scholars – for instance by Todd (2005) and Wimmer (2008) in the study of race and ethnicity (for an update on the more recent research, see Pachucki, *et al.*, 2007). During this period, the study of boundaries moved closer toward the center of gravity of our discipline and was featured as the theme of the 2007 meetings of the American Sociological Association.

My study of the French and American upper-middle class was followed in 2000 by another book on the French and the American working class titled *The Dignity of Working Men: Morality and the Boundaries of Race, Class, and Immigration*. This book drew on 160 interviews with African-American and white blue-collar and white-collar workers living in the New York area, and with North African immigrants and white French workers living around Paris. As in *Money, Morals, and Manners*, I asked respondents to produce boundary work in the context of the interviews and considered the criteria they used to determine the worth of others. Here also, Bourdieu helped shape the questions I pursued. While he described those who valued morality as 'losers' (my term) who make virtue of necessity, I showed how workers use morality to maintain their dignity and draw boundaries toward 'people above' and 'people below', as well as toward members of racial minority groups and immigrants. Nevertheless, this book was far less engaged with Bourdieu, in part because he had not written on ethno-racial boundaries.

While writing *The Dignity of Working Men*, I was also moving closer to the work of Bruno Latour (1989, on black boxing) as I studied the types of evidence mobilized by individuals to sustain their beliefs that ethno-racial groups are similar/different and equal/non-equal (what my former student Ann Morning (2009) came to call 'racial conceptualization'). I was also inspired and stimulated by the work of the *Groupe de sociologie politique et morale* (GSPM) at the *École des hautes études en sciences sociales*, which was animated by Luc Boltanski and Laurent Thévenot, two former students of Pierre Bourdieu who had left his *Centre de sociologie Européenne* in the 1980s to develop an ambitious agenda focused on the frames of action (see Boltanski and Thévenot, 1999). That agenda became one of the two most influential 'post-Bourdieu' lines of research in French sociology (together with Actor-Network Theory developed by Michel Callon and Bruno Latour). GSPM researchers aimed to study the blind spots of Bourdieu's work, which they saw as the study of how ordinary people understand their engagement with the world and how they go about making universalistic claims, including concerning morality (Boltanski, 1984; Boltanski and Thévenot, 2006).[15] Like me, they were also researching socially shared ways of classifying the world and in competing principles of justification (a type of cultural structure). Their approach overlapped significantly with my own interest in understanding competing criteria of evaluation. Thus, I began a four-year collaborative project co-directed with Laurent Thévenot, which brought together 11 researchers from Princeton University (where I taught) and the GSPM to engage jointly in comparative research projects on various principles of evaluation at work across national settings around conflicts surrounding sexual harassment, the protection of the environment, journalistic neutrality, racism, contemporary art, voluntarism, and literary studies. We produced a collective volume titled *Rethinking Comparative Cultural Sociology: Repertoires of Evaluation in France and the United States* (2000), which considered the relative availability of various types of cultural repertoire across national contexts and provided case studies to analyze the use of criteria of evaluation and/or principles of justification in France and the United States (with a focus on moral, cultural and socio-economic criteria and with civic, industrial, market and other justifications). For this book I analyzed the rhetoric of racism and anti-racism in France and the United States, which led me to consider whether, how, and why ordinary French and American men believe that racial groups are equal, focusing on principles of equivalence (of interest to the GSPM), but also on recognition, and definitions of social membership[16] – this project grew into another international collaborative project on anti-racism and destigmatization strategies and the boundedness of ethno-racial identities in Brazil, Israel, and the United States.[17] Compared with the research conducted by the GSPM, my focus was the inductive analysis of boundary work (whose content is open ended) instead of regimes of worth (or '*grandeurs*') and the 'qualifications' they required. Although I was and remain very engaged by their work, I am also more concerned with the relative embeddedness of repertoires in institutions as well as with their relative availability and presence across various groups (in contrast to Bourdieu, the GSPM tended to downplay the social location of actors – Lamont (2008) describes the convergences and divergences between my research and that of the GSPM).

I returned to Bourdieu in *How Professors Think* (2009) which analyses how academics go about evaluating the work of their colleagues and students. Drawing on 81 interviews with panelists involved in five different multidisciplinary funding competitions over a two-year period, this book focuses on the meaning given to criteria of evaluation by panelists as well as to the conditions that make it possible for academics to think about the evaluation process as fair. Bourdieu (1975, 1984, 1996b) is among the few scholars who provide bases on which to ground a comparison of academic evaluation. However, like others who have written on the topic, Bourdieu does not consider the varied meanings given to criteria of evaluation. These largely follow from his standard model of field analysis which mechanistically opposes heteronymous and autonomous principles of structuration. In contrast, my book provides a detailed empirical analysis of the criteria on which U.S. scholars rely to distinguish 'excellent' and 'promising' research from less stellar work. I do not predefine the content of criteria of evaluation, but leave open the question of their relative salience and presence among a wider range of alternative criteria.

There is another point around which my analysis of academia is essentially divergent from Bourdieu's. He views academic fields as animated by a competition for influence and power. Indeed, in *Homo Academicus*, he analyzes scientists as engaged in a struggle to impose their vision of the world – and their definition of high-quality scholarly work – as legitimate. He tells us that scholars compete to define excellence, and points to the co-existence of competing criteria of evaluation. Whereas Bourdieu's academics are presumed to engage in opportunity hoarding and the imposition of their definition of legitimate scholarship, I studied empirically their orientations. My approach revealed their pluralistic orientation in their role as evaluators.

How Professors Think points to other new directions for the study of academics. The interviews I conducted reveal that the self-concept of evaluators is central to the process of assessment and especially to the conditions required for producing evaluation that they perceive as fair. Self-concept is absent from Bourdieu's work on academics, as from his other writings, because he assumes that academics are moved by a quest for maximizing their position within fields (Lamont, 2001; and Gross, 2008; for another interpretation of Bourdieu, see Steinmetz, 2006). In contrast, my interviews demonstrate the importance of pleasure and curiosity as alternative types of motivation. Moreover, I argue that the customary rules that evaluators draw on as they deliberate, especially their respect for disciplinary expertise and their views on the importance of bracketing of self-interest, sustain their identity as experts and as fair and broadminded academics. These conclusions resonate with recent work in science studies that emphasizes how the selfhood of academics is central to the evaluation of knowledge, as opposed to being an extraneous and corrupting influence (Shapin, 1994). Equally important, panelists' comments and observations reveal evaluation to be an eminently social and emotional undertaking, rather than a cognitive process corrupted by extra-cognitive factors. Emotions are also crucial to the functioning of the interdisciplinary research networks I am currently studying (with Veronica Boix-Mansilla and Kyoko Sato) – at the Santa Fe Institute, the MacArthur Foundation, and the Canadian Institute for Advanced Research. In all cases, preliminary findings suggest that emotions are crucial to the creation of shared socio-cognitive platforms that individuals construct together for the purpose of collaboration.

How Professors Think also continues to be influenced by the work of the GSPM to the extent that I consider the production of agreements through interaction and how panelists justify their judgments.[18] I show how actors create a sense of justice that is not only a compromise between types of norm (a theme central to Boltanski and Thévenot, 2006) but also an outcome of following customary rules. Thus, I identify a number of pragmatic constraints that panelists have to take into consideration as they go about deliberating, such as the customary rules that are viewed as collective goods. But I also acknowledge the strategies panelists use – such as establishing credibility and respect – in order to get what they define as good work funded. These rules act as constraints and regulators of behavior, but they are also justifications that create feelings of justice and that emerge from how evaluative practices are performed. While for Lévi-Strauss (1958) rules are unconscious, and while for Bourdieu (1990b) they are strategic codes used by actors, for *How Professors Think* they are rules pragmatically created by actors as they participate in a given situation.

Bourdieu, good to think with?

All in all, I have cultivated simultaneously multiple relationships with Bourdieu's work. I have made empirical correctives to it (for instance, concerning the place of morality and high culture in the culture of the French upper-middle class). I have been inspired by it and extended Bourdieu's intellectual agenda (with my empirical examination of various forms of high-status signals). I have also used Bourdieu's work as a springboard to open new vistas and ask new questions (concerning, for instance, the porousness of group boundaries). Finally, I have criticized its metatheoretical assumptions (concerning the zero-sum character of social relations inherent in the notion of fields).

Because of my own life experience, I remain persuaded that pleasure, curiosity, and a need for community and recognition are powerful engines for human action, certainly as powerful as the quest for power and the maximization of one's position in fields of power that are privileged by Bourdieu. These essential meta-theoretical differences put me at odds in a fundamental way with his work and with that of some of his followers. Thus, taking distance from Bourdieu was not simply a matter of drifting away or pursuing questions he had not considered. It meant proposing a different approach focused on boundary work which, if it did not supersede Bourdieu's, was fundamentally 'other': I took novel angles on new and different issues, and several of these angles required rejecting some of the keystones of Bourdieu's theoretical apparatus.

Against the experience of this complex relationship, I remain committed to a cumulative, or at least a path-dependent, view of knowledge development: i.e., to an understanding of intellectual change that emphasizes how new developments are constrained and channeled by what preceded them. At the same time, at the start of the twenty-first century, I am convinced that broadening the study of inequality and social reproduction to systematically compare patterns of inclusion, recognition, and social membership has become unavoidable given the challenges of diversity faced by post-national societies. Moreover, it is also unavoidable from the perspective of the development of a discipline concerned with understanding fundamental mechanisms for the production and transformation of the social order. Exclusion and inclusion, differentiation and recognition, spatial segregation and self-segregation are increasingly acknowledged to be complementary pieces of the inequality puzzle. Thus I now see myself moving even further away from Bourdieu, tempted by new and entirely different challenges. In 2003, I became involved in a long-term interdisciplinary collaboration on the conditions that lead to the production of *Successful Societies* (Hall and Lamont, 2009), which is concerned with the role of institutions and culture in mediating the impact of inequality on health outcomes. I have been studying the individual and collective resilience of members of stigmatized groups and how societies provide cultural and institutional scaffoldings that sustain this resilience. I have also become much more interested in the bridging of boundaries than in social exclusion, and particularly in the ways members of stigmatized groups contribute to the transformation of group boundaries and influence their social categorization.[19] These questions are for the main outside Bourdieu's paradigm, yet essential if we are to understand what we (collectively and individually) can do to prevent the daily wear and tear of experiencing inequality from getting under the skin of our most vulnerable populations.

Notes

1 I thank Elizabeth Silva and Alan Warde for providing insightful comments on an earlier draft. I also thank the following colleagues for their reactions and suggestions: Christopher Bail, Bruno Cousin, Frank Dobbin, Jane Mansbridge, Claude Rosental, Jeffrey Sallaz, George Steinmetz, and Mitchell Stevens. The intellectual developments described here were made possible by constant dialogues and exchanges with a wide network of friends and colleagues, both in Europe and North America. Regrettably, the dialogic character of these intellectual developments cannot be conveyed by the linear narrative of this particular paper, which is focused on a single individual, instead of on the cognitive and social network of relations that made my contributions possible (on intellectual social movements, see Frickel and Gross, 2005).

2 For a more exhaustive discussion of the importation of Bourdieu's work to the United
   States, see Sallaz and Zavisca (2007). On Bourdieu's social and intellectual trajectory
   in France, see Heinich (2007) and Reed-Danahay (2004), as well as Bourdieu (2004b).
   This chapter adds to a corpus of writings on Bourdieu's influence on the work of a
   number of French sociologists (see Encrevé and Lagrave, 2003).
3 Bourdieu's inadequacy as a mentor of women resonates with his ignorance of the feminist scholarship and literature on gender inequality that was available at the time (Silva,
   2005).
4 This transition is described in Lamont (1988).
5 Although DiMaggio also came to use Bourdieu as a springboard for new theoretical
   developments (see especially DiMaggio, 1988).
6 Looking back, I now realized that Annette was more engaged at the time with the
   Bourdieu of *Reproduction* while for me *Distinction* was more crucial. Her work has
   centered on the intersection between family life and school, whereas my earlier work
   aimed at understanding high-status cultural signals in a comparative perspective. She
   also adopted an ethnographic approach to study how capital is turned into profit, whereas
   I used in-depth interviews to analyze high-status cultural signals – what counted as cultural capital – across classes.
7 To mention only a few: Hall (1992), Halle (1993), Bryson (1996), Erickson (1996)
   and Carter (2005). Holt (1997) reviewed some of this literature and defended Bourdieu
   against his critics.
8 See especially his posthumous *Esquisse pour une socio-analyse* (Bourdieu, 2004a).
9 The methodological approach which consists in conducting a large number of interviews
   was essential to establish the various types of high-status signal valued among professionals and managers. Others scholars have used ethnographic approaches for analyzing
   the use of high-status signals in a range of contexts (e.g. Sherman, 2007; Rivera, 2009).
   I view these questions and approaches as complementary.
10 At the time I was also influenced by Grignon and Passeron (1989). Lahire (1998), which
   took Bourdieu as a point of departure for an empirical exploration of habitus, was to be
   published a few years later.
11 This influence also spread through the combined effect of a number of critical and less
   critical publications on Bourdieu's work, which essays were published before (e.g.
   Brubaker, 1985) or after (e.g. Alexander, 1995; Calhoun, *et al.*, 1993; Schwartz, 1997)
   Money, Morals and Manners. See Sallaz and Zavisca (2007) for a detailed account.
12 In contrast, the success of symbolic interactionism was hindered by its anti-quantitative
   culture and almost exclusive reliance on ethnography, while the diffusion of cultural
   studies was hindered by its weaker culture of systematic empirical inquiry.
13 Personal communication with Michael Murphy, American Sociological Association.
14 The group was concerned with topics such as the salience of boundaries, their stability, spatial, temporal, and visual boundaries, signaling through expressive forms and
   consumption, the public/private boundary, the changing institutional character of
   boundaries, the bridging of boundaries, and the management of group boundaries.
   Co-ordinated by Bethany Bryson and myself, it included at various times scholars such
   as Richard Alba, Howard Aldrich, Elizabeth A. Armstrong, Mabel Berezin, Albert
   Bergeson, Sarah Corse, Michelle Dillon, Penny Edgell, Nina Eliasoph, Cynthia Fuchs
   Epstein, Bonnie Erickson, Roger Friedland, Chad Goldberg, John Hall, Maria Kefalas,
   Paul Lichterman, Christina Nippert-Eng, Michèle Ollivier, Peggy Levitt, John Ryan,
   Abigail Saguy, Suzanne Shanahan, John Schmalzbauer, Art Stinchcombe, Charles Tilly,
   Diane Vaughan, Al Young, Robin Wagner-Pacifici, and Eviatar Zerubavel.
15 Luc Boltanski and Elisabeth Claverie had spent a year at the Institute for Advanced
   Studies in the early 1990s, which created the opportunity for many exchanges and
   discussions around these topics.
16 Thévenot (2006) also became interested in the question of what makes people equal
   or compatible in his research on 'regimes of proximity'. The political management of

diversity and definitions of communities are now one of the main axes of research of the GSPM. (Available online at: http://gspm.ehess.fr/sommaire.php?id=170)

17 Available online at: http://www.wcfia.harvard.edu/weatherhead_initiative/07_discrimination/projects.

18 In analyzing peer review as connoisseurship, I have also been influenced by the work of Nathalie Heinich, who has long been associated with the GSPM (see Danko (2008) on her work), and by that of Antoine Hennion (2007) on taste (including taste in wine and classical music).

19 My approach to bridging contrasts with that of Robert Putnam for whom 'bridging' refers to engaging in joint activities with people with whom one has little in common (fans of a football team, for instance). For a critique of Putman, see Portes (1998) and Hall and Lamont (2009).

11 Bourdieu in a multi-dimensional perspective

Frédéric Lebaron

The present book illustrates the vitality and the accuracy of Bourdieu's work in contemporary debates and research in the field of sociology, and more generally in the field of social sciences. The simple fact that some of the critical assessments of his scientific conceptions, which this book contains, re-organize or re-activate what previous critical accounts originally illustrated, testifies to the still provocative content of these conceptions. This book also shows that new 'lines' or 'forms' of critique and new controversial points express a large and moving set of complex interactions between Bourdieu's theory and the contemporary global sociological field, evident in processes of import and export of concepts, themes and methods.

These interactions can result in new foci and in attempts to create adequate instruments for capturing emerging social realities (for example, through a 'hybridization' between Bourdieu and other theoretical traditions). This particular outcome of his work is consistent with Bourdieu's conception of sociological theory as a collective patrimony or as an intellectual 'toolbox' at the disposal of the researcher (Bourdieu and Wacquant, 1992): for him, one should take from and leave in this universal toolbox according to the stakes, the sociological problems, the interpretative needs of empirical research, the limits of existing theoretical conceptions, and so on. After years of various synthetic publications following his death (in French, see especially the synthesis by Mauger, 2005), as Elizabeth Silva and Alan Warde show in the introduction, Bourdieu still generates scientific controversy and can hardly be ignored in a large number of sub-fields where his theory is discussed, applied and criticized.

This dynamism is partially related to what I call the *multidimensionality* of Bourdieu's work itself. This is so because: (1) the theoretical and empirical contributions are diverse and creative in various ways; (2) the contributions are interrelated by a complex, and often ignored, web of theoretical and methodological links; (3) the body of work is framed, since the first texts on Algeria,[1] by a common theoretical perspective or orientation despite some variation in lexicon, polemical focus and methodology. One could describe this 'framing' theory as a particular sort of 'grounded theory' (in Glaser and Strauss's definition (1967)) in the sense that Bourdieu's theoretical conception is at least partially the result of an inductive process of 'generalization', going from limited empirical observation to systematic comparisons, through the transpositions of schemes or concepts from one field to another (see Lebaron, 2004). 'Bourdieu's theory' has a dual form, as an evolutionary, context-oriented, flexible network of theoretical objects or operations, but also, from another point of view, as a limited and stable set of concepts which 'concentrates' sociological theory into a model that is both simple and universally applicable. The concepts (habitus, field, capital and others) were consciously constructed, after a long process of trials and errors, for the need of empirical 'generalization' or for practical comparisons between different constructed research objects. They were also invented in order to help to produce a large amount of new consistent observations; for Bourdieu's methodology, which is more a sociological practice than a formalized 'canon', is systematically integrated in his theoretical reflection and it is a part of his innovative posture (Bourdieu and Wacquant, 1992).

After describing Bourdieu's work as a space in itself, I will briefly analyse the space of reception of his work in order to situate the contributions in this book. I will evoke Bourdieu's work as the product of particular theoretical and practical choices, as those discussed in this book. In the last section, I will focus on Bourdieu's very specific definition of sociological practice as the articulation of quantitative objectification and ethnographic fieldwork. I will argue that this articulation is still in its infancy in formulating a general research programme as envisaged from the development of Bourdieu's work.

Bourdieu's work as a space

Since his early work in Algeria, Bourdieu developed a 'relational' vision of the social world, which he applied to various sorts of problems and objects. These included the transition from a traditional to a capitalist society; the tendencies to social reproduction related to cultural capital inequalities; the genesis and functioning of specific social universes devoted to symbolic goals (especially the literary and philosophical fields); the social conditions of sociological knowledge, taste and class; the social suffering resulting from the transformation of the welfare state, economic and social policies; and the market of private housing.

The range of subjects investigated by Bourdieu is closely related to his social and scientific trajectory. He began his career with a rupture from speculative philosophy through a deep dive into ethnographic work in Algeria. He then practised large survey quantitative research, combining it with the use of various qualitative techniques in the collective dynamics of his research group at the *Centre de Sociologie Européenne*. He developed his theoretical apparatus in close connection with various empirical investigations, and never ceased to multiply empirical case studies, embedded in a more and more systematic – and also, to some extent, 'concentrated' – theory. He never ceased to cross the fields of academic thought and never thought of himself as the academic expert of a well-delimited domain, but more as a theoretical inventor making 'fire from any sort of wood' (*faire feu de tout bois*, as the French say (Lebaron, 2004)).

A large part of his better known books – like *An Invitation to Reflexive Sociology*, which was central for the international reception of his work (Bourdieu and Wacquant, 1992) – aimed at diffusing a *modus operandi* related to what he calls a scientific habitus: sociology is first of all a *practice* of empirical research, where theory is always framing concrete operations, like observing a particular ordinary life situation, interacting with people during an interview, writing an ethnographic journal, coding the results of a questionnaire, interpreting axes from a Multiple Correspondence Analysis, producing an article as the particular focused synthesis of empirical results, and so on.

The first issues of the journal he created in 1975, *Actes de la Recherche en Sciences Sociales*, show that he did not conceive the presentation of the final results of a project as the ultimate goal of sociological research. He also considered it important, if not necessary, to formulate research programmes, propagate sociological practice and extend the powers of the 'sociological eye' through practice and examples taken from the most heterogeneous, and contrasting, social realities.

When he entered a theme of enquiry, Bourdieu was particularly aware of the space of dominant interpreters in competition to 'tell the truth' about the particular problem or object under scrutiny. Many of his writings attempt to counter-balance a dominant conception or *doxa*, as he reacted against a scientific 'deviation' or a 'bias' that he considered particularly dangerous or misleading, as the product of field-specific social conditions (Pinto, 2002). He situated himself in dialectical and controversial relations to other social scientists. Part of his work has therefore a strong polemical charge aimed in three key directions: (1) against the limits of a structural(ist) theory of action, countering the objectivist and positivist vision of class derived from Marxism or Weberian stratification studies and developed in large survey research; (2) against the a-sociological and imaginary prophecies of postmodernism; (3) against the false anthropology of rational choice theory. Depending on the object and the specific figuration of leading sociological discourses about it, his posture could move and focus on one or another polemical stake without losing its specific purposes. For example, he was very critical of Robert K. Merton's too idealistic vision of science in a well-known article about the scientific field ('La spécificité du champ scientifique …' (Bourdieu, 1975a)). However, with the success of relativist accounts of science since the 1980s, especially following Bruno Latour, the target became, in his last writings on science (Bourdieu, 2001c), much more the tendency to reduce science activity to power relations in the 'new' sociology of science (Merton becoming an 'ally'). Yet over time his conception of scientific autonomy remained unchanged: the polemical stakes changed but not the scientific line of argument.

The space of Bourdieu's reception: international contexts

Since the first publication of his survey results about metropolitan France, especially in the 1964 book *Les héritiers* (*The Inheritors*) with Jean-Claude Passeron, which was based on official data about inequalities in higher education and can be seen as the basis of the theory of cultural reproduction, Bourdieu's work has been under the fire of a very large variety of critiques, coming from different social and intellectual positions in the scientific – and also the political – field, changing according to contexts, the appearance of new theoretical hypotheses and methodological fashions or 'new research tools'. A systematic sociology of the reception of his work would require a very large and complex empirical survey, which should try to avoid oversimplification, interpreting a sufficient number of relevant dimensions (to speak like data analysts), strata or levels. One should at least distinguish between direct confrontations to 'Bourdieu's theory' and more specific, often also more nuanced and detailed, discussions of the interpretations he proposes for particular objects or themes in his empirical analyses. There is a certain gap between both types of discussion, related to the segmentation of the international sociological field, between 'sociological theory' and particular domains of research, which tend to pursue their programmes with disregard for, or in competition with, 'pure' theoreticians. A second and more damaging confrontation with Bourdieu is often implicitly made between his theory and his methodological choices or practices, especially when he tries to articulate quantitative survey data (using Geometric Data Analysis) and ethnographic or qualitative material in order to 'quantify' his theory (Robson and Sanders, 2009).

Some aspects of Bourdieu's reception are related to the international and disciplinary traditions in which he is read, cited and used for empirical or theoretical purposes. We have in this book a good illustration of the ways the British and, to a lesser extent, the North-American sociological fields have recently developed their own reception and interpretation of Bourdieu, which are partially disconnected from the broad literature on Bourdieu in French, which remains largely not translated into English.

In the UK this reception is for example very much related to the way Bourdieu's writings challenge both the sociological narrative about the decline of class *and* largely ignore the growing debate about class identity and 'dis-identification', as argue Mike Savage, Elizabeth Silva and Alan Warde in Chapter 5. These debates were never really present as such in Bourdieu's 'polemical space', where, on the contrary, historical accounts for the symbolic and political existence, or non-existence, of 'class' or 'groups' (cf. E. P. Thompson) was central. This historical approach would be his way to grasp and, above all, criticize the notion of 'identity' (whatever its use). Bourdieu would hardly discuss class self-identification without a long account of the way the representatives of different groups – and also 'legitimate' social discourse producers, including the media and political actors – create and manipulate categories and never cease to struggle, in order to impose their categories in various fields. The sociology of classification, as part of the sociology of knowledge and political sociology, is for Bourdieu a precondition for a study of spontaneous self-identification discourses of any kind, but it cannot be isolated from the study of the various fields in which dominant classifications are produced and diffused by particular social agents.

Another illustration of this international reception process concerns the intellectual debate with Foucault, which is here presented and analysed by Tony Bennett in Chapter 8. Close colleagues at the Collège de France, Bourdieu and Foucault never really engaged in a systematic theoretical confrontation between 'philosophical systems', as *normaliens* would traditionally do. Bourdieu used Foucault in his writings as the illustration of an epistemic pole associated to what he saw as a more general discursive-reducing conception of 'fields', in line with the traditional (and socially determined) philosophical focus on texts, which largely ignore the social properties of intellectual producers and their interrelations, and, of course, thereby implicitly refuse empirical sociological methodology. Foucault was part of the more general polemics of Bourdieu against philosophical biases (which he called later, more generally, 'scholastic biases') and Foucault was not really discussed as a contributor to a specific research object. The creation *post-mortem* of this polemical space can appear a bit artificial, though interesting and stimulating as an attempt to hybridize close but distinct theories. In his focus on 'neo-liberal governmentality' and the stakes it generates for social sciences, the positions presented by Bennett in the British context seem surprisingly the reverse of the French one, where Bourdieu, together with Foucault's biographer Didier Eribon (2001), tried to save Foucault from a vulgar enterprise of political recuperation at the end of the 1990s. François Ewald, former close collaborator of Foucault, had become a theoretician of the Confederation of French Industries (the *Mouvement des Entreprises de France*) without abandoning his Foucauldian allegiance and legitimacy. He referred to Foucault in an attempt to reorganize the balance of corporations' power in favour of the managers and company leaders at the expense of the unions. Bourdieu with Eribon organized a conference about Foucault reaffirming the radicality of Foucault's thought against this misuse (Eribon, 2001). In the UK, Foucault is probably more often seen as a 'radical thinker' and Bourdieu as a 'survey' sociologist, which means closer to official statistical production. In France, on the contrary, Bourdieu, and not Foucault, is often associated with the most recent social contestations, including feminist or gay and lesbian movements (Eribon, 2007).

David Swartz's account of Bourdieu's political sociology in Chapter 4 presents his theoretical contribution as being largely ignored by mainstream international political science, and insists on his various contributions to understanding power and domination as a decisive breakthrough in this field. In France, the situation is much more ambivalent than that observed by Swartz in the Anglo-Saxon American world, since a very large reception and appropriation of Bourdieu has already radically changed the landscape of French political science. Bourdieu's constructivist claims on class formation, the role of a *porte-parole* (spokesperson), and his focus on symbolic struggles and stakes, have largely penetrated the field of political science, affecting areas of electoral research (focused on the biographical determinations of vote and abstention and the critique of opinion polls biases) and the sociology of political parties (the social bases of political organizations, and the relations between these properties and their symbolic modes of existence and political resources). Empirical systematic investigations about the characteristics of élite groups (like the European civil servants and lobbyists) have also helped to understand shifts in public policies and the development of 'socio-history' as a field crossing into political science. All the mainstream fields of political science in France have been more or less deeply influenced by Bourdieu's conception of sociological practice and, to some extent, by his theoretical apparatus and empirical findings. It would be interesting, in line with Swartz, to understand why this French renewal of the discipline seems largely not to have been exported. This certainly relates to the functioning of the international academic fields, the domination of English language in scientific communication and the imposition of specific intellectual traditions in political sociology, which remain untouched by Bourdieu's sociological practice.

The space of Bourdieu's reception: theoretical choices

Most of the critiques developed in this book relate to the space of theoretical choices in which Bourdieu can be situated, but often at the price of abstraction from his empirical case-studies. The present book reactivates persistent critical assessments of Bourdieu's theory, introduces new ones (see above on class 'disidentification'), as well as it illustrates some of the remaining lines of defence developed by Bourdieu and his followers. Certainly, some contributors also produce empirical analyses strongly inspired by Bourdieu's research programme, as occurs in Chapter 3, where Rick Fantasia makes an excellent illustration of the potential of Bourdieu's theory of symbolic goods when it is applied to the field of gastronomy. Following Michael Grenfell's argument in Chapter 2, namely that one can classify the critiques along various lines and levels, I note that the critiques share the implicit idea that Bourdieu's presence in contemporary sociological debates is challenging other theoretical or empirical enterprises. I focus on some of the dominant features of this challenge.

The basic and dominant critiques of Bourdieu usually insist on distinguishing between what his apparatus may shed light on *and* on what it deliberately ignores, completely fails to grasp, distorts, or makes invisible. These critiques often operate by reactivating classical philosophical oppositions like freedom/determinism, reflexivity/unconscious, subject/object, and so on. Bourdieu's theory is often associated with one of the philosophical poles of the epistemic couples that he, very precisely, wanted to avoid. His theory is commonly seen as offering a too mechanistic and deterministic vision of social action, and various authors try to enlarge it by introducing a stronger focus on ethics, reflexivity, consciousness, disidentification, social ambiguities or ambivalences. This is the case in Diane Reay's contribution (Chapter 6). Another critical approach involves moving clearly away from Bourdieu's 'limited' French perspective to adopt an alternative theoretical framework (Lamont's contribution (Chapter 10), is an example), which can be combined, in a more 'Bourdieu-style' kind of polemical confrontation, to explain its attraction. Antoine Hennion (Chapter 9) follows this approach based on an alternative perspective which presupposes a generalized social intuition of social groups, despite the theoretical limits and biases of such conception.

The assimilation of Bourdieu to one pole of the philosophical space can be interpreted, following Louis Pinto (2002), as an indicator of the strength of the philosophical habitus which frames the reader's perception of his work. This imposes a certain perception of his key concepts on the basis of pre-existing dominant traditional taxonomies. These critiques too often isolate sociological concepts from three main aspects which Bourdieu held as essential for sociological practice:

(1) the social and intellectual context, or the 'polemical space' as I coined it, in which concepts were produced; (2) the practical use of concepts precisely in order to avoid scholastic oppositions; and finally, (3) the survey results, observations, qualitative data, of which the concepts were first supposed to make sense. These three operations are precisely related to what Bourdieu critically dismissed in his notion of 'scholastic bias'.

Intellectual strategies, illustrated here in different chapters, are often based on an attempt to *enlarge* Bourdieu's theory to less automatic and reproductive behaviour, allowing a larger place for reflexivity, conscious action, and ethical deliberation. The notion of the habitus is of course the most discussed in this perspective. One can here recall that habitus was the new formulation of the notion of *ethos* which Bourdieu explicitly took from Weber after his Algerian period and rethought in more Marxist and Durkheimian terms (Lebaron, 2009a). Habitus is a systematic operator of practices, related to past social experience, which largely determines the way people react in an ordinary situation (reproducing its conditions of formation) or in radically new situations (like strong economic changes, where habitus also frames the way people react, adapt and invent). The main issue is here the degree of predictability of social behaviour and perceptions that the notion of habitus posits. If one leaves aside a strictly deterministic view, which was never in Bourdieu's mind, this issue can be formulated in terms of *probability* (of a particular practice, a choice, a position taking). Is 'self-reflexivity' itself not a part of a transformation of habitus into more strategic and rationalized automatism, observable in specific groups or fields? If one admits that the notion of the habitus, embedded in a corporal conception of action, much stressed by Bourdieu and Wacquant (1992), relates to the process of social cognition and to the way the human brain is socially 'constructed', one can associate it with the importance of 'neuronal plasticity' and with the re-evaluation of 'procedural memory' in any – more or less – rationalized/expert competence or action. This would mean that Bourdieu did account for aspects which Andrew Sayer (Chapter 7) accuses him of disregarding. If one associates habitus not strictly with the reproduction of original conditions but also with adaptation and invention in new situations, the various empirical observations of concrete habitus and their changes open a large space for a sociological research programme. This has only partially begun to be developed.

Bourdieu's sociological programme and its future

One could argue that Bourdieu's conception of sociological theory is, first of all, 'pragmatic', in the sense that sociological theory is for him a 'toolbox' helping to interpret sociological observations. For him sociological 'laws' are the product of an accumulation of converging observations which allow progressive and slow generalization towards more and more solid theoretical propositions.

If this general epistemology of sociology ('theory of the social (world)', following the terms of *Le métier de sociologue*, reactivated by Pinto (2002)) is accepted, a discussion of Bourdieu's work depends more on the degree of 'robustness' of the empirical conclusions resulting from the careful application of notions like habitus, capital and field, than on the intrinsic virtues of these concepts in an abstract space. At this level of empirical findings, it is necessary to recall that Bourdieu's work itself is a 'multi-level' and multi-faceted operation of sociological formalization.

To understand the peculiar status of Bourdieu's theory, which may explain its strength despite the remaining – though partially changing – logical or philosophical critiques, one has to recall that since the 1950s he had tried to construct this theory by combining different approaches. He sought to articulate 'thick' ethnographic descriptions (in the French 'Maussian' tradition, which he supported all his life, as illustrated in articles in his journal *Actes* or work like that of his follower Loïc Wacquant), with the interpretation of quantitative data. His quantitative leanings were much influenced by neo-classical economics and econometrics, but with a strong awareness of the limits of positivism, and a persistent need for a structural vision of society, which led him to use Geometric Data Analysis (GDA) methods after 1970 (Lebaron, 2009b).

His theoretical conception can be seen as a general frame, in the sense that it describes the various fundamental components of any social space on the basis of previous empirical observations and theoretical conclusions. But, of course, Bourdieu does not propose a precise model of each particular social space or field; rather, each should be investigated following his general perspective not by means of a mechanical application of static concepts. His perspective actually offers a rather open and broad vision of the components to be included in the structural analysis of a society, a group or a field. Homologies between two national figurations can be more or less important, and the *degree* of similarity is itself a matter of sociological debates. Yet, the main operation of sociological formalization rests in the definition of social distance (a very concrete operation in GDA), which allows the construction of a relevant space and the interpretation of its particular structure, leading to the analysis of its predictive aspects.

Qualitative observations make sense when the researchers keep in mind the entire 'construction of the research object' as a structural frame. It is dangerous to separate the analysis of an interaction or behaviour from the global structure in which it creates or expresses some difference or some meaning. In structural linguistics the difference between phonemes is at the basis of the creation or expression of meanings. The social structure itself needs concrete elements to be fully interpreted. In the general research programme derived from Bourdieu's work, sociological theory should be incorporated inside each concrete research operation and only developed more at the stage of the writing of the sociological interpretation.

One could conclude, following these few brief observations, that a theoretical discussion of Bourdieu's work is, at this stage of the history of the sociological field, less useful than the collective creation of a new dialectics between the empirical results emerging from a research programme inspired by Bourdieu, and the various challenging or contradictory results or theoretical generalizations coming from other traditions or research programmes. The contributions of this book clearly go in this direction; they open themselves a large 'space'. This book should be followed by new steps in a now collective, critical, and necessarily international, scientific field process to enlarge and solidify the sociological understanding of contemporary practices.

Note

1 Recent publications recall the conditions in which Bourdieu developed a theoretically ambitious perspective, through a very specific empirical investigation, during the liberation war in Algeria. See for example, Martin-Criado (2008) and Bourdieu (2008a).

12   Habitus and classifications

Fiona Devine

You do not have to be a devotee of Pierre Bourdieu to acknowledge the awesome influence of his work on the social sciences across the globe over the last half century. The enormous impact of Bourdieu's theoretical ideas is a little surprising in one respect. Over the same period, sociologists (at least) have started to move away from so-called grand theory: namely, big theories that attempt to understand the whole of social life. Disquiet has been expressed about the relationship between theoretical developments and the seemingly growing distance from empirical research on everyday life. Theorists stand accused of engaging in grand speculative thinking and making predictions about epic social change uninformed by past empirical research (Goldthorpe, 2007a, 2007b; Savage and Burrows, 2007; Smart, 2007; see also Devine and Heath, 2009). Bourdieu is a big theorist albeit one mostly interested in stability rather than change. Yet, his theoretical ideas have inspired a vast amount of empirical research that has extended way beyond his native France and continental Europe to include the UK (Bennett, *et al.*, 2009); America (Lamont, 2000, see also Lamont's contribution to this collection (Chapter 10)); Australia (Bennett, *et al.*, 2001), and, more recently, Latin America (Mendez, 2008). This is why Bourdieu, as Lamont suggests in chapter 10 (pp. 128–41), is one of the 'very small pantheon of individuals who have determined the shape of the social sciences'.

The chapters in this collection capture the significance of Bourdieu's work on one particular social science: namely, sociology. The range of substantive topics that are covered here – from politics, ethics, emotions and educational choices to food, cooking and class identity – illustrate his considerable influence across various sub-disciplines within sociology too. As one of the final contributions to the discussion of Bourdieu's analysis of culture and the legacy of his work, I explore some of the key issues and challenges for the future raised by the chapters in this book. The remainder of this short chapter is organized as follows. First, I pick up on the partial appropriation and critical revisions of the concept of habitus, drawing on Diane Reay and Andrew Sayer, and reflect upon whether the limitations of habitus can be overcome while retaining the concept (or not). Second, I discuss issues of identity, dis-identification and classification struggles by drawing on the partial appropriation of Bourdieu's work by Mike Savage, Elizabeth Silva and Alan Warde, and the (partial) repudiation of his work by Michèle Lamont. I consider ways in which interesting work on classification and identity could proceed. In conclusion, I make an overall assessment of Bourdieu's theoretical concepts and empirical research, and how future generations of scholars may engage with his work.

Extending our understanding of habitus and human actions

The concept of habitus, as Reay rightly notes in her chapter, is a 'rich generative conceptual tool' (p. 85), and key to Bourdieu's theory of the reproduction of social inequalities across time and space. She is appreciative of the concept for the way in which it captures a person's embodiment of their past and present positions – both in an individual and collective sense – through their dispositions. Contrary to the critics' view that the notion of habitus is highly deterministic, Reay stresses the transformative nature of habitus, since experiences can challenge the habitus and thereby reproduce it in both similar and different ways. She considers moments of tension and transformation of the habitus in her empirical work (Reay, *et al.*, 2007; 2009). Reay shows how white middle-class parents who send their children to mixed-race inner-city schools 'were more likely to generate a protective reinforcement of white middle-class habitus and a mobilization of capitals in order to defend against the discomforts of the field rather than any long-lasting change in habitus' (p. 83). In contrast, working-class students applying to élite universities experience a refashioning of their dispositions in sometimes new, exciting and challenging ways. While a prior habitus is never completely usurped, and unfamiliarity is often associated with anxiety and discomfort, such experiences are the source of new learning, self-improvement and change. Overall, Reay concludes, 'it is in the ruptures, the disjunctures, the edges of coherence between habitus and field that the most interesting theory lies' (p. 85).

Reay's reworking of habitus offers much food for thought, although her discussion highlights additional (albeit very familiar) limitations with Bourdieu's concept. Reay works with notions of a middle- and working-class habitus which are tightly bounded and distinct from each other, noting differences while similarities in dispositions are left unacknowledged. This is a major problem with the concept: namely, it is used to explain the reproduction of inequalities but it is too tight a concept, which overstates reproduction and ignores change. The idea of focusing on tensions where there is a disjuncture between habitus and field is, therefore, a fruitful one. That said, Reay's discussion of middle-class experiences of misalignment could be pushed further. To be sure, white middle-class parents who send their children to mixed-race inner-city schools will still mobilize their resources. It is possible to acknowledge that the experiences of tension will have some impact on middle-class dispositions too. Some change has to be acknowledged. The discussion on the changing habitus of working-class children going to élite universities is exciting because change in the habitus is appreciated. It shows young people exploring new ways of being, adapting their dispositions and creating hybrids of dispositions which can be a source of advantage too. Embracing the possibility of such transformations, however, poses a difficulty for Reay. Does this reworking stretch Bourdieu's concept too far? Is it worth holding onto the concept? There could be some radical implications arising out of the answers to these questions for the concept of habitus.

Andrew Sayer also praises Bourdieu for strengthening our sociological understanding of domination through the concept of habitus. He has strong misgivings, however, about the implicit views of human nature that underpin Bourdieu's discussion of how habitus influences everyday practices. The morality of human beings and their actions needs to be acknowledged in the study of inequality (see also Sayer, 2005). Like others, he believes that Bourdieu's concepts of habitus and practice are too deterministic. For Bourdieu, in different fields, people are engaged in a game, are preoccupied with getting a feel for the game and, ultimately, are engaged in strategic calculations about how to win the game. Sayer argues that an understanding of human actions needs to be modified to embrace human reflexivity and the ethical dispositions that are an important component of reflections. That is to say, people reflect (through inner conversations) on their experiences, and respond to the situation in which they find themselves in both predicable and unpredictable ways. Choices are made. Moreover, it is important to understand emotions as intelligent responses to objective circumstances. Emotions are part of reasoning and such emotional intelligence is a crucial part of how people feel about inequalities, for example. Finally, Sayer argues that it is important to move away from a notion of all actions as self-interested. People have a strong capacity for fellow feeling, and have strong commitments and attachments to others, which they value. Such concern for our own and others' well-being is about an acknowledgement of human vulnerability, which is part of the human condition.

Sayer's contribution is thus critical of the micro-sociological foundations of Bourdieu's theory and concepts. Interestingly, his desire to get away from 'bland accounts of social life' are similar to Carol Smart's (2007) concerns (noted in the introduction) about how big theories – in her case, that of individualization (Giddens, 1992; Beck and Beck-Gernsheim, 1995) – fail to capture the richness and complexity of everyday life. Thinking about family relationships and personal life, she prefers an approach that embraces the way in which people are connected and related to one another. Smart also highlights the importance of emotional bonds between individuals so that the multi-dimensional character of people is fully appreciated. The parallel in these arguments suggests that Bourdieu is far from alone in his tendency to portray individuals as one-dimensional rational actors, where action is based on conscious, systematic deliberations, and economistic evaluations of the pros and cons of action are always viewed in strategic terms. Arguably, it is a problem that besets sociology as a discipline (see my comments with regard to rational action theory (Devine, 1998; 2004b)) and other social sciences like economics. Given that Bourdieu was preoccupied with self-interested power and advantage, it is a considerable challenge to take his understanding of the reproduction of advantage and disadvantage forward with a more sophisticated theory of the micro-foundations of action and social interaction.

154   F. Devine

Identities, dis-identifications and classifications

Sociologists have long been concerned with the relationship between 'objective' and 'subjective' class positions, and Bourdieu is no exception, despite his pronouncement otherwise. As Savage, Silva and Warde note, his views of the dualism are somewhat contradictory: namely, he emphasizes that class identities cannot be 'read off' from class positions (defined in terms of capitals), yet his concept of habitus implies a strong correspondence between class position, identities and practices (Bourdieu, 1984; 1987). Be that as it may, his theory has been hugely influential in the discussion of class identification and dis-identification in the UK. Savage and his colleagues explore whether forms of dis-identification, found among the working classes (Skeggs, 2004a), are evident among the middle classes. Drawing on survey data from the Cultural Capital and Social Exclusion (CCSE) project, they found that class identification is generally low and that, when pressed, most people identify more with the working class (53 per cent) than with the middle class (39 per cent). In qualitative interviews, they found that people distanced themselves from the label of 'middle class' (see also Devine, 2005). The interviewees were willing to acknowledge that they were middle-class if they had an opportunity to tell a mobility story, emphasizing their disadvantaged roots and the virtues of working-class culture. These stories were a way of showing they are 'not really' middle-class, or not like the middle class of yesteryear. Savage, et al. rightly note that people are well aware of the 'politics of classification', and this awareness influences how they engage with classificatory systems like those of class.

The virtue of the chapter by Savage, Silva and Warde is the way in which it links a specific debate on class identities to the wider issues of classification as raised by Bourdieu. As they say, people know they live in an unequal world and are accordingly sensitive to the 'wider politics of positioning and classification' (p. 72). Interestingly, they argue that the discussion on dis-identification may now have run its course. The concept has always been beset with the problems of suggesting 'false consciousness' and, furthermore, it implies a 'deficit view' of identity. More attention should be devoted, they argue, to classification processes and the role of culture in those processes more generally. This idea sounds like a promising research agenda although some of their empirical findings point to possible limitations with the current discussion on classifications. The examples of 'shifts in self-identification' highlight, as Savage, Silva and Warde rightly note, that 'the distinction between middle class and working class may be less salient to people than sociologists might like to think' (p. 67; see also Savage, et al., 2001). Thus, the study of classifications should not only be about distinctions that people draw between themselves and others, but about similarities and alliances that are imagined and forged with other people. With regard to culture, this is to recognize that people will have similar as well as different tastes in reading, films and so on, and these might not matter so much to people either. As ever, the key is to think about the context in which these things are important and unimportant, and to find the best methods possible to explore these issues.

In the autobiographical reflections in her chapter, Michèle Lamont also points to the importance of Bourdieu's work on overcoming the dualism of object and subject, which had plagued Marxist discussions of false consciousness, and the structure and agency dichotomy that allowed her to come down firmly on the side of agency. This led Lamont to study valuation processes, how different (class) groups of people define a worthy person, group boundaries and so forth, in her two groundbreaking books (Lamont, 1992; 2000). As she recounts, her distinctive comparative approach led her to acknowledge something very different from Bourdieu's France: namely, a loosely bounded, less hierarchical American culture where even upper-middle-class people do not care much for high culture (although this is not to say Americans do not use cultural signals as sources of distinction). Pursuing new challenges has led Lamont to consider more deeply the nature of classification struggles – what is core and what is periphery – to explore the permeability of group boundaries and to understand inclusions as well as exclusions – and, increasingly, to link the issues to that of identity (just as, in the other direction, questions of identity have led Savage, Silva and Warde to consider classification struggles more broadly). These issues have been well explored in Lamont's work on the dignity of working men, how working-class men maintain their sense of moral worth and social standing, and establish boundaries between themselves and those above and below them. An additional beauty of this research, of course, is the focus on ethno-racial boundaries on which Bourdieu was surprisingly silent.

Lamont honestly discusses her travels to and from Bourdieu, her most recent work on knowledge production (Lamont, 2009) and her enduring 'interest in questions of inequality, and more specifically with the resilience of members of stigmatized groups and how societies provide a cultural and institutional scaffolding that sustains this resilience' (p. 139). Arguably, this is one of the big challenges facing all Bourdieu scholars: namely, to explore the extent to which his theoretical ideas can be used to explain the everyday lives and struggles of the disadvantaged as well as the advantaged. It requires finding a way of understanding working-class habitus which has often eluded academic scholars of inequality (Savage, Bagnall and Longhurst, 2005). The challenge is to not simply focus on the seemingly relentless misery and suffering of working-class lives (Charlesworth, 2000). To be sure, it is imperative to understand the 'hidden injuries of class', and this has proved a rich seam of enquiry (Sennett and Cobb, 1973; Skeggs, 1997). At the same time, however, it is imperative to understand, as both Reay and Lamont suggest in their chapters, the dignity of ordinary people's lives, their pleasures in life as well as their pains, their hopes and dreams as well as their setbacks and losses. Many of the contributors of this book have emphasized the importance of one of Bourdieu's last publications – *The Weight of the World* (Bourdieu, *et al.*, 1999). Given that most of Bourdieu's work was focused on the reproduction of advantage, the extent to which his theoretical architecture can explain the reproduction of disadvantage will shape an important research agenda in the next few years.

Some final remarks

The contributions to this collection have captured the tremendous impact of Bourdieu's cultural analysis in sociology and the social sciences over the last fifty years. He has certainly been a dominant figure – even in a global sense – and his way of describing and explaining the social world will shape future generations of sociologists to be sure. Of course, as the contributors here note, it is important not to be slavish to one way of thinking, but to critically engage with Bourdieu's theory and concepts, to subject his work to empirical enquiry, and to take the findings from research to adapt and refine his theoretical ideas. Bourdieu would not want it any other way! Over time, and after a period of intense interest in his work, it may be that scholars will challenge Bourdieu's ideas more fundamentally, develop alternative ways of doing theory and research, and move some distance away from him. Some of these things are to be found in this edited book. It is hard to imagine, however, that his way of seeing the world will be simply abandoned in years to come; rather there will be an enduring legacy which will shape sociology – theoretically and empirically – during this coming century.

I am not a Bourdieu scholar, and I have used his work in a pluralistic way alongside the work of others in the study of class inequalities and how advantages and disadvantages get reproduced over time and space. Nevertheless, I will continue to draw on and engage with Bourdieu's work and especially his discussion of classes as bundles of capitals of an economic, cultural and social kind (Savage, Warde and Devine 2005). I remain intrigued by the links between economic, cultural and social capital and, although those links might be looser than previously imagined, they are still there (Bennett, *et al.*, 2009; Le Roux, *et al.*). I think that it is still interesting to explore links between economy and culture (Crompton and Scott, 2005), and to find sophisticated ways of exploring the connections between them; how they are intertwined and transformed into and by each other. Similarly, I am increasingly interested in the ways in which cultural capital and social capital are entwined with each other, and the ways in which social capital is crucial to the making of cultural capital (Devine, 2008). These concluding remarks suggest that even scholars who have not privileged Bourdieu's work will find their theoretical and empirical work influenced by him in one way or another. This is testimony to Bourdieu's reach in sociology and the social sciences over the last fifty years.

13 Epilogue

Bourdieu's legacy?

Elizabeth Silva and Alan Warde

A dozen chapters, no matter how insightful, can make only a limited contribution to a thorough assessment of Bourdieu's legacy. The varied concerns and contrasting evaluations indicate the complexity of the subject matter and its capacity to arouse disagreement. But arguably, controversy is productive, and the best way to establish a platform from which to go forward to exploit the inheritance of the currently most influential sociologist of the last quarter of the twentieth century. Perhaps also, it is explicable.

As Frédéric Lebaron insists, Bourdieu's work, as well as being vast, is multi-dimensional. Although one man's multi-dimensionality may be another woman's ambivalence, people are able to take many different elements from his work, fashion them into novel configurations and generate new research questions. Certainly, multi-dimensionality produces openness to different lines of interpretation and hence, disputation. More than that of most other major contributors to sociological theory, his work lends itself to partial appropriation and empirical application. These are features which make Bourdieu constantly useful in the present, at a time when, only a few years after his death, the overall value of a multitude of works with a complex architecture is still neither fully known nor appreciated beyond the circles of his closest collaborators and most vituperative critics.

This book, we hope, not only represents the range of opinion concerning Bourdieu's current standing, but will be complementary to others attempting to evaluate the full significance of his work. In this case, we have surveyed the options it makes available for the sociology of culture. Out of the disagreements we might yet distil some worthwhile lessons. It now looks as if the interpretations of Bourdieu which have been specific to national sociological traditions, to which Lebaron refers, are becoming less of an obstacle. Although translation of his works is no guarantee of this, the growth of his reputation in the USA over the last decade will ensure that they will get increasingly wide international exposure. Disagreements and counter-evaluations will become less dependent on national traditions.

The American reception of Bourdieu has tended to focus on the application of his key concepts, among them habitus, cultural capital, field, legitimate culture, disinterestedness, and practice. His work has thereby provided a significant foil for clarification, modification and re-conceptualization across many sub-areas of sociology. The close examination of the concept of habitus is one example.

There have been attempts to partially rehabilitate or refine it (e.g. Crossley, 2001; Lizardo, 2004; Reay and Sayer, both this volume); and others have sought to specify it more closely for critical purposes (e.g. Archer, 2007; Crossley, 2001; Lahire, 2003), and have added significantly to the understanding of recurrent social action. Another example is the uniquely Bourdieusian concept of cultural capital which has likewise inspired detailed conceptual clarification and diverse application (e.g. Bennett, *et al.*, 2009; Lamont and Lareau, 1988; Lareau and Weinenger, 2003; Lizardo, 2008). Perhaps most encouraging is the fact that not only are his key concepts being refined but that they find wide application in substantive sociological analysis. This is no doubt the reason why Bourdieu has become so much cited in American journals in recent years (Sallaz and Zavisca, 2007). Of course, raids to capture discrete concepts may violate the integrity of the conceptual schema which some detect as core to his work. To a purist, such forays may smack of indiscipline, but in practice they provide a focus for cumulative empirical research on topics of cultural practice in the context of power.

As Fiona Devine observed, Bourdieu was a master of the art of combining theory with empirical research. Bourdieu was particularly effective because his work has sufficient of a theoretical core to hold the œuvre together – there are concepts that are recognizable, which can be redeployed in different contexts, and a framework of concepts which provide a platform for coherent concrete analyses – but without ever subsiding into pure theory. For those who either loyally subscribe to the Bourdieusian corpus or who are simply satisfied with the intimations of the overall meta- and middle-range theoretical assumptions, his framework provides a point of departure from which to undertake empirical analysis without having to rework the fundamentals of the discipline. This is something not to be disregarded lightly; laying aside questions of theoretical axioms, basic assumptions and orientations towards data is often very necessary to the conduct of social research. *Pace* Michael Burawoy (2005a), sociologists have many important things to do in addition to sharpening their concepts and integrating them into a meta-theoretical framework. Nevertheless, for sociology, the key to becoming a cumulative social science requires scholars to be working with identifiable paradigms on sets of problems which are explored thoroughly. It probably requires scholars like Bourdieu, who both organize sociological research programmes *and* have to hand a malleable meta- and middle-range theoretical framework, to establish a platform for cumulative knowledge building in social sciences.

Bourdieu also made a significant, if unsystematic, contribution to methodology. While we might not necessarily go so far as Lebaron in claiming this as his major contribution or legacy, his flexible adaptation and inspired experimentation with a wide range of investigative techniques makes his appeal a wide one (Silva, *et al.*, 2009; Warde, 2008a). To review Bourdieu's opus as a giant sociological toolkit would reveal enormously versatility. There perhaps lies the rub, for one can do both good and bad things with his instruments; they allow both congenial and objectionable ways of approaching the analysis of the social world.

Bourdieu has also proved extremely valuable as a target for critique. This is partly because he held distinctive and challenging positions on key issues. He was, in retrospect, very prescient regarding what was likely to become a significant sociological or political issue. Consistently combative in style, he always tried to separate his position from others in a debate, often by refusing either side of a polarized debate and claiming to break down obstructive dichotomies and create more sustainable syntheses. In some instances he was applauded for success, in other cases it left many readers with a sense of ambiguity, confusion and exasperation. As a prominent figure in the French intellectual field he personally inspired loyalty, admiration and affection from some, and disdain and hostility from others. Emotional reactions continue to be heated. However, one might expect the personal animosities to soon be forgotten. Hopefully, attempts to reconstruct his ambiguities and ambivalences into some form of consistent, and therefore necessarily oversimplified, coherent theoretical edifice – an activity which both his friends and foes seem to do in equal measure – will cease. Because his contribution does not depend massively upon a grand and abstract theoretical schema, it is more amenable to adaptation for new purposes.

We expect that social change and new evidence will require modification of his concepts and methods, though this is nothing that he would not readily acknowledge. Topics which he ignored will inevitably increase with the passage of time. Of course as Grenfell (Chapter 2, this volume) points out, it is perverse to criticize a social scientist for not having answered every possible interesting question, past or present. Nevertheless, some types of analysis and some sorts of question may be uncongenial to particular traditions of thought – they are not considered to be relevant questions, or they are thought to be improperly formulated, or they are impossible to ask within a particular theoretical frame. In this regard, some have been unconvinced that Bourdieu gives any worthwhile purchase on newly emergent processes in contemporary social life that demand alternatives. Key areas where new and necessary concepts have emerged include the heterogeneity of multiple cultural hierarchies that challenge the primacy of class, such as gender, age and ethnicity (see Bennett, *et al.*, 2009), international mobilities and the impact of multiculturalism (Hage, 1998) and the effects of changing commitments of personal relationships on the relationality of the social (where the notion of 'emotional capital' is a related concern, cf. Reay, 2000; Silva, 2000). Attempts to apply the established concepts in international comparative analysis have not always met with obvious success; the example of legitimate culture in the UK and the USA might be an example. The effects of environmental degradation on social life will be another relevant area of contemporary concern requiring rigorous analysis for which there has been little preparation within a Bourdieusian perspective.

Contributions to this book show that the richness of Bourdieu's work has potential for grasping current social issues. We have little doubt that his orientation to sociology and his methods and concepts will be deployed extensively in the near to mid-term future. Indeed, since he has only recently become widely appreciated among sociologists outside France, there should be much further mileage in the technical and theoretical apparatus. A loose theoretical framework which contains concepts and procedures so readily applicable in empirical analysis and explanation is likely to have continued impact. Of course, reformulation and enlargement will be required to account for the new dynamics of contemporary life. Bourdieu (1999b: 225) noted that as academics we are deeply marked by the contexts in which we find ourselves. Our misunderstandings are sometimes resources for social position in a highly competitive field. Perhaps as the force of his personality and its influence on relationships with other schools of thought diminishes, and personal loyalties and animosities subside, the potential that so many of our contributors see in various aspects of his work will be released and realized. This may well result in many aspects of his account being revised and superseded, but given his conviction that the theoretical and the empirical should be intricately associated this should have caused him neither surprise nor distress.

References

Accardo, A. (1983) *Initiation à la sociologie de l'illusionnisme social*, Bordeaux: Editions le Mascaret.

Alexander, J. (1995) 'The Reality of Reduction: The Failed Synthesis of Pierre Bourdieu', in *Fin de Siècle Social Theory: Relativism, Reduction, and the Problem of Reason*, London: Verso, pp. 128–217.

Allatt, P. (1996) 'Becoming privileged', in I. Bates and G. Riseborough (eds) *Youth and Inequality*, Buckingham: Open University Press.

Anderson, B. (1983) *Imagined Communities: Reflections on the Origin and Spread of Nationalism*, London: Verso.

Archer, M. S. (2000) *Being Human*, Cambridge: Cambridge University Press.

—— (2003) *Structure, Agency and the Internal Conversation*, Cambridge: Cambridge University Press.

—— (2007) *Making Our Way Through the World*, Cambridge: Cambridge University Press.

Aristotle (1980) *The Nicomachean Ethics*, Oxford: Oxford University Press.

Aronoff, M. J. (2000) 'Political Culture', in E. F. Borgatta (ed.) *Encyclopedia of Sociology*, Vol. 3, Detroit: Macmillan, pp. 11640–4.

Arpaly, N. (2003) *Unprincipled Virtue: An Inquiry into Moral Agency*, Oxford: Oxford University Press.

Atkins, L. and Skeggs, B. (2004) *Feminism after Bourdieu*, London: Blackwell.

Bachelard, G. (1949) *Le rationalisme appliqué*, Paris: Presses Universitaires de France.

—— (1980) *La Formation de l'esprit scientifique: Contribution à une psychanalyse de la connaissance objective*, Paris: J. Vrin.

—— (1984) *The New Scientific Spirit*, New York: W. W. Norton.

Bal, M. (1992) 'Telling, showing, showing off', *Critical Inquiry*, 18 (3).

Barbalet, J.M. (2001) *Emotions, Social Theory and Social Structure*, Cambridge: Cambridge University Press.

Barnett, C. (1999) 'Culture, government and spatiality: Reassessing the "Foucault effect" in cultural-policy studies', *International Journal of Cultural Studies*, 2 (3): 369–97.

Barth, F. (1969) *Ethnic Groups and Boundaries*, Boston, MA: Little Brown.

Bauman, Z. (1989) *Modernity and the Holocaust*, Cambridge: Polity.

—— (1998) *Globalization: The Human Consequences*, Cambridge, Polity.

Beck, U. and Beck-Gernsheim, E. (1995) *The Normal Chaos of Love*, Cambridge: Polity.

Becker, H. (1983) *Art Worlds*, Chicago: University of Chicago Press.

Bellah, R. N., Madsen, R., Sullivan, W. M., Swidler, A. and Tipton, S. M. (1984) *Habits of the Heart: Individualism and Commitment in American Life*, Berkeley, CA: University of California Press.

Benda, J. (1927) *La trahison des clercs*, Paris: Grasset.

Bennett, T. (1998) *Culture: A Reformer's Science*, Sydney: Allen and Unwin; London and New York: Sage.

—— (2004) *Pasts Beyond Memories: The Evolutionary Museum and Colonial Science*, London: Routledge.

—— (2005) 'The historical universal: The role of cultural value in the historical sociology of Pierre Bourdieu', *British Journal of Sociology*, 56 (1), 141–64.

—— (2006) 'Civic seeing: Museums and the organisation of vision', in S. MacDonald (ed.) *Companion to Museum Studies*, Oxford: Blackwell, pp. 263–81.

—— (2007) 'Habitus clivé: Aesthetics and politics in the work of Pierre Bourdieu', *New Literary History*, 38 (1): 201–28.

—— (2008/9) 'Aesthetics, government, freedom', *Key Words: A Journal of Cultural Materialism*, 6: 76–91.

Bennett, T., Emmison, M. and Frow, J. (2001) *Accounting for Taste, Australian Everyday Cultures*, Cambridge: Cambridge University Press.

Bennett, T., Savage, M., Silva, E. B., Warde, A., Gayo-Cal, M. and Wright, D. (2009) *Culture, Class, Distinction*, London: Routledge.

Benson, R. (1999) 'Field theory in comparative context: A new paradigm for media studies', *Theory and Society*, 28: 463–98.

Benson, R. and Neveu, E. (eds) (2005) *Bourdieu and the Journalistic Field*, Cambridge, UK and Malden, MA: Polity.

Bloemraad, I. (2001) 'Outsiders and insiders: Collective identity and collective action in the Quebec Independence Movement, 1995', in B. A. Dobratz, L. K. Waldner and T. Buzzell (eds), *The Politics of Social Inequality*, New York: JAI, pp. 271–305.

Boltanski, L. (1981) 'America, America … Le plan marshall et l'importation du *management*', *Actes de la recherche en sciences sociales*, 38: 19–41.

Boltanski, L. (with Yann Darre et Marie-Ange Shiltz) (1984) 'La dénonciation', *Actes de la recherche en sciences sociales*, (51): 3–40.

Boltanski, L. and Thévenot, L. (1999) 'The sociology of critical capacity', *European Journal of Social Theory*, 2 (3): 359–77.

—— (2006, 1991 French edn) *On Justification: Economies and Worth*, Princeton, NJ: Princeton University Press.

Bottero, W. (2005) *Stratification: Social Division and Inequality*, London: Routledge.

—— (2009, forthcoming) 'Intersubjectivity and Bourdieusian approaches to identity', *Cultural Sociology*.

Bourdieu, P. [1964] (1979) *The Inheritors: French Students and Their Relations to Culture*, Chicago: University of Chicago Press.

—— (1967) 'Systems of education and systems of thought', *Social Science Information*, 14: 338–58.

—— (1969) 'Intellectual Field and Creative Project', *Social Science Information*, 8 (2): 89–119.

—— (1972) 'Les Doxosophes', *Minuit*, 1: 26–45.

—— (1975a) 'La spécificité du champ scientifique et les conditions sociales du progrès de la raison', *Sociologie et Sociétés*, 7 (1): 91–118.

—— (1975b) 'The specificity of the scientific field and the social conditions of the progress of reason', *Social Science Information* 14 (6): 19–47.

—— (1979) *La Distinction*, Paris: les Éditions de Minuit.

—— (1981) 'Décrire et préscrire. Note sur les conditions de possibilité et les limites de l'efficacité', *Actes de la recherche en sciences sociales*, 38 (May): 69–73.

—— (1984) [1979] *Distinction: A Social Critique of the Judgement of Taste*, London: Routledge; Cambridge MA: Harvard University Press.

—— (1986) 'The forms of capital', in J. G. Richardson (ed.) *Handbook of Theory and Research for the Sociology of Education*, London: Greenwood, pp. 241–58.

—— (1987) 'What makes a social class? On the theoretical and practical existence of groups', *Berkeley Journal of Sociology*, 32: 1–18.

—— (1988) [1984] *Homo Academicus* (trans. P. Collier), Cambridge: Polity.

—— (1989a) 'The corporatism of the universal: The role of intellectuals in the modern world', *Telos*, 81: 99–110.

—— (1989b) *La Noblesse d'Etat. Grandes Corps et Grandes Ecoles*. Paris: Les Éditions de Minuit.

—— (1989c) 'Social space and symbolic power', *Sociological Theory*, 7 (1): 14–25.

—— (1990a) [1984] *Homo Academicus*, Palo Alto CA: Stanford UP.

—— (1990b) [1980] *The Logic of Practice* (trans. R. Nice), Cambridge: Polity; Stanford, CA: Stanford University Press.

—— (1990c) *In Other Words: Essays Towards a Reflexive Sociology*, Cambridge: Polity.

—— (1993a) 'Concluding remarks: For a sociogenetic reading of intellectual works', in C. Calhoun, E. Lipuma and M. Postone (eds) *Bourdieu: Critical Perspectives*, Oxford: Polity.

—— (1993b) 'Esprits d'État: Genèse et structure du champ bureaucratique', *Actes de la recherche en sciences sociales* (96/97): 49–62.

—— (1993c) *The Field of Cultural Production: Essays on Art and Literature*, New York: Columbia University Press; Cambridge: Polity.

—— (1993d) 'Principles of a sociology of cultural works', in S. Kemel and I. Gaskell (eds) *Explanation and Value in the Arts*, Oxford: Polity.

—— (1993e) *Sociology in Question*, Thousand Oaks, CA and London: Sage.

—— (1994) [1987] *In Other Words: Essays Towards a Reflexive Sociology* (trans. M. Adamson), Cambridge: Polity.

—— (1996a) [1992] *The Rules of Art: Genesis and Structure of the Literary Field*, Stanford CA: Stanford University Press; Cambridge: Polity.

—— (1996b) [1989] *The State Nobility: Elite Schools in the Field of Power*. Stanford, CA: Stanford University Press.

—— (1998a) *On Television*. New York: New Press.

—— (1998b) [1994] *Practical Reason*, Oxford: Polity.

—— (1999a) [1993] 'The Contradictions of Inheritance' in Bourdieu, P., *et al. The Weight of the World: Social suffering in contemporary society*, Cambridge: Polity, pp. 507–13.

—— (1999a) *The Weight of the World: Social suffering in contemporary society*, Cambridge: Polity.

—— (1999b) 'The social conditions of the international circulation of ideas', in R. Shusterman (ed.) *Bourdieu: A Critical Reader*, Oxford: Blackwell.

—— (2000a) 'Making the economic habitus. Algerian workers revisited' (trans. R. Nice and L. Wacquant), *Ethnography*, 1 (1): 17–41.

—— (2000b) 'Monopolisation politique et révolutions symboliques', in *Propos Sur Le Champ Politique*, Lyon: Presses Universitaires de Lyon: 99–107.

—— (2000c) 'Move over shrinks', *Times Higher Educational Supplement*, 14 April: 19.

—— (2000d) [1997] *Pascalian Meditations*, Cambridge: Polity.

—— (2000e) *Propos sur le Champ Politique*, Lyon: Presses Universitaires de Lyon.

—— (2001a) *Masculine Domination*, Stanford, CA: Stanford University Press.

—— (2001b) *Si le monde social m'est supportable, c'est parce que je peux m'indigner*, Paris: Editions de l'Aube.

—— (2001c) 'Science de la science et réflexivité', Cours du Collège de France 2000–2001, Paris: Éditions Raison d'Agir.

—— (2002a) *Interventions, 1961–2002. Science sociale et action politique*, Marseille: Agone.

—— (2002b) 'Les chercheurs et le mouvement social', in *Interventions, 1961–2001. Science sociale & action politique*, Marseille: Argone, pp. 465–9.

—— (2002c) 'Pour une Internationale des intellectuels', in *Interventions, 1961–2001. Science sociale & action politique*. Marseille: Agone, pp. 257–66.

—— (2002d) Principes pur une réflexion sur les contenus d'enseignement. *Pierre Bourdieu: Interventions, 1961–2001*. F. Poupeau and T. Discepolo. Marseille, Agone: 217–26.

—— (2002e) Propositions pour l'enseignement de l'avenir. *Pierre Bourdieu: Interventions, 1961–2001*. F. Poupeau and T. Discepolo. Marseille, Agone: 199–201.

—— (2004a) *Esquisse pour une auto-analyse*, Paris: Éditions Raison d'Agir.

—— (2004b) *Essai pour une socio-analyse*, Paris: Liber.

—— (2005a) 'Habitus', in J. Hillier and E. Rooksby (eds) *Habitus: A Sense of Place*, Aldershot: Ashgate.

—— (2005b) [2000] *The Social Structures of the Economy*, Oxford: Polity.

—— (2007) [2004] *Sketch for a Self-Analysis*, Cambridge: Polity.

—— (2008a) *Esquisses Algériennes* (textes édités et présentés par Tassadit Yacine), Paris: Seuil.

—— (2008b) [2002] *Political Intervention: Social Science and Political Action* (selected and introduced by F. Poupeau and T. Discepolo), London: Verso.

Bourdieu, P. and Grenfell, M. (1995) *Entretiens: Pierre Bourdieu et Michael Grenfell*. Occasional Paper No. 35. Southampton: University of Southampton.

Bourdieu, P. and Hahn. O. (1970) 'La théorie', *VH*, 101 (2) (Summer): 12–21.

Bourdieu, P. and Passeron, J. C. (1964) *Les Héritiers*, Paris: Minuit.

—— (1977) [1970] *Reproduction in Education, Society and Culture* (trans. R. Nice), London: Sage.

—— (1990) [1970] *Reproduction in Education, Society and Culture*, Thousand Oaks CA: Sage.

Bourdieu, P. and Wacquant, L. (1989) 'Towards a reflexive sociology: a workshop with Pierre Bourdieu', *Sociological Theory*, 7 (1): 26–63.

—— (1992) *An Invitation to Reflexive Sociology*, Chicago IL: University of Chicago Press.

Bourdieu, P., Boltanski, L., Castel, R. and Chamboredon, J. C. (1990a) [1965] *Photography: A Middle-brow Art* (trans. S. Whiteside), Oxford: Polity.

Bourdieu, P., Chamboredon, J. C. and Passeron, J. C. (1990b) [1980] *The Craft of Sociology*, New York: Aldine de Gruyter.

Bourdieu, P., Darbel, A. and Schnapper, D. (1990c) [1966] *The Love of Art: European Art Museums and their Public* (trans. C. Beattie and N. Merriman), Oxford: Polity.

Bourdieu, Pierre and Alain Accardo, Gabrielle Balazs, Stephane Beaud, Francois Bonvin, Emmanuel Bourdieu, Phillippe Bourgois, Sylvain Broccolichi, Patrick Champagne, Rosine Christin, Jean-Pierre Fauguer, Sandrine Garcia, Remi Lenoir, Francoise Oeuvrard, Michel Pialoux, Louis Pinto, Denis Podalydes, Abdelmalek Sayad, Charles Soulie Loic, J. D. Wacquant (1999) *Weight of the World: Social suffering in contemporary society*, Cambridge: Polity.

Bradley, H. (1996) *Fractured identities: Changing patterns of inequality*, Cambridge, Polity.

Bridge, G. (2001) 'Bourdieu, rational action and the time-space strategy of gentrification', *Transactions of the Institute of British Geographers*, 26: 205–24.

Brown, N. and Szeman, I. (eds) (2000) *Pierre Bourdieu: Fieldwork in culture*, Boulder CO: Rowman and Littlefield.

Brown, W. (2006) *Regulating Aversion: Tolerance in the Age of Identity and Empire*, Princeton NJ: Princeton University Press.

Brubaker, R. (1985) 'Rethinking classical theory: The sociological vision of Pierre Bourdieu', *Theory and Society*, 14: 745–75.

—— (1992) *Citizenship and Nationhood in France and Germany*, Cambridge, MA: Harvard University Press.

Bruguière, André (1980) [Article], *Nouvel Observateur* 810: 160–6 (19 May).

Bryson, B. (1996) 'Anything but heavy metal: Symbolic exclusion and musical dislikes', *American Sociological Review*, 61 (5): 884–99.

Burawoy, M. (2005a) 'For public sociology', *American Sociological Review*, 70(1): 4–28.

—— (2005b) Response: Public sociology: populist fad or path to renewal? *The British Journal of Sociology*, 56 (3): 417–32.

Butler, J. (1990) 'Gender trouble: Feminist theory and psychoanalytic discourse', in L. J. Nicholson (ed.) *Feminism/Modernism*, New York: Routledge.

Butler, T. and Savage, M. (eds) (1995) *Social Change and the Middle Classes*, London, UCL Press.

Calhoun, C. (2005) 'Centralité du social et possibilité de la politique', in J. DuBois, P. Durant, Y. Winkin (eds) *Bourdieu: Le colloq Cerisy*, Liège: Éditions de l'Université de Liège.

Calhoun, C., LiPuma, E. and Postone, M. (eds) (1993) *Bourdieu: Critical Perspectives*, Chicago: University of Chicago Press.

Callewaert, S. (2006) 'Bourdieu, critic of Foucault: The case against double-game-philosophy', *Theory, Culture and Society*, 23 (6): 73–98.

Callon, M. and Law, J. (1982) 'On interests and their transformation: Enrollment and counter-enrollment', *Social Studies of Science* 12: 615–25.

Callon M., Bastide F., Bauin S., Courtial J. and Turner, W. (1984) 'Les mécanismes d'intéressement dans les textes scientifiques', *Cahiers STS* 4.

Capatti, A. (1999) 'The Taste for Canned and Preserved Food', in J. L. Flandrin and M. Montanari (eds) *FOOD: A culinary History from Antiquity to the Present*, New York: Columbia University Press.

Carter, P. L. (2005) *Keepin' It Real: School Success Beyond Black and White*, New York: Oxford University Press.

Certeau, L. (1980) *Lire: un braconnage. L'Invention du quotidien, Arts de faire*. Paris: UGE.

Champagne, P. (1979) *Faire l'opinion. Le nouvel espace politique*, Paris: Éditions de Minuit.

—— (1990) *Faire l'opinion: le nouveau jeu politique*. Paris: Éditions de Minuit.

Chan, T. W. and Goldthorpe, J. H. (2004) 'Is there a status order in contemporary British society?: Evidence from the occupational structure of friendship', *European Sociological Review*, 20 (5): 383–401.

Charles, M. (2008) 'Culture and inequality: Identity, ideology, and difference in "Post-Ascriptive Society"', *The Annals of the American Academy of Political and Social Science*, 619: 59–77.

Charlesworth, S. (2000) *A Phenomenology of Working Class Experience*, Cambridge: Cambridge University Press.

Cicourel, A. V. (1993) 'Aspects of structural and processual theories of knowledge', in C. Calhoun, E. Lipuma and M. Postone (eds) *Bourdieu: Critical Perspectives*, Cambridge: Polity.

Clifford, J. (1988) *The Predicament of Culture: Twentieth-Century Ethnography, Literature, and Art*, Cambridge MA: Harvard University Press.

Collectif Révoltes logiques (eds) (1984) *L'Empire du sociologue*. Paris: La Découverte.

Cordier, F. (1989) 'Michel Guérard: Comme Un Poisson Dans l'Industrie', *Neo Magazine* (precursor of *Neo Restauration*) 199, Juin.

Corthay, A. (1902) *La Conserve Alimentaire*, Paris: Rety.

Coxon, A. and Fisher, K. (2003) 'Criterion validity and occupational classification', in D. Pevalin and D. Rose (eds) *A Researcher's Guide to the National Statistics Socio-economic Classification*, London: Sage, pp. 107–30.

Crompton, R. (2008) *Class and Stratification* (3rd edn), Cambridge, Polity.

Crompton, R. and J. Scott (2005) 'Class analysis: Beyond the cultural turn', in F. Devine, M. Savage, J. Scott and R. Crompton (eds) *Rethinking Class, Culture, Identities and Lifestyles*, Basingstoke: Macmillan.

Crossley, N. (1999) 'Fish, Field, Habitus and Madness: The first wave mental health users movement in Great Britain', *British Journal of Sociology*, 50: 647–70.

—— (2001) *The Social Body: Habit, Identity and Desire*, London: Sage.

—— (2002) *Making Sense of Social Movements*. Buckingham: Open University Press.

Cultural Studies (2003) special edition on Bourdieu, 17 (3–4).

Danko, D. (2008) 'Nathalie Heinich's Sociology of Art – and Sociology from Art', *Cultural Sociology* 2 (2): 242–56.

Davydova, I. and Sharrock, W. (2003) 'The rise and fall of the fact/value distinction', *The Sociological Review*, 51 (3): 357–75.

Dean, K. (2003) *Capitalism and Citizenship: The Impossible Partnership*, London: Routledge.

De Certeau, M. (1984) [1980] *The Practice of Everyday Life*, Berkeley CA: University of California Press.

Devine, F. (1998) 'Class analysis and the stability of class relations', *Sociology*, 32: 23–42.

—— (2004a) *Class Practices*, Cambridge: Cambridge University Press.

—— (2004b) 'Talking about class in Britain', in *Social Inequalities in Comparative Perspective*, Oxford: Blackwell.

—— (2005) 'Middle class identities in the United States', in F. Devine, M. Savage, R. Crompton and J. Scott (eds) *Rethinking Class, Identities, Cultures and Lifestyles*, Basingstoke: Palgrave.

—— (2008) 'Class reproduction and social networks in the USA', in L. Weis (ed.) *The Way Class Works*, New York: Routledge.

Devine, F. and Heath, S. (2009) *Doing Social Science: Evidence and Methods in Empirical Research*, Basingstoke: Macmillan.

Devine F. and Savage, M. (2005) 'The cultural turn, sociology and class analysis', in F. Devine, M. Savage, J. Scott and R. Crompton (eds) *Rethinking Class: Culture, Identities and Lifestyles*, Basingstoke: Palgrave, pp. 1–23.

Devine, F., Savage, M., Crompton, R. and Scott, J. (eds) (2005) *Rethinking Class, Identities, Cultures and Lifestyles*, Basingstoke: Palgrave.

DiMaggio, P. (1977) 'Social capital and art consumption: Origins and consequences of class differences in exposure to the arts in America', *Theory and Society*, 5: 109–32.

—— (1979) 'Review essay on Pierre Bourdieu', *American Journal of Sociology*, 84: 1460–74.

—— (1982a) 'Cultural capital and school success: The impact of status culture participation on the grades of U. S. high school students', *American Sociological Review*, 47: 189–201.

—— (1982b) 'Cultural entrepreneurship in nineteenth century Boston: The creation of an organizational base for high culture in America', *Media, Culture and Society*, 4: 33–50.

—— (1988) 'Classification in art', *American Sociological Review*, 52: 440–55.

Dornenburg, A. and Page, K. (2003) *Becoming A Chef* (rev. edn), Hoboken NJ: Wiley.

Douglas, M. (1973) *Rules and Meanings*, Harmondsworth: Penguin.

DuBois, J., Durant, P. and Winkin, Y. (eds) *Bourdieu: Le colloq Cerisy*, Liège: Éditions de l'Université de Liège.

Durkheim, E. (1966) *The Rules of Sociological Method*, New York: The Free Press.

Echikson, W. (1995) *Burgundy Stars: A Year in the Life of a Great French Restaurant*, Boston: Little Brown and Company.

Eco, U. (1979) *Lector in Fabula*, Milan: Bompiani. [Note: Parts of the book are translated in *The Role of the Reader* (1979), Bloomington: Indiana UP.].

Emirbayer, M. and Johnson, V. (2008) 'Bourdieu and organizational analysis', *Theory and Society*, 37: 1–44.

Encrevé, P. and Lagrave, R. M. (eds) (2003) *Travailler avec Bourdieu*, Paris: Flammarion.

Eribon, D. (ed.) (2001), *L'infréquentable Michel Foucault: renouveaux de la pensée critique*, Paris: Eppel.

Eribon D. (2007) *D'une révolution conservatrice et de ses effets sur la gauche française*, Paris: Variations V/Editions Leo Scheer.

Erickson, B. H. (1996) 'Class, Culture, and Connections', *American Journal of Sociology*, 102: 217–51.

Evans, G. (1992) 'Is Britain a class divided society? A reanalysis and extension of Marshall, *et al.*'s study of class consciousness', *Sociology*, 26 (2): 233–58.

—— (2006) *Educational Failure and the White Working Class*, Basingstoke: Palgrave.

Eyal, G. (2003) *The Origins of Postcommunist Elites: From the Prague Spring and the Breakup of Czechoslovakia*, Madison MN: Minnesota University Press.

—— (2005) 'The making and breaking of the Czechoslovak political field', in L. Wacquant (ed.) *Pierre Bourdieu and Democratic Politics: The Mystery of Ministry*, Cambridge, UK and Malden, MA: Polity, pp. 151–77.

Fabiani, Jean-Louis (2001) 'Les règles du champ' in Bernard Lahire (ed.) *Le travail sociologique de Pierre Bourdieu: Dettes et critique*, Paris: Éditions la Découverte, pp. 75–91.

Fantasia, R. (1995) 'Fast Food in France', *Theory and Society*, 24: 201–43.

—— (2000) 'Restaurants rapides pour "société sans classes"', *Le Monde Diplomatique*, 554 May: 6–7.

Farnell, B. (2000) 'Getting out of the Habitus: An alternative model of dynamically embodied social action', *Journal of the Royal Anthropological Institute*, 6: 397–418.

Featherstone, M. (1991) *Consumer Culture and Postmodernism*, London: Sage.

Fedele, P. (2003) 'Bocuse met le cap à l'Ouest', *Néorestauration*, 396 Mars: 60–1.

Ferguson, P. (1998) 'A cultural field in the making: Gastronomy in nineteenth century France', *American Journal of Sociology*, 104 (3) November: 597–641.

—— (2004), *Accounting for Taste: The Triumph of French Cuisine*, Chicago IL: University of Chicago Press.

Filonowicz, J. D. (2008) *Fellow-Feeling and the Moral Life*, Cambridge: Cambridge University Press.

Flandrin, J. L. (1999) 'From dietetics to gastronomy', in J. L. Flandrin and M. Montanari (eds) *FOOD: A Culinary History from Antiquity to the Present*, New York: Columbia University Press.

Foucault, M. (1970) [1966] *The Order of Things: An Archeology of the Human Sciences*, Paris: Gallimard.

—— (1972) *The Archaeology of Knowledge*, London: Tavistock.

—— (1988) 'Technologies of the self', in L. H. Martin, H. Gutman and P. H. Hutton (eds) *Technologies of the Self: A Seminar with Michel Foucault*, London: Tavistock, pp. 16–49.

—— (1989 [1984] 'An aesthetics of existence', in *Foucault Live*, New York: Semiotext(e).

—— (1991) 'Govermentality' in Graham Burchell, C. Gordon and P. Miller (eds) *The Foucault Effect: Studies in Govermentality*, London: Harvester/Wheatsheaf, pp. 87–104.

—— (1997) 'Polemics, politics and problematization: An interview', in P. Rabinow (ed.) *Essential Works of Foucault*, New York: New Press.

—— (2000) [1968] 'On the archaeology of the sciences: Response to the Epistemology Circle', in M. Foucault *Aesthetics, Method, and Epistemology*, London: Penguin, pp. 297–334.

—— (2008) *The Birth of Biopolitics: Lectures at the Gollège de France, 1978–9*, London: Palgrave Macmillan.

Fowler, B. (2000) (ed.) *Reading Bourdieu on Society and Culture*, Oxford: Blackwell.

Frickel, S. and Gross, N. (2005) 'A general theory of scientific/intellectual movements', *American Sociological Review*, 70 (2): 204–32.

Friedmann, J. (2005) 'Place-making as project? Habitus and migration in transnational cities', in J. Hillier and E. Rooksby (eds) *Habitus: A Sense of Place*, Aldershot: Ashgate.

Frow, J. (2010) 'Matter and materialism: a brief history of the present', in T. Bennett and P. Joyce (eds) *Material Powers: Culture, History and the Material Turn*, London and New York: Routledge.

Fuller, S. (2006) 'France's last sociologist', *Economy and Society*, 35 (2) 314–23.

—— (2008) 'Conatus', in M. Grenfell (ed.) *Pierre Bourdieu: Key Concepts*, Stocksfield: Acumen.

Gaxie, D. (1978) *Le Cens caché. Inégalités culturelles et ségrégation politique*, Paris: Seuil.

Giddens, A. (1991a) *The Consequences of Modernity*, Cambridge, Polity.

—— (1991b) *Modernity and Self-Identity: Self and Society in the Late Modern Age*, Cambridge: Polity.

—— (1992) *The Transformation of Intimacy*, Cambridge: Polity.

Glaser, B. G. and Strauss, A. (1967) *The Discovery of Grounded Theory: Strategies for Qualitative Research*, Chicago: Aldine.

Glover, J. (2001) *Humanity: A Moral History of the Twentieth Century*, London: Pimlico.

Golan, G. (1995a) 'Paul Bocuse: la gastronomie comme un humanisme', *Le Chef*, 83 Decembre: 18–21.

—— (1995b) 'Qui Consulte les Guides?' in *Le Chef*, 75 janvier–février.

Goldberg, C. A. (2003) 'Haunted by the specter of communism: Collective identity and resource mobilization in the demise of the workers alliance of America', *Theory and Society*, 32 (5–6): 725–73.

Goldthorpe, J. H. (2007a, 2nd edn) *On Sociology: Volume One: Critique and Program*, Stanford, CA: Stanford University Press.

Goldthorpe, J. H. (2007b, 2nd edn) *On Sociology: Volume Two: Illustrations and Retrospect*, Stanford, CA: Stanford University Press.

Goldthorpe, J. H. and Marshall, G. (1992) 'The promising future of class analysis – a response to recent critiques', *Sociology*, 26: 381–400.

Goodman, N. (1978) *Ways of Worldmaking*, Indianapolis: Hackett.

Goody, Jack (1982) *Cooking, Cuisine and Class*, Cambridge: Cambridge University Press.

Goswami, M. (2004) *Producing India: From Colonial Economy to National Space*, Chicago: University of Chicago Press.

Gouldner, A. W. (1979) *The Future of Intellectuals and the Rise of the New Class*, New York: Oxford.

Grenfell, M. (1993) 'The linguistic market of Orléans', in M. Kelly and R. Bock (eds) *France: Nation and Regions*, Southampton: ASM & CF, pp. 77–92.

—— (1996) 'Bourdieu and the initial training of modern language teachers', *British Educational Research Journal*, 22 (3): 287–303.

—— (2003) 'Language: Constructing an object of research', in M. Grenfell and M. Kelly (eds) *Bourdieu: Language, Culture and Education*, Bern: Peter Lang.

—— (2004a) 'Bourdieu in the classroom', in M. Olssen (ed.) *Language and Culture*, New York: Greenwood.

—— (2004b) *Pierre Bourdieu: Agent Provocateur*, London: Continuum.

—— (2005) *Pierre Bourdieu: Agent Provocateur*, London: Continuum.

—— (2006) 'Bourdieu in the field: From the Béarn to Algeria – a timely response', *French Cultural Studies*, 17 (2): 223–40.

—— (2007) *Pierre Bourdieu: Education and Training*, London: Continuum.

—— (2008a) *Pierre Bourdieu: Key Concepts*, Oxford: Acumen.

—— (2008b) 'Social classes? Bourdieu and a practical epistemology of social classification'. Keynote Paper at the Conference, Reproductions: Social Class in Theory and Practice, University of Warwick, July.

Grenfell, M. and Hardy, C. (2007) *Art Rule: Pierre Bourdieu and the Visual Arts*, Oxford: Berg.

Grignon, C. and Passeron, J. C. (1989) *Le savant et le populaire*, Paris: Seuil.

Gross, N. (2008) *Richard Rorty: The Making of an American Philosopher*, Chicago: University of Chicago Press.

Hage, G. (1998) *White Nation: Fantasies of White Supremacy in a Multicultural Society*, Annandale, NSW: Pluto.

Hall, J. (1992) 'The capital(s) of cultures: A non-holistic approach to status situations, class, gender, and ethnicity', in M. Lamont and M. Fournier (eds) *Cultivating Differences: Symbolic Boundaries and the Making of Inequality*, Chicago: University of Chicago Press, pp. 257–85.

Hall, P. A. and Lamont, M. (2009) *Successful Societies: How Institutions and Culture Affect Health*, New York: Cambridge University Press.

Halle, D. (1993) *Inside Culture: Art and Class in the American Home*, Chicago: University Chicago Press.

Halsey, A. H. (2004) *A History of Sociology in Britain*, Oxford: Oxford University Press.

Hartmann, M. (2000) 'Class-specific habitus and the social reproduction of the business elite in Germany and France', *Sociological Review*, 48: 241–61.

Heath, A., Curtice, J., Andersen, R. and Thomson, K. (2008) 'Are traditional identities in decline?' End of Award Report, ESRC Identities Programme, Swindon: ESRC.

Heinich, N. (2002) 'Sociologie de l'art, avec et sans Bourdieu', *Sciences Humaines*, special number *L'œuvre de Pierre Bourdieu*.

—— (2007) *Pourquoi Bourdieu?* Paris: Gallimard.

Helm, B. W. (2001) *Emotional Reason: Deliberation, Motivation and the Nature of Value*, Cambridge: Cambridge University Press.

Hennion, A. (1981) *Les Professionnels du disque, une sociologie des variétés*, Paris: A-M. Metailié.

—— (1985) 'Esthétique populaire ou théâtralité théorique?' in Collectif Révoltes logiques (eds) *Esthétiques du people*, Paris: La Découverte: pp. 249–65.

—— (1989) 'An intermediary between production and consumption: The producer of popular music', *Science, Technology and Human Values*, 14 (4): 400–24.

—— (2007) 'Those Things that Hold Us Together: Taste and Sociology', *Cultural Sociology*, 1 (1): 97–114.

Hey, V. (1997) *The Company She Keeps. An ethnography of girls' friendships*, Buckingham: Open University Press.

Hillier, J. and Rooksby, E. (eds) (2005) *Habitus: A Sense of Place*, Aldershot: Ashgate.

Holt, D. B. (1997) 'Distinction in America? Recovering Bourdieu's theory of tastes from his critics', *Poetics*, 25: 93–120.

Hunter, I. (1988) *Culture and Government: The Emergence of Literary Education*, London: Macmillan.

Jacquemond, F. (2001) 'Projet de Bernard Loiseau en Haute-Garonne', *Néo Restauration*, 378, juillet–août: 14.

James, D. (1995) 'Mature studentship in higher education: Beyond a "species" approach', *British Journal of Sociology of Education*, 16: 451–66.

Jenkins, R. (1992) *Pierre Bourdieu*, London: Routledge.

—— (1996) *Social Identity*, New York: Routledge.

Kauppi, N. (2005) *Democracy, Social Resources and Political Power in the European Union*, Manchester: Manchester University Press.

Kingston, P. W. (2001) 'The unfulfilled promise of cultural capital theory', *Sociology of Education*, 74, extra issue: 88–99.

Knight, C. (2004) 'Blending fame and flavors: A chef's art lies in marketing', *International Herald Tribune*, 16–17 October: 13.

Lahire, B. (1998) *L'homme pluriel. Les resorts de l'action*, Paris: Nathan.

—— (1999) *Le Travail Sociologique de Pierre Bourdieu. Dettes et Critiques* (2nd edn), Paris: La Découverte.

—— (2003) 'From the habitus to an individual heritage of dispositions: Towards a sociology at the level of the individual', *Poetics*, 31: 329–55.

Lakatos, I. (1978) *The Methodology of Scientific Research Programs*, New York: Cambridge University Press.

Lamont, M. (1987) 'How to become a dominant French philosopher: The case of Jacques Derrida', *American Journal of Sociology*, 93 (3): 584–622.

—— (1988) 'From Paris to Stanford: A sociological reconversion from French to American sociology', *Politix*, 3–4: 22–9.

—— (1989) 'The power-culture link in a comparative perspective', *Comparative Social Research*, 11: 131–50.

—— (1992) *Money, Morals, and Manners: The Culture of the French and the American Upper-Middle Class*, Chicago: University of Chicago Press.

—— (2000) *The Dignity of Working Men: Morality and the Boundaries of Race, Class, and Immigration*, New York: Russell Sage Foundation; Cambridge MA: Harvard University Press.

—— (2001) 'Three questions for a big book: Collins, The Sociology of Philosophies', *Sociological Theory*, 19 (1): 86–91.

—— (2004) 'The theory section and theory satellites', *Perspectives. Newsletter of the ASA Theory Section*, 27 (1) (January) 5.

—— (2008) 'Critères d'évaluation et structures culturelles: réflections sur un parcours de recherches', in Marc Breviglieri, Claudette Lafaye and Daniel Trom (eds) *Sens de la critique, sens de la justice*, Paris: Economica.

—— (2009) *How Professors Think? Inside the Curious World of Academic Judgment*, Cambridge, MA: Harvard University Press.

Lamont, M. and Fournier, M. (eds) (1992) *Cultivating Differences: Symbolic Boundaries and the Making of Inequality*, Chicago: University of Chicago Press.

Lamont M. and Lareau, A. (1988) 'Cultural capital: Allusions, gaps and glissandos in recent theoretical developments', *Sociological Theory*, 6 (2): 153–68.

Lamont, M. and Molnár, V. (2002) 'The study of boundaries across the social sciences', *Annual Review of Sociology*, 28: 167–95.

Lamont, M. and Small, M. (2008) 'How culture matters: Enriching our understanding of poverty' in A. Lin and D. Harris (eds) *The Colors of Poverty: Why Racial and Ethnic Disparities Persist*, New York: Russell Sage Foundation.

Lamont, M. and Thévenot, L. (eds) (2000) *Rethinking Comparative Cultural Sociology: Repertoires of Evaluation in France and the United States*, London: Cambridge University Press; Paris: Presses de la Maison des Sciences de l'Homme.

Lamont, M. and Zuckerman, E. (forthcoming) 'Toward a sociology of valuation: convergence, divergence and synthesis', *Annual Review of Sociology*.

Lareau, A. (1989) *Home Advantage: Social Class and Parental Intervention in Elementary Education*, New York: Rowman, and Littlefield.

—— (2003) *Unequal Childhoods: Class, Race, and Family Life*, Berkeley and Los Angeles CA: University of California Press.

Lareau, A. and Weininger, E. (2003) 'Cultural capital in educational research: a critical assessment', *Theory and Society*, 32, 567–606.

Latour, B. (1983) 'Comment redistribuer le Grand Partage?' *Revue de Synthèse*, 110 (2): 203–36.

—— (1989) [1987] *Science in Action*, Cambridge MA: Harvard University Press.

Latour, B. and Bastide, F. (1984) 'Essai de Science-Fabrication', *Études Françaises*, pp.19–2.

Latour, B. and Woolgar, S. (1979) *Laboratory Life: the Social Construction of Scientific Facts*, London: Sage.

Law, J. and Urry, J. (2004) 'Enacting the social', *Economy and Society*, 33 (3): 390–410.

Lawler, S. (2000) *Mothering the Self*, London: Routledge.

—— (2008) 'The middle classes and their aristocratic others: Culture as nature in classification struggles', *Journal of Cultural Economy*, 1 (3): 245–62.

Le Roux, B., Rouanet, H., Savage, M. and Warde, A. (2008) 'Class and cultural division in the UK', *Sociology*, 42 (6): 1049–71.

Lebaron, F. (2004) 'Pierre Bourdieu: Economic models against Economism', in D. Swartz and V. Zolberg (eds) *After Bourdieu. Influence, Critique, Elaboration*, Dordrecht-Boston-London: Kluwer Academic, pp. 87–101.

—— (2009a) 'Ethos capitaliste, ethos de classe. Quelques remarques autour des notions d'éthos, habitus et sens moral', in Sandra Laugier (dir.) *Normativités du sens commun*, Paris: PUF, CURAPP.

—— (2009b) 'How Bourdieu "quantified" Bourdieu. The geometric modelling of data', in K. Robson and C. Sanders (2009) *Quantifying Theory: Pierre Bourdieu*, Dordrecht/London/Boston: Springer.

Lee, O. (1998) 'Culture and democratic theory: Toward a theory of symbolic democracy', *Constellations*, 5 (4): 433–55.

Lescourret, M. A. (2008) *Pierre Bourdieu. Vers une économie du bonheur*, Paris: Flammarion.

Levi-Strauss, C. (1958) *L'anthropologie structurales*, Paris: Plon.

Lin, N. (2001) *A Theory of Social Structure and Action*, New York: Cambridge University Press.

Lizardo, O. (2004) 'The cognitive origins of Bourdieu's *habitus*', *Journal for the Theory of Social Behavior*, 34: 375–401.

—— (2005) 'The puzzle of women's "highbrow" culture consumption: Integrating gender and work into Bourdieu's class theory of taste', *Poetics* 34: 1–23.

—— (2008) 'The question of culture consumption and stratification revisited', *Sociologica: Italian Online Sociological Review*, 2.

Longhurst, B. and Savage, M. (1996) 'Social Class, consumption and the influence of Bourdieu: Some critical issues', in S. Edgell, K. Hetherington and A. Warde (eds), *Consumption Matters*, (Sociological Review Monograph), Oxford; Blackwell, pp. 274–301.

Loosely, D. L. (2004) 'The development of a social exclusion agenda in French cultural policy', *Cultural Trends*, 13 (2): 1–13.

Loveman, M. (2005) 'The modern state and the primitive accumulation of symbolic capital', *The American Journal of Sociology*, 110 (6): 1651–83.

MacIntyre, A. (1985, 2nd edn) *After Virtue: A Study in Moral Theory*, London: Duckworth.

MacIntyre, A. (1998) *A Short History of Ethics*, London: Routledge.

McNay, L. (1999) 'Gender, habitus and the field: Pierre Bourdieu and the limits of reflexivity', *Theory, Culture and Society*, 16 (1), 95–117.

—— (2001) 'Meditations on Pascalian Meditations', *Economy and Society*, 30: 139–54.

McRobbie, A. (2002) 'A mixed bag of misfortunes? Bourdieu's Weight of the World', *Theory, Culture and Society*, 19 (3): 129–38.

Marshall, G., Newby, H., Rose, D. and Vogler, C. (1988) *Social Class in Modern Britain*, London; Hutchinson.

Martin-Criado, E. (2008) *Les deux Algéries de Pierre Bourdieu*, Bellecombe-en-Bauges: Croquant.

Martin, J. L. (2003) 'What is field theory?', *American Journal of Sociology*, 109 (1): 1–49.

Marx, K. (1978) 'Theses on Feuerbach', in R. C. Tucker (ed.) *The Marx-Engels Reader*, New York: W. W. Norton, pp. 143–5.

Mauger, G. (ed.) (2005) *Rencontres avec Pierre Bourdieu*, Bellecombe-en-Bauges: Croquant.

Mendez, M. L. (2008) 'Middle class identities in a neo-liberal age: Tensions between contested authenticities', *Sociological Review*, 56 (2): 220–37.

Mennell, S. (1996) *All Manners of Food* (2nd edn), Urbana IL: University of Illinois Press.

Mesplède, J. F. (1998) *Trois Etoiles au Michelin: Une histoire de la haute gastronomie francaise*, Paris: Grund.

Midgley, M. (2003) *Heart and Mind*, London: Routledge.

Miller, D. (1995) (ed.) *Acknowledging Consumption: A Review of New Studies*, London: Routledge.

Morning, A. (2009) Toward a sociology of racial conceptualization for the 21st century', *Social Forces*, 87 (3): 1167–92.

Mouzelis, N. (2008) *Modern and Postmodern Social Theorizing*, Cambridge: Cambridge University Press.

Murdoch, I. (1970) *The Sovereignty of Good*, London: Routledge.

Nichols, S. (2004) *Sentimental Rules: On the Natural Foundations of Moral Judgment*, Oxford: Oxford University Press.

Noble, G. and Watkins, M. (2003) 'So, how did Bourdieu learn to play tennis? Habitus, consciousness and habituation', *Cultural Studies*, 17 (3/4): 520–38.

Noisette, T. (1998) 'Bernard Loiseau parie sur la Bourse', *Néo Restauration*, 346, septembre.

Nord, P. (1986) *Paris Shopkeepers and the Politics of Resentment*, Princeton, NJ: Princeton University Press.

Nussbaum, M. C. (2001) *Upheavals of Thought: The Intelligence of Emotions*, Cambridge: Cambridge University Press.

Oakley, J. (1993) *Morality and the Emotions*, London: Routledge.

Ouellette, L. and Hay, J. (2008) *Better Living through Reality TV*, Oxford: Blackwell.

Pachucki, M. A., Pendergrass, S. and Lamont, M. (eds) (2007) 'Cultural Lines; Emerging Research on Boundaries', *Poetics*, 35 (6).

Payne, G. and Glew, D. (2005) 'Unpacking class ambivalence: Some conceptual and methodological issues in accessing class cultures', *Sociology*, 39 (5): 893–910.

Pedrocco, G. (1999) 'The food industry and new preservation techniques', in J. L. Flandrin and M. Montanari (eds) *FOOD: A Culinary History from Antiquity to the Present*, New York: Columbia University Press.

Pels, D. (1995) 'Knowledge politics and anti-politics: toward a critical appraisal of Bourdieu's concept of intellectual autonomy', *Theory and Society*, 24: 79–104.

Peterson, R. A. (2005) 'Problems in comparative research: The example of omnivorousness,' *Poetics*, 33: 257–82.

Philips, D. (2005) 'Transformation scenes: The television interior makeover', *International Journal of Cultural Studies*, 8 (2): 213–29.

Pinto, L. (2002) *Pierre Bourdieu et la théorie du monde social*, Paris: Seuil.

Portes, A. (1998) 'Social capital: Its origins and applications in modern sociology', *Annual Review of Sociology*, 24: 1–24.

Poulot, Dominique (2005) *Une histoire des musées de France, XVIII–XX siècle*, Paris: Éditions la Découverte.

Poupeau, F. and Discepolo, T. (2004) 'Scholarship with commitment: On the political engagements of Pierre Bourdieu', *Constellations*, 11 (1): 76–96.

Prieur, A. (2008) 'Disidentification from class', paper presented at the Workshop 'Putting Bourdieu to Work', CRESC, Manchester, May.

Pudlowski, G. (2000) 'Le syndrome de "l'annexité"', *Le Point*, 1455, 4, août.

Rancière, J. (1983) *Le Philosophe et ses Pauvres*, Paris: Fayard. [Note: in English, *The Philosopher and his Poor Relations*.]

—— (2004a) *The Philosopher and His Poor*, Durham and London: Duke University Press.

—— (2004b) *The Politics of Aesthetics: The Distribution of the Sensible*, London and New York: Continuum.

Reay, D. (1998a) '"Always Knowing" and "Never being sure": Institutional and familial habituses and higher education choice', *Journal of Education Policy*, 13 (4): 519–29.

—— (1998b) *Class Work: Mothers' Involvement in Children's Schooling*, London: University College Press.

—— (2000) 'A useful extension of Bourdieu's conceptual framework?: Emotional capital as a way of understanding mothers' involvement in their children's education', *Sociological Review*, 48 (4): 568–85.

—— (2004) '"It's all becoming a habitus": Beyond the habitual use of Pierre Bourdieu's concept of habitus in educational research', *British Journal of Sociology of Education* (special issue on Pierre Bourdieu) 25 (4): 431–44.

—— (2005) 'Beyond consciousness: The psychic landscape of social class', *Sociology*, 911–28.

Reay, D., Crozier, G. and Clayton, J. (2009a, forthcoming) '"Fitting in" or "standing out": Working-class students in UK higher education', *British Educational Research Journal*.

—— (2009b, forthcoming) '"Strangers in Paradise"? Working-class students in elite universities', *Sociology*.

Reay, D., David, M. E. and Ball, S. (2005) *Degrees of Choice: Social Class, Race and Gender in Higher Education*, Stoke-on-Trent: Trentham.

Reay, D., Hallingworth, S., Williams, K., Crozier, G., Jamieson, F., James, D. and Beedell, P. (2007) 'A darker shade of pale: Whiteness, the middle classes and multi-ethnic inner-city schooling', *Sociology*, 41: 1041–60.

Reed-Danahay, D. (2004) *Locating Bourdieu*, Bloomington, IN: Indiana University Press.

Remy, P. (2004) *L'inspecteur se met à table*, Paris: Éditions des Équateurs.

Rivera, L. (2009) 'Hiring and Inequality in High Prestige Professions', dissertation, Department of Sociology, Harvard University.

Robbins, D. (1991) *The Work of Pierre Bourdieu: Recognizing Society*, Boulder and San Francisco: Westview.

—— (2000) *Bourdieu and Culture*, London: Sage.

—— (2005) 'The origins, early development and status of Bourdieu's concept of "cultural capital"', *British Journal of Sociology*, 56 (1): 13–30.

—— (2006) 'Introduction: A social critique of judgement', *Theory Culture & Society*, 23 (6): 1–24.

Robson, K. and Sanders, C. (2009) *Quantifying Theory: Pierre Bourdieu*, Dordrecht/London/Boston: Springer.

Rose, J. (2002) *The Intellectual Life of the British Woking Classes*, New Haven and London: Yale University Press.

Rose, N. (1996) 'Authority and the genealogy of subjectivity', in P. Heelas, S. Lash and P. Morris (eds) *Detraditionalisation: Critical Reflections on Authority and Identity*, Oxford: Blackwell.

Rowse, T. (1998) *White Flour, White Power: From Rations to Citizenship in Central Australia*, Melbourne: Cambridge University Press.

Sallaz, J. J. and Zavisca, J. (2007) 'Bourdieu in America, 1980–2004', *Annual Review Sociology*, 33: 21–41.

Savage, M. (2000) *Class Analysis and Social Transformation*, Buckingham, Open University Press.

—— (2005a) 'Revisiting Classic Qualitative Studies', *Historical Social Research/Historische Sozialforschung*, 30 (1): 118–39.

—— (2005b) 'Working class identities in the 1960s: revisiting the affluent worker study', *Sociology*, 39 (5): 929–46.

—— (2007) 'Changing social class identities in post-war Britain: Perspectives from mass-observation', *Sociological Research Online*, 12 (3) 29 May.

Savage, M. and Burrows, R. (2007) 'The Coming Crisis of Empirical Sociology', *Sociology*, 41 (5): 885–99.

Savage, M., Bagnall, G. and Longhurst, B. J. (2001) '"Ordinary, ambivalent and defensive": class identities in the northwest of England', *Sociology*, 35: 875–92.

Savage, M., Bagnall, G. and Longhurst, B. J. (2005) 'Local Habitus and Working Class Culture', in F. Devine, M. Savage, J. Scott and R. Crompton (eds) *Rethinking Class: Culture, Identities and Lifestyle*, London: Palgrave.

Savage, M., Warde, A. and Devine, F. (2005) 'Capital, assets and resources: Some critical issues', *British Journal of Sociology*, 56 (1): 31–48.

Sawchuck, P. (2003) *Adult Learning and Technology in Working-Class Life*, Cambridge: Cambridge University Press.

Sayer, A. (1999) 'Bourdieu, Smith and disinterested judgement', *The Sociological Review*, 47 (3): 403–31.

—— (2005) *The Moral Significance of Class*, Cambridge: Cambridge University Press.

—— (2008) 'Understanding lay normativity', in S. Moog and R. Stones (eds) *Nature, Social Relations and Human Needs: Essays in Honour of Ted Benton*, Basingstoke: Palgrave Macmillan, pp.128–145.

Schinkel, W. (2007) 'Sociological discourse of the relational: the case of Bourdieu and Latour', *Sociological Review*, 55 (4): 707–29.

Scott, J. C. (1990) *Domination and the Arts of Resistance: Hidden Transcripts*, New Haven, CT: Yale University Press.

Sennett, R. and Cobb, J. (1973) *The Hidden Injuries of Class*, New York: Vintage.

Shapin, S. (1994) *A Social History of Truth: Civility and Science in Seventeenth-century England*, Chicago: University of Chicago Press.

Sherman, R. (2007) *Class Acts: Service and Inequality in Luxury Hotels*, Berkeley, CA: University of California Press.

Shusterman, R. (ed.) (1999) *Bourdieu. A Critical Reader*, Malden MA: Backwell.

Silva, E. B. (2000) 'The politics of consumption at home: practices and dispositions in the uses of technologies', *Pavis Papers* 1, Milton Keynes: The Open University.

—— (2005) 'Gender, home, and family in cultural capital theory', *British Journal of Sociology*, 56 (1): 83–102.

Silva, E. B. and Wright, D. (2005) 'The judgement of taste and social position in focus group research' *Sociologia e Ricerca Sociale*, special double issue, 76/77: 241–53. Milan: Angeli. Available online at: http://www.open.ac.uk/socialsciences/includes/__cms/ download.php?file=w4lkl1zo6ef8h2c0b0.pdf&name=judgement_of_taste_and_social_position_in_focus_group_research.pdf.

—— (2009) 'Display, desire and distinction in housing', *Cultural Sociology*, 3(1): 31–50.

Silva, E. B., Warde, A. and Wright, D. (2009) 'Using mixed methods for analyzing culture: The Cultural Capital and Social Exclusion Project', *Cultural Sociology*, 3(2): 299–316.

Skeggs, B. (1997) *Formations of Class and Gender*, London: Sage.

—— (2004a) *Class, Culture, Self*, London: Routledge.

—— (2004b) 'Context and Background: Pierre Bourdieu's analysis of class, gender and sexuality', in L. Adkins and B. Skeggs (eds) *Feminism After Bourdieu*, Oxford: Blackwell.

Smart, C. (2007) *Personal Life*, Cambridge: Polity.

Smith, A. (1984) [1759] *The Theory of Moral Sentiments*, edited by D. D. Raphael and A. L. Macfie, Indianapolis: Liberty Fund.

Steinmetz, G. (1999) 'Introduction: Culture and the state', in *State/Culture: State-Formation after the Cultural Turn*, Ithaca and London: Cornell University Press, pp. 1–49.

—— (2006) 'Bourdieu's Disavowal of Lacan: Psychoanalytic Theory and the Concepts of "Habitus" and "Symbolic Capital"', *Constellations*, 13 (4): 446–63.

Stout, A. (2008) *Creating Prehistory: Druids, Ley Hunters and Archaeologists in Pre-war Britain*, Oxford: Blackwell.

Swartz, D. L. (1997) *Culture and Power: The Sociology of Pierre Bourdieu*, Chicago: The University of Chicago Press.

—— (1998) 'Universalism and parochialism: How Gouldner and Bourdieu understand the interests of intellectuals', Annual Meeting of the American Sociological Association, San Francisco.

—— (2003a) 'From critical sociology to public intellectual: Pierre Bourdieu and politics', *Theory and Society*, 32 (5–6): 791–823.

—— (2003b) 'Pierre Bourdieu's political sociology and governance perspectives', in H. P. Bang (ed.) *Governance as Social and Political Communication*, Manchester and New York: Manchester University Press, pp. 140–58.

—— (2006) 'Pierre Bourdieu and North American political sociology: Why he doesn't fit in but should.' *French Politics*, 4: 84–9.

—— (2008) 'Bringing Bourdieu's master concepts into organizational analysis', *Theory and Society*, 37: 45–52.

Swartz, D. L. and Zolberg, V. L. (eds) (2004) *After Bourdieu. Influence, Critique, Elaboration*, Dordrecht: Kluwer Academic.

Sweetman, P. (2003) 'Twenty-first century dis-ease? Habitual reflexivity or the reflexive habitus', *Sociological Review*, 51 (4): 528–49.

Swidler, A. (1986) 'Culture in action: Symbols and strategies', *American Sociological Review*, 51 (2): 273–86.

Swinbank, V. (2002) 'The sexual politics of cooking: A feminist analysis of culinary hierarchy in Western culture', *Journal of Historical Sociology*, 15 (4) December: 464–94.

Taylor, C. (1985) *Human Agency and Language*, Cambridge: Cambridge University Press.

Terence, I. (1996) *Le monde de la grande restauration en France*, Paris: Harmattan.

Thévenot, L. (2006) *L'action au pluriel. Sociologie des regimes d'engagement*, Paris: La Découverte.

Thiault, B. (1999) 'Je veux render acessible notre savoir-faire culinaire', *Néo Restauration*, 350, janvier.

Tiles, M. (1984) *Bachelard: Science and Objectivity*, London: Cambridge University Press.

Todd, J. (2005) 'Social transformation, collective categories and identity change', *Theory and Society*, 34: 429–63.

Topper, K. (2001) 'Not so trifling nuances: Pierre Bourdieu, symbolic violence, and the perversions of democracy', *Constellations*, 8 (1): 30–56.

Trubeck, A. (2000) *Haute Cuisine: How the French Invented the Culinary Profession*, Philadelphia: University of Pennsylvania Press.

Valverde, M. (1996) '"Despotism" and ethical liberal governance', *Economy and Society*, 25 (3).

Villette, M. (2005) 'Portrait de Pierre Bourdieu en capitalist sauvage', in G. Mauger (ed.) *Rencontres avec Pierre Bourdieu*, Bellecombe-en-Bauges: Éditions du Croquant, pp. 219–24.

Wacquant, L. J. D. (1992) 'Toward a social praxeology: The structure and logic of Bourdieu's sociology', *An Invitation to Reflexive Sociology*, Chicago: The University of Chicago Press, pp. 2–59.

—— (1998) 'Pierre Bourdieu' in Stones, R. (ed.) *Key Sociological Thinkers*, New York: New York University Press.

—— (2004) 'Pointers on Pierre Bourdieu and democratic politics', *Constellations*, 11 (1): 3–15.

Wacquant, L. J. D. (ed.) (2005) *Pierre Bourdieu and Democratic Politics*, Cambridge: Polity.

Walkerdine, V., Lucey, H. and Melody, J. (2001) *Growing Up Girl. Psychosocial Exploration of Gender and Class*, Basingstoke: Palgrave.

Warde, A. (2004) *Practice and Field: Revising Bourdieusian Concepts*, CRIC Discussion Paper No. 65, Manchester: University of Manchester.

—— (2008a) 'Dimensions of a social theory of taste', *Journal of Cultural Economy*, 1 (3): 321–36.

—— (2008b) 'Does taste still serve power?', *Sociologica: Italian Online Sociological Review*, 3: 1–26.

Warde, A. and Savage, M. (forthcoming, 2010) 'Cultural capital and the sociological analysis of culture: a re-assessment' in Marco Santoro (ed.) *Cultura in Italia*, Vol. 2, Bologna: Il Mulino.

Warde, A., Wright, D. and Gayo-Cal, M. (2007) 'The meaning of cultural omnivorousness, or the myth of the cultural omnivore', *Cultural Sociology*, 1 (2): 143–64.

Weber, M. (1978) 'The distribution of power within the political community: Class, status, party', in G. Roth and C. Wittich (eds) *Economy and Society: An Outline of Interpretative Sociology*, Vol. 2, Berkeley, CA: University of California Press, pp. 926–40.

Weininger, E. (2004) 'Pierre Bourdieu on social class and symbolic violence', in E. Colin Wright (ed.) *Alternative Foundations of Class Analysis*, New York: Bedminster.

—— (2005) 'Foundations of Pierre Bourdieu's class analysis', in E. O. Wright (ed.) *Approaches to Class Analysis*, Cambridge, Cambridge University Press.

White, M. (2005) 'The liberal character of ethnological governance', *Economy and Society*, 34 (3): 474–94.

Wilder, G. (2005) *The French Imperial Nation-State: Negritude and Colonial Humanism between the two World Wars*, Chicago: University of Chicago Press.

Wilkinson, I. (2005) *Suffering: A Sociological Introduction*, Cambridge: Polity.

Wimmer, A. (2008) 'The Making and Unmaking of Ethnic Boundaries: A Multilevel Process Theory', *American Journal of Sociology*, 13 (4): 970–1022.

Young, M. (ed.) (1971) *Knowledge and Control*, London: MacMillan.

Zunz, O. (ed.) (2002) *Social Contracts Under Stress*, New York: Russell Sage Foundation.

Index

Page numbers in **bold** denote references to tables.